BUFFY AND THE ART OF STORY SEASON ONE

WRITING BETTER FICTION BY WATCHING BUFFY

L. M. LILLY

Copyright © 2020 by L. M. Lilly

All rights reserved.

No part of this book may be reproduced in any form or by any electronic or mechanical means, including information storage and retrieval systems, without written permission from the author, except for the use of brief quotations in a book review.

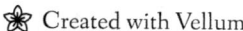 Created with Vellum

CONTENTS

Introduction	v
1. Key Plot Points And Turns For Your Story	1
2. Welcome To The Hellmouth	5
3. The Harvest	24
4. The Witch	50
5. Teacher's Pet	72
6. Never Kill A Boy On The First Date	91
7. The Pack	107
8. Angel	125
9. I, Robot... You, Jane	151
10. The Puppet Show	175
11. Nightmares	195
12. Out of Mind, Out of Sight	213
13. Prophecy Girl	240
14. Season One Overview	262
Appendix	281
About the Author	287
Also by L. M. Lilly	289

INTRODUCTION

The first time I watched Buffy the Vampire Slayer it was for sheer enjoyment. I loved the clever dialogue, the strong character development, and the partly scary, partly funny plots. At the time, most network television shows lacked any season-long story arc. They were written so that you could drop in and out at any time. That Buffy was an exception and told novel-length stories through TV didn't hit me at first.

That's partly because I didn't see the early seasons completely in order until the DVD box sets released years later. That's when I really grasped just how well structured and well written the show is. After that, I rewatched the entire series time and again.

When podcasts came around I discovered one that broke down each Buffy episode and talked about its story elements. Examining Buffy that way opened my eyes to issues in my own stories. It helped me better understand structure, characterization, tone, genre, and theme. I loved it. But the podcast disappeared when the two hosts divorced. While there are other fantastic Buffy podcasts out there, I haven't found one that looks closely at Buffy from a story perspective.

So I did what I've done with so many other things in my life. Started one myself: Buffy and the Art Of Story.

Who Am I?

I am L. M. Lilly, an author, attorney, and adjunct professor of law. (And a lot of other things, but I really like that alliteration with the three As.) A few years back, I founded WritingAsASecondCareer.com to share information with people juggling writing novels with working at other jobs or careers.

My non-fiction includes books on writing craft, including story structure, character development, and novel writing. (More on those in the Appendix.)

As Lisa M. Lilly, I'm the author of the bestselling four-book Awakening supernatural thriller series. The Awakening books have been downloaded over 90,000 times in over 35 countries. The first book in my current series, the Q.C. Davis Mysteries, debuted as the No. 1 female private eye novel on Amazon in Canada. The second Q.C. Davis Mystery was a 2019 Finalist in The Wishing Shelf Book Awards.

The plot elements I cover in Buffy and the Art of Story are the same ones I use to guide my own writing, and that I explain in the next chapter.

Is This Book For You?

As I say at the start of each podcast episode, if you love Buffy the Vampire Slayer and you love writing stories – or just taking them apart to see how they work – you're in the right place. In these pages, you'll find a breakdown of every episode of Season One of Buffy the Vampire Slayer, plus a Season One overview.

Much of this content is transcribed from podcast, edited

minimally for better flow and organization. You'll also find specific questions to consider about your own writing based on each episode.

By putting the podcast content in book form, I hope to reach people who would rather read than listen. I also decided to publish the book because I often find it helpful to see certain concepts and ideas on a page even after I've listened to them. While you can find a rough transcript of each podcast episode on my website LisaLilly.com, it's a bit harder to follow there. Personally, I usually prefer reading an ebook or paperback rather than scrolling through dozens of website pages.

How This Book Handles Spoilers

The main part of each chapter, like each podcast episode, is spoiler-free. After a spoiler warning, though, I discuss foreshadowing, which requires talking about future Buffy episodes. While I try not to spoil anything major that's more than a season out, occasionally it's relevant. So if you haven't watched the whole series, proceed with caution.

Getting The Most From This Book

There are two ways to read this book. (Or at least two that I can think of. You might be able to find more.) One is to read it straight through. I recommend this method if you haven't listened to the podcast already or if you're looking forward to revisiting Buffy Season One in order.

The other way is to look over the bullet points at the beginning of each chapter and the questions at the end. Doing so will give you a pretty good idea which story elements each chapter covers. That way, if you're struggling with a particular issue, let's say point of view, you can read those chapters first.

Whichever way you read I hope that, like me, you'll find

that taking apart Buffy episodes to see how they work (and very occasionally don't) will help you improve your own writing.

First, though, let's talk about those key plot points I mentioned. In the next chapter, I'll cover them quickly.

CHAPTER ONE

KEY PLOT POINTS AND TURNS FOR YOUR STORY

WHEN PLOTTING A NOVEL — and when discussing Buffy episodes – I look at seven key plot points and turns.

If you've already read either Super Simple Story Structure: A Quick Guide To Plotting And Writing Your Novel or The One-Year Novelist: A Week-By-Week Guide To Writing Your Novel In One Year, you may want to skip to the next chapter. On the other hand, a little review never hurts!

Opening Conflict

Every good story starts with conflict. That conflict can relate to the main plot or it can involve something else entirely. What matters is that it draws the reader immediately into the story.

If everything is going smoothly on Page 1 and your protagonist wants for nothing, most readers won't turn the page. Similarly, we'll see in Buffy that whether it's a monster of the week, Buffy's personal life clashing with her Slayer duties, or a scary voiceover in a darkened room, we always start with conflict.

Story Spark (a/k/a Inciting Incident)

Around 10% into a movie, book, or television episode you will usually see something happen that sets off the main plot. This event is known as the Inciting Incident or, as I call it, the Story Spark (which will be literal in the episode The Witch).

Most Buffy episodes are about 42-44 minutes long – standard for network television at the time.

In almost every episode, we'll see the Story Spark somewhere between 4 and 5 minutes in. That makes Buffy a great show to watch to study how seasoned writers quickly get their stories moving in an engaging way.

The One-Quarter Twist

The first major plot turn in any story should spin it in a new direction. Typically whatever does that comes from outside the protagonist. In most movies and novels (at least in commercial fiction, but often in literary fiction as well) you will find this turn right around one quarter of the way through. Thus, my very creative naming of it as the One-Quarter Twist.

Now and then in Buffy, and in other television shows, you'll see that major plot turn come just a little bit later, more like around one third through the story. Either way, though, it comes from outside the protagonist. Usually, it makes life harder for her.

The Midpoint

It's common to hear advice that conflict needs to escalate throughout the story. That's great advice as far as it goes.

But it can also lead to seeing plot as simply "and then this happens and this happens and this happens...."

As a result, a lot of writers find their plot losing steam at the middle of a novel, screenplay, or other story. They may have a great beginning and a great ending, and perhaps a first major plot turn. But they're just not sure how to get from there to the end. Conflict may be escalating, but they feel bored. (A guarantee that the audience will be bored.)

If you look at a well-structured story, though, you will almost always find one of two things at its midpoint. Either the protagonist commits fully to the quest, often throwing caution to the wind, or the protagonist suffers a major reversal. In some of my favorite stories, including the pilot of Buffy, both things happen.

This type of strong midpoint drives the story forward. It also ensures that the protagonist takes action rather than being batted about by outside forces. That's key to readers or audience members engaging with and caring about your protagonist and, by extension, your story.

The Three-Quarter Turn

Unlike the first major plot turn, which comes from outside the protagonist, the next major plot turn grows from the protagonist's action. Specifically, the commitment at the Midpoint or the response to the Midpoint reversal.

Like that first plot turn, though, the Three-Quarter Turn also spins the story in yet another new direction. This, too, helps keep the plot engaging and exciting rather than simply escalating the same type of conflict over and over.

As you probably guessed, I call it the Three-Quarter Turn because it typically happens about three quarters of the way through the story. In some books or television episodes, though, you will see it around two thirds of the way through.

The Climax

The climax is the culmination of the main plot. The protagonist wins (sometimes at a great cost) or loses, the antagonist is defeated, sometimes to return another day, or prevails. One way or another, the main plot ends.

Falling Action

We then have the Falling Action. That is the end of the

story where we tie up all the loose ends and any subplots that didn't resolve during or before the climax.

Sometimes here we also see a game changer. This is something that happens that significantly changes the landscape going forward.

Other Key Story Elements

In addition to the above plot points and turns, in each Buffy episode I'll talk about subplots, character development, theme, and other story elements. And, of course, dialogue.

Okay, let's dive into the Hellmouth. Starting with Season One, Episode One, Welcome to the Hellmouth.

CHAPTER TWO

WELCOME TO THE HELLMOUTH

This chapter talks about Welcome to the Hellmouth, Part 1 of the pilot, written by Joss Whedon and directed by Charles Martin Smith.

In particular, we'll look at:

- **A prologue that sets the tone**
- **An opening conflict that signals the show's theme**
- **Keeping exposition compelling by revealing it through conflict**
- **How Buffy commits to her quest at the Midpoint and suffers an immediate reversal**
- **Keeping the stakes high (no pun intended)**

Okay, let's dive into the Hellmouth.

A Prologue That Subverts Tropes

We start with what looks like two high school students breaking into a high school. Neither of these two characters is the protagonist. The events here come before the story starts, which is what makes this a prologue.

The girl seems nervous. The boy is reassuring her and kind of luring her further into the high school, which is deserted. She keeps saying, "I think I hear something," or "are you sure there's no one here?"

He's the one who seems so confident about being here and wanting to get her alone. Then it all turns on its head, and the girl goes into vamp face and attacks him.

So immediately we have this subverting of the horror movie trope. Even though we don't see Buffy, we do see that this is going to be part of what this show is — or the heart of what the show is. This pretty blonde who we traditionally had thought of as the victim becomes the one whom others fear.

And then we cut.

There is a lot of controversy among authors and readers about the use of prologues. Because by definition they come before our story starts. As a reader I sometimes have to push myself to read a book with a prologue.

Because I know if I become really engaged with these characters and this story it's going to end shortly and yank me into probably a different time. Maybe a different place. Very likely totally different characters.

Often, however, we see an antagonist in the prologue. Here, Darla (the girl) is part of what I would call the antagonistic force. The Master is our overall antagonist.

One author at a writing conference that I went to said he

does use prologues in his books, but he always calls them Chapter One. Probably to avoid people like me who look at a prologue and say, "Oh, I don't I don't know if I want to read that."

All that being said, here I think the prologue is very nicely done.

It serves a purpose of telling us the tone of the series. Because it is horror, and it's a little bit funny because it is not what we're expecting.

Dramatic Irony

The prologue here also creates dramatic irony. That occurs when the audience or reader knows something that our protagonist doesn't. We will see Darla later, and we as the audience will know she's a vampire. But the character talking to her does not know that. So it creates tension because we're aware that Darla is a threat.

On the side of those who might say you don't need this prologue, you truly could, other than that dramatic irony, lift this prologue right out. It would not make any difference to the plot. We would certainly figure out that there are vampires. We see this boy's dead body fall out of a locker later. And we would infer what happened, though we wouldn't know it was Darla.

Opening Conflict And Exposition

On to our opening conflict, which is the first point that I look at when I'm starting a story. Or if I'm examining someone else's to see how well it works for me.

First, we see Buffy having nightmares. This is the one place where I find the exposition just a little bit clunky because we have these vampires, these crosses, this imagery that doesn't move our plot forward. That being said, because it's the beginning of the series, I think this works.

In the DVD commentaries, I think it's in an interview

with Joss Whedon, he talks about how he did this because it was a way to sum up the events of the movie for those people who had not seen it.

(I had seen it. I thought it was kind of fun, but it wouldn't necessarily have drawn me back into the show. But a friend who is a screenwriter, and who knows what kind of things I like, worked at Warner Brothers at the time. He kept saying to me, "I think you would really like this show." And I loved it obviously or I wouldn't be doing the Buffy and the Art of Story podcast.)

One thing I really love about that nightmare sequence is that Buffy wakes up and we as viewers are expecting her to be afraid about the nightmares.

In fact, we find out almost immediately what she's afraid about is the first day of high school.

Exposition Through Conflict: Buffy And Joyce

We then get some wonderful exposition with Buffy and Joyce (Buffy's mom). Joyce drops Buffy off at school. She is mostly reassuring Buffy, saying she thinks Buffy will do great and this is going to be a good school.

But as Buffy gets out of the car, Joyce says, "Honey, try not to get kicked out."

And Buffy says, "I promise."

This so nicely gives us that back story of Buffy having been kicked out. It also tells us a lot about the relationship between these two. Joyce is being supportive, and yet she is worried about Buffy. And she does throw in this comment, which is something of a criticism, obviously pointing out to Buffy something that Buffy knows.

But she does it in a playful way.

So I don't get the sense that this is ongoing — Joyce angry at Buffy or expecting her to fail. She's just saying, "hey, be careful." Buffy's response tells us that she takes it that way because she says, "I promise."

It also tells us Buffy really wants to do well at this new school. She does not want to have confrontation with her mom. She wants her mom to be happy with her.

So it tells us a lot about both of them.

Exposition Through Conflict: Principal Flutie

We then move to Buffy and Principal Flutie. It's another great example of working in exposition while moving the story forward.

And Principal Flutie, I love him as a character. Because we see that he wants to be this great principal who is on the students' side. He wants to be on Buffy's side. And he's telling her she has a clean slate; she got kicked out of her old school, but she gets a fresh start here. He says, "We want to serve you."

And yet we get this internal conflict. That is shown by Flutie's actions when he looks at why she got kicked out and sees that she burned down the gym.

He is still saying these kinds of supportive things, but his tone changes. And while he previously was ripping up her paper record about her old school to demonstrate how she has this fresh start, now he's taping it back together.

Buffy in response is trying to explain what happened. We get her internal conflict with being the Slayer but having to cover that up. And we see how much she wants to get along and do well in this school and how hard it is for her.

She starts to say, "You know, that gym was filled with vampires," and switches to "asbestos."

And this tells us how much Buffy really wants to be seen as that girl that she was before this happened. She wants to be able to explain to the principal. But she knows that she can't. So she is stuck with being in this spot where people see her as a potential danger.

Principal Flutie wants to support her, but he also has a responsibility to his other students. And this student coming in who burnt down her gym is a danger.

So we've got the conflict between the two of them.

Internal Conflict

And we have each of their internal conflicts. Even though Principal Flutie is talking about things that Buffy knows — that she got kicked out and she burned down the gym — there is a narrative purpose for that to come out.

That's the difference between a compelling scene where we learn about these characters and we move the story forward and a scene that screeches to a halt and just tells us stuff we need to know. The latter would be something like:

"As you know Buffy, you burnt down the gym at your old school."

"Yes, Principal Flutie. I know that and I'm very sorry."

That would do the same thing. But it would not be very interesting. We probably wouldn't be engaged with it.

The next few scenes continue to move us up to our one-quarter point in the story. So the opening conflict needs to be enough that it propels the character forward to that plot turn.

More Obstacles For Buffy

Before we get there, we're going to see Buffy encountering more obstacles. Mainly with school.

We see her meet Cordelia. Cordelia initially is very nice to Buffy but mean to Willow at the water fountain. She criticizes her clothes. Willow basically runs away.

We see this conflict for Buffy here because she's been enjoying talking to Cordelia. She's been feeling like she's fitting in. She seems happy. And then she sees Cordelia be mean to Willow, and Buffy's face shows that she's uncomfortable with that.

Now Buffy goes to the library, pursuing her goal of fitting in at school. She is going to get textbooks. Giles instead gives her the vampire book.

Her interactions with Giles show that she is a reluctant hero. The story structure of The Hero's Journey involves our hero getting a call to action and rejecting the call. And we see Buffy do that here. Because initially she is just walking out on the vampire book and saying, "No, that is not what I came here for," and leaving.

Story Spark Or Inciting Incident

Next we have what I call the Story Spark. Which is also known as the Inciting Incident.

It's what sets the main plot in motion. It typically happens about 10% into the story, which is what we see here. We see this boy's dead body fall out of a locker.

And who tells Buffy about it? Cordelia.

This is a wonderful choice for tension. Because it goes right to the heart of what Buffy is struggling with.

She wants to be friends with Cordelia. And yet when Cordelia tells her about the "extreme dead guy" in the locker, despite having insisted to Giles that she does not want to be the Slayer, Buffy immediately asks all these questions about the death.

Cordelia finds her morbid. This is the beginning of that process of alienating Cordelia from Buffy.

So this is the Inciting Incident where the vampire world intrudes into Buffy's normal life. She now has to face a specific threat, not just the abstract idea of taking up her Vampire Slayer duties.

Heading Toward The One-Quarter Twist

The one-quarter point in a well-structured story usually

comes from outside of the protagonist and spins the story in a new direction.

Here, Buffy is unaware of what is being put in motion. It is the Master's plan. He is this very powerful vampire. And he is trapped underground and wants to get out. There is this moment, this mystical upheaval. This is the one time that the Master can get out if he does certain things. We don't know specifically what they are yet. But right around the one-quarter point of our two-episode arc, so 20 to 22 minutes in of an 84-minute or so story, we see a few things happening.

We see the Master in his lair. How powerful he is. We see Luke. He's this powerful vampire who is going to try to raise the Master. We have Giles talking about a mystical upheaval.

And we have Angel, who comes in and talks about the Harvest.

Buffy's Progress

Even before that, though, we get more events that are pushing Buffy towards accepting her duties as a Slayer. The main one being this dead body falling out of the locker. And we see immediately a slight change in Buffy. Or maybe it's more than slight.

She's been trying so hard to fit in, but now when she hears about this dead guy, she starts asking: "Well, how did he die?" All these details that make Cordelia think that Buffy is really strange.

Buffy just ignores that, goes to the gym, and looks at the body. She sees that he has been bitten and knows that yes, there are vampires here. It's not just the creepy new librarian.

She goes back to the library to tell Giles what happened.

He says to her, "Well, I thought you didn't care." She tells him she doesn't, and that's what she came to tell him. (It's much better dialogue than that because it's Joss Whedon, but that is the push and pull there.)

So again, we have Giles pushing her to accept her duties. And she is pushing back and saying, "No, I am not going to do this."

A Personal One-Quarter Twist

Around that one-quarter point we also see a personal turn that spins the story in the new direction for Buffy. Up to that point it has been all about school. Doing well her first day, talking to Principal Flutie, trying to make friends.

But at the one-quarter point we see her struggling with what to wear to go to the Bronze. This is a new social setting. We get her saying to herself, "I used to be so good at this."

So we know that she also personally feels she has lost some of her social skills.

She heads for the Bronze. That's when Angel intercepts her on the way and talks about the Harvest. She doesn't know what this is yet, but it is another part of that turn that is going to spin the story.

So now it is not going to be about just one vampire being killed. It is about Luke's and the Master's plan to bring about the Harvest. Buffy from this point to the Midpoint will be reacting to that plan despite that she doesn't know exactly what it is.

We next see Buffy at the Bronze.

She's talking to Willow. I love this about Buffy because she really wants to be Willow's friend and hang out with her even though she first came to Willow for help with homework. Cordelia and Willow are not in the same social circle. But Buffy doesn't care.

She and Willow have his conversation about seizing the day. Buffy encourages Willow to get out and talk to boys and says, "What's the point of being so shy because tomorrow you might die."

And she means that literally. Willow of course doesn't know that.

Buffy sees Giles and leaves Willow to talk to him. And he is again pushing her to take up her Slayer duties. She's rejecting that until she looks down and she sees Willow dancing with a vampire. And Buffy has to react to that.

Pressure On Buffy

There are two things going on here that propel Buffy forward. One is the Master's and Luke's plan. They have sent vampires in to gather people so that the Master can feed and become stronger.

So it is directly the Master's plan to get Willow. Obviously, he doesn't know who Willow is. But she is one of the people swept up in the net.

We also have this amazing internal pressure on Buffy. Because she is the one who encouraged Willow to go out there and talk to boys. That is why Willow is out there dancing. Giles says something like, "What's she doing?" Buffy says either "seizing the moment" or "seizing the day." So we know that Buffy feels this personal responsibility.

And this is part of what I mean by the protagonist still reacting. Because it's not that Buffy changes her mind and says, "Okay, I'm going to go forward and be the Slayer." But she reacts because she's a decent person.

We have to think any even somewhat decent person, having accidentally put someone else in peril, would try to save that person. Particularly when, like Buffy, she has the power to do that. And at this point Buffy is still thinking she's dealing with one vampire.

In fact, she says, "One vampire I can handle."

So she is going to go and save Willow.

Putting Characters In Peril

This is also something that Joss Whedon talks about in the DVD scene-by-scene commentary. He says they have to put Buffy's friends in peril because Buffy is so strong and she's the hero. It's hard to put her in peril all the time. We certainly do it to some extent. But the audience is not for the most part going to believe that Buffy is going to lose big time or die because it's her show.

So they have to put Buffy's friends in peril.

He also commented they have to put Buffy in peril emotionally because it's hard to put her in physical peril. And there will be more of that in the future. I'll talk about it at the time. Sometimes I have some trouble with how that emotional peril is done.

Also, Joss Whedon commented that they learned early on that putting Willow in peril was a surefire way to engage the audience. Not just physical peril, but when Willow is hurt emotionally. Partly because Alyson Hannigan (the actress who plays Willow) is so good at showing that.

So we have Buffy still essentially in reaction mode going after Willow. And she encounters Xander. I'm going to talk more about the characterization of Xander and Willow and Cordelia in the next chapter because there's just so much to cover here. I promise I will get to that.

Xander goes along with Buffy and they get to the crypt. And Buffy encounters these vampires.

Commitment And Reversal At The Midpoint

And we finally have, as Buffy is fighting, that Midpoint where the protagonist commits to her quest. That typically happens in a strong Midpoint. We see the protagonist making a vow, throwing caution to the wind, going all-in after her quest for the Holy Grail or whatever it is. Or we see the character suffer a reversal.

We can also see both happen. A commitment and a reversal for the protagonist. We're going to see both here.

So Buffy commits in a couple ways.

One is by her words. Until the Midpoint (which comes at the end of this part of the pilot), throughout this episode Buffy has been pushing her Slayer identity away. She's hiding it. Saying "I don't want that" to Giles. "I don't want to do this." She only is drawn in reluctantly. She goes in to help Willow, but she has not embraced it.

And she expresses frustration that people know about her identity. That Giles knows knows she's a Slayer. When Xander says, "Oh because you might have to slay the vampires," she says something like, "What, did they put out an APB?"

She is very upset that she can't come in to this new school and just be a normal girl. That people know she's the Slayer.

The Midpoint of Welcome to the Hellmouth

But now when Buffy's facing these vampires and she's saving her new friend, the vampires are surprised. Darla is surprised by Buffy being strong compared with her. And Buffy says, "Don't you know who I am?"

I love this moment because it is her saying, "Yes, I am the Slayer, Don't you know who I am?"

Also, it's the first time we actually see Buffy fighting vampires. I picked up on that when I watched. What I didn't notice until I listened to the scene-by-scene DVD commentary is it is also the first time we see her dust a vampire.

(I guess that's obvious because it's the first time we see her fight. But because I've seen the series and rewatched it so many times, that didn't really have the same impact that it probably did on first viewing.)

So this is Buffy embracing who she is. Becoming the Slayer again. Then immediately we get a reversal.

Because she says, "Don't you know who I am?" And behind her is Luke, but she doesn't hear him. Despite Slayer senses that we've already heard a bit about, she doesn't hear him. She doesn't pick up on him being there.

And Luke says, "I don't care."

They fight. He throws her into the coffin, lunges on top of her, is about to bite her. We don't see a way she's going to get out. And cut. Cliffhanger. To Be Continued.

So Buffy has suffered this major reversal. She has been overpowered by this vampire when up to this point she has been almost casual and cocky about it. So I think this is just amazing storytelling and such a strong Midpoint.

The Middle Of Your Story

Part of why I love this strong Midpoint in the pilot episode is because the halfway mark in a novel was something that I certainly struggled with when I was a new writer. And not just as a new writer.

Many writers struggle with it.

You hear people talk about the saggy middle or the soggy middle. And here you see this example of this strong Midpoint commitment and reversal that's so dramatic. It definitely grabs us and keeps us engaged, which is really good because back when this series aired I'm pretty sure you had to wait a whole other week for the second part.

Why I Include DVD Commentary Highlights

Before spoilers, I want to talk about a couple other things from the DVD commentary.

If you're watching streaming, I don't think there's any way to access these commentaries. As a writer, I find them so valuable, particularly for Buffy. I have listened to or watched DVD features for other shows, including scene-by-scene commentary, and it is not always that insightful.

But with the Buffy ones, I learn so much. Because the

commentaries are by the writers or directors, including Joss Whedon. You really get insight into how they put together Buffy. Why they made the choices that they did. Including production issues that I would not have guessed at, not knowing that much about how TV shows are produced.

So I love these features and that's why I include them in the podcast. If you want to get the DVDs, you can look at the links in the show notes for each episode. But I will try to tell you what I think is most useful from them.

Or just fun and interesting.

Why A Hellmouth

Joss commented on why Sunnydale is on a Hellmouth. That was his answer to, "Why does everything happen in Sunnydale?"

And the reason I like that is I feel like a lot of horror stories or mysteries don't really have an explanation for that. Some will kind of make a joke about it. Like the small town where there are so many murders per capita because that's where our amateur sleuth happens to live.

It's somewhat of a convention of the genre. You just have to go with it.

If you like reading a particular series or watching it, that's okay. Yeah, it's not realistic but we're going to go with it because we love this character and the setting. So we're going to imagine that this many murders would happen in this one place.

But I love that in Buffy they gave a reason for it: that we're on a Hellmouth. And that's also why you're going to get all kinds of monsters, not just vampires.

High School Characters

The other thing from a writing perspective that Joss said: He thought people over high school age still respond to Buffy because, in his words, "I don't think you ever get over high school."

I think that's a really interesting observation. I was in law school when I was watching Buffy. And I found it just as engaging and fun, even though high school was obviously far behind me. And I'm sure many people who were older than that also really liked Buffy.

Also on the DVD, if you are going to get the set, there is an interview with Joss Whedon and David Boreanaz about Angel and Buffy. But it's an overview of Season One, so there are spoilers in there. So just proceed with caution. They must have assumed that everyone who bought the DVD set had already watched the show. (Probably that was a safe assumption at the time.) But I was a little surprised when watching that they had spoilers.

Spoilers

HERE WE ARE with our spoilers for Welcome To The Hellmouth.

Story Questions About Angel

Very minor point on Angel. Well, it's a major spoiler but a minor hint at it. When he and Buffy first meet, she pins him. He says, "I don't bite." Apparently some people started already thinking he might be a vampire.

I have to say that did not occur to me. I wondered who he was. But I think that's the point.

He's this mysterious stranger. We want to know what his deal is. But I did not think he was a vampire then. I did think when he was kind of stalking Buffy and following her that he might be a vampire. But when she pinned him and he didn't go into vamp face, and he at least seemed to be trying to help her, I didn't think he was a vampire.

So I was very surprised in the episode where that's revealed. I was completely drawn in by that.

Buffy, Giles, And Foreshadowing

I love the Buffy and Giles scene. Well, I love all the Buffy and Giles scenes. But one in particular where he says to her, "I don't understand why you won't take up your Slayer duties again. You've done it before."

And he's talking about his role as the Watcher and says, "I'm there to prepare you." And she says, "Prepare me for what? To get kicked out of school? To lose all my friends?" She goes through this list of what she has lost. It's another example of great exposition coming out through conflict because this is a genuine and real conflict between her and Giles.

It is also a foreshadowing.

It foreshadows their conversation in the season finale where she overhears him telling Angel about the prophecy. That she'll face the Master and she will die. And she says something to him like, "Read me my fortune." She's basically saying the same thing, something like: "What good are you? How can you help me? I'm sixteen. I have to face this, and I don't want to die."

So it's the same kind of conversation, the same dynamic. But it is ratcheted up times a hundred in the finale. And I love the season arc we have with the two of them, how she comes to trust him and rely on him.

They have this great relationship.

Yet there is still this dynamic that they in a way cannot ever get around. Because she is always the one in the forefront fighting. He is always the one in the background helping. While he becomes more active in that role, he can't step into her shoes. And they will always have that despite a great respect and love for one another.

It's something that cannot be fixed. She will always be in danger of dying. And it will always be his role to try to prepare her as best he can. Yet it is not within his power to completely protect her. He is the protector and yet there is this limit.

A great recipe for conflict.

So I love that we get that in the very first episode. And then we see its most extreme form in that season finale.

Keeping The Stakes High

We have this signal of what the show will be in that Jesse gets killed. Initially we think that he will be one of the gang. He seems like maybe he's going to be this ongoing character, and he gets killed.

Which tells us that everyone is at risk.

In the commentaries Joss said he had wanted to have a credit sequence with Jesse in it to further emphasize that. And then a second sequence after the pilot where there is no Jesse. But there weren't the funds to do two credit sequences.

He also commented on how the idea that no one is safe is done in an even stronger way when Principal Flutie is killed several episodes in. Because we really think he's going to be an ongoing character right from the start.

He has that back-and-forth with Buffy. We like him. We see him a few more times and Wham, he's gone. And so we know that there is this great tension here because people can die. And remember that wasn't something that Joss Whedon was known for at that point.

Now, we might expect that going into a show by him or a movie by him.

But at that time this was new. And I think it was fairly new in television at the time as well. The network wasn't going to allow a core character to be killed off. This is particularly important in a show where you have a protagonist whom the show is named for. The show is Buffy the Vampire Slayer.

You're not going to have the main character die because the show goes away then. So that lowers the tension and fear on the part of the audience.

Killing off someone we think is a core character ratchets that fear up again. And of course Joss will subvert even that trope of you can't kill the main character.

I think we do see this even in the opening episode. We get that clue that, hey, this is a writer who is going to undermine those expectations. And there are times when viewers are going to be very unhappy about that.

Okay, that is it for our spoiler and foreshadowing section. Thank you for staying with me.

Questions For Your Writing

- **Does your first scene (whether it's a prologue or not) quickly convey the tone and genre of your piece? If not, can you revise it so that it does?**
- **Examine anywhere in your story that includes exposition that comes in through dialogue. Are your characters telling each other things they already know? Are they merely giving one another information?**
- **If yes to either question, can you revise**

using genuine character conflict to bring out the information?
- **What type of major commitment can or does your protagonist make in your story?**

Next: The Harvest

NEXT IS THE HARVEST, the second half of the pilot. I'll talk more about the Midpoint and will cover the remaining major plot turns. We'll also cover character development for some of our favorite characters: Xander, Willow, Cordelia, plus a little more about Buffy's character.

CHAPTER THREE

THE HARVEST

THIS CHAPTER TALKS about The Harvest, the second half of the pilot episode, written by Joss Whedon and directed by John T. Kretchmer.

In particular, we'll look at:

- **Doubling down on the Midpoint Commitment**
- **Showing a character's vulnerability and strengths**
- **More exposition through strong conflict**
- **How the plot turn at the three-quarter point grows from the Midpoint**
- **Story questions in the Falling Action to keep the audience hooked**

Okay, let's dive into the Hellmouth.

THE MIDPOINT

The Harvest picks up right at the Midpoint. So, remember, the protagonist at the Midpoint typically throws caution to the wind and goes all in on her quest or suffers a reversal or both.

We saw both last time. Buffy embraced being the Slayer both in her words and her actions, doing her first dusting and saying, "Don't you know who I am?"

She then immediately suffers a reversal when Luke comes from behind her. She doesn't hear him. He says, "I don't care." And he throws her into this coffin. He's about to kill her and — cut.

We pick up right there in The Harvest.

Buffy is able to push Luke away partly because of that cross she's wearing that Angel gave her. Which she chose to wear. But I like to think regardless she would have found a way to get Luke off of her.

However, she isn't able to kill him or pursue him. He disappears. She goes after the other vampires to try to get Jesse and Willow back. Xander is with her.

They're able to save Willow but not Jesse. So he has been taken away with the vampires within a few minutes of the Midpoint at the start of this episode.

Buffy Affirms Her Commitment

We see Buffy in the library, and she further affirms her commitment now to being the Slayer. She says Jesse is her responsibility.

No one else is going to go after him because she's the one who got him killed. I'm pretty sure she says killed even though we don't know yet that Jesse has been killed. But she is going to go after him. And she is definitely at this point embracing being the Slayer and feeling guilty for not doing it sooner. No doubt thinking that maybe she would have been able to prevent this.

From this point on Buffy drives the story forward rather than just reacting to what is happening around her.

Story Questions

Our next major Buffy scene is in the crypt again. She has figured out that Luke must have come from a passageway in it.

We see her encounter Angel. Once more this scene doesn't really move the plot forward. He doesn't tell her enough to make a big difference. In some ways, it's just Angel showing up being cryptic. You could really lift this right out of the episode and it wouldn't change anything.

And yet the scene works because it does move the subplot. It may be an exaggeration to call it an episode subplot. But I would say it is a season subplot of Buffy and Angel and how they will interact. What will their relationship be?

These are strong story questions. Who is Angel? What is the deal with him?

There is chemistry between them. But is that a good thing? A bad thing? Is anything going to happen with that or is he just going to show up and give information and disappear?

The other thing that happens here, which for me makes the scene compelling, is we have a little more than just the Buffy-Angel chemistry question. We get a little insight into who he is.

Character Development: Angel

Buffy makes this sarcastic comment about, "Do you know what it's like to have a friend?" The way Angel responds – the silence, the look on his face – shows that he doesn't. Buffy realizes that, and it is the first time that we see Angel vulnerable.

Up to this point when we've seen him at all, he has seemed very in control.

He's only sharing what he wants to share. He's not letting Buffy know very much about him. But here he reacts, and he can't help it. He is vulnerable, and this is part of what makes us like a character and engage with a character.

So that also, at least for me, makes that scene engaging and is why I would not want to see it lifted out of the story. Despite that for the main plot we don't need it.

And I love that. As a writer, because I write genre fiction (thrillers and suspense), generally I'm really trying to make each scene move the story forward. That's what helps keep a fast pace. At the same time, this scene shows there is a place for a quiet scene that shows a relationship developing. As long as there is enough tension within the scene to keep it interesting in itself, every single scene does not have to move that main plot or even a clearly defined subplot.

(Because, as I mentioned, at this point there isn't really a Buffy-Angel story arc for this pilot episode.)

Characterization: Xander

We also get to learn quite a bit about Xander in the first half of the pilot. When we meet Xander, he is a bit awkward. He says the wrong thing. He's aware he says the wrong thing.

Also, we see that Xander is very loyal.

Most of that first episode he's focused on trying to impress Buffy, seemingly mainly just because she's the new girl and she's cute. Also we see him skeptical when he overhears her and Giles talking about her being the Slayer. And when Buffy says she has to find Willow and he says, "Oh, 'cause you might have to slay a vampire."

But as soon as he grasps that Willow is truly in danger, all that goes out the window. And he is right there. He's not caring about how Buffy's pretty, and he's got to impress her. He's not caring that he doesn't believe in the whole idea of vampires.

He is right there to help Willow.

We see that again, and perhaps more so, with Jesse. Now he knows Jesse is in danger. He has seen the vampires and he wants to help. And he does help. He goes down into the tunnels.

And this is where we see that Xander also is courageous because while he's petrified, and he really has no particular skills to offer, he still goes down into the tunnels.

I love that he is self-aware about that. We also see his humor come through. Buffy asks if he brought anything with to help fight. And he says, "You know, the part of my brain that would have told me to bring those things was too busy telling me not to do this."

This makes Xander a person we can identify with because it really speaks to those times when we plow ahead with something that we know is a bad idea, and we're little bit in denial about that, and it keeps us from being fully prepared for what we're doing.

We also see another aspect of Xander. His very deep insecurity and strong feelings of inadequacy. Because, yes, he follows Buffy because of loyalty. But he also responds to her saying, "Look I do this, not you, because I'm the Slayer" by saying something like, "I knew you were going to throw that back at me."

That applies to everybody, that's not a specific thing to Xander. Buffy's the Slayer and nobody else is. Yet to him it feels very personal. He also links it with masculinity. He says something like, "I'm not enough of a man."

He's I think a sophomore in high school at this time. Most

adolescents are struggling with questions like: What does it mean to be an adult? How do I become an adult?

Often that also is tied up with gender and sexuality. So it's probably not unique to Xander that he has these fears, these feelings of inadequacy that he relates to what it means to be a man. But the fact that Buffy being a Slayer stirs this up when really that's so unrelated to any of those things tells us a lot about Xander.

More Exposition Through Conflict

Xander and Buffy in the tunnel is another great example of getting exposition in through conflict. In a tense situation, Buffy explains more of the rules of how to slay vampires to Xander. Including this line I love where she says there was the football player, and he'd been turned into a vampire, and she beheads him with "a little little exacto knife."

It's such a great line. It's sort of funny, and it tells us more about Buffy's strength, what she can do. And how the vampires can be killed.

All within this very tense time because at any moment they could encounter vampires. Xander is definitely vulnerable. Buffy is reassuring him.

So again, there is a reason for her to be telling him these things. He does not know them, and he may need to know them in a second or two.

Character Development: Willow

Also, we have some really nice Willow characterization.

We see her in the computer lab. Cordelia is commenting on Buffy, saying bad things about her. And Willow – who did not previously stick up for herself with Cordelia in the first episode — does stick up for Buffy. Plus she gets revenge by tricking Cordelia into deleting the computer program she's working on.

In the commentary Joss said he saw this as Willow's first

empowering moment, and it shows the beginning of her character arc and the influence of her friendship with Buffy. Not just that Buffy encourages her to be less timid generally. But because Willow has been through this experience with the vampires with Buffy and has survived. So she feels more confidence.

Which brings us to Cordelia.

Character Development: Cordelia And Buffy

In these two episodes, there is a lot of Cordelia as the classic mean girl. So she doesn't have a lot of layers in this pilot.

We see her being very nice to Buffy. And Cordelia is popular. She has friends who follow her around. She is a foil for Buffy. We get this sense, even if we didn't know the story already, that Buffy was kind of a Cordelia. One of the popular girls. I like to think Buffy was not a mean girl, though, because of the way she reacts when Cordelia treats Willow the way she does.

Also, Buffy then makes a point that she is going to be friends with Willow whether Cordelia likes it or not, even though Buffy clearly does want Cordelia to like her. Buffy is very upset when in the Bronze she is looking for Willow, and she almost stakes Cordelia. Cordelia says, "I have to call everybody I know."

Buffy's upset about that. She comments to Giles about her social life being on the critical list.

So Buffy does care, but she is still going to be friends with Willow.

Cordelia, though, does something in this pilot that I really like. Whether I picked up on it the first time I watched I'm not sure. But I see it as I look back on it and see her interacting with Jesse.

Jesse As A Foil For Xander

Just as Cordelia is a foil for Buffy, I see Jesse as a foil for Xander.

They both are obsessed with the new girl. And the initial attraction seems to be just it's a new girl and she's pretty. It's not about who Buffy is.

Likewise, all we really see from Jesse is he is pursuing Cordelia. We don't get any sense of that it's about who Cordelia is as a person. Maybe it is, maybe it's not. All we see is him very aggressively encroaching on her space, saying obnoxious things, not taking a hint, not listening when she is clearly saying, "Get away from me. I am not interested in you."

So in that sense, I see Jesse as the stepped-up version of the things that we don't love about Xander.

And Jesse is the unaware version. Xander says to Buffy when he first meets her, "Can I have you?" And he meant to say, "Can I help you?" He feels awkward and embarrassed that he said, "Can I have you?"

Jesse seems beyond embarrassment. He says things to Cordelia, he keeps pursuing her though she's not interested, and he doesn't seem to have self-awareness about that.

Cordelia's Strengths

What I like about Cordelia is that she is so clear. I feel like all of us have had those moments where we have what's going in our head and we don't say it because we think that will be too mean. Or someone is approaching us — particularly for women and girls (this must happen to non-females as well, but I'm primarily familiar with it from talking to other girls and women) – which is where a guy comes up to you, and you are not interested. Most of us have had that happen on a bus or on the street.

And there is this line to walk. You need to push this person away because you don't want to encourage him to hang around and to stay there. Yet if you are too insistent, you are too cutting, even too clear, there could be a violent reaction.

So it is kind of fun to watch Cordelia just shut Jesse down. To see her say, basically, "I am not putting up with this guy who keeps coming over, who is encroaching on my space and doesn't want to take no for an answer."

After The Midpoint

All of this has grown from the Midpoint. Specifically, from Buffy's commitment at the Midpoint to go after Jesse and do everything she can to save him and prevent more harm.

She goes down into the tunnel. Xander follows her because she made the decision to do that. The Master also acts in response to Buffy's commitment. Because remember he and Luke are talking. The Master is upset that Luke, Darla, and the others have not brought back more humans for him to feed off of. And Luke says there was a girl. "She fought me and she lived." He and the Master agree that Buffy probably is the Slayer.

This is the first time they have faced a Slayer in a long time.

The fact that Buffy embraced being the Slayer and fought off Luke triggers the Master to turn Jesse into bait instead of feeding off him.

Buffy is already coming down into the tunnels, and she doesn't know this has been done. The key is she will think Jesse is still human, and he will be able to lead her into a place of more danger. Which is exactly what happens.

All of this has grown from Buffy's actions at the Midpoint.

In a well-structured story like this we see that strong Midpoint propelling the story forward, the protagonist's action propelling the story forward, to the Three-Quarter Turn. And here that is exactly what happens.

From the Midpoint to the three-quarter point the mission is to save Jesse.

Everything is done in pursuit of that. And then it all changes.

The Three-Quarter Turn

Right around 20-22 minutes into this episode, which would be about 62 minutes into the roughly 86-minute double episode arc, Xander and Buffy are in a tight space in the tunnel. Jesse vamps out. So he has turned into a vampire, and is now going to help the other vampires trap them.

The entire story shifts because we can't save Jesse anymore.

First Buffy and Xander have to survive and get away, which they do. They barely get out. Now they move forward, and none of it is about saving Jesse. It is all about stopping the Harvest.

So the Harvest has been there in the background. But now that becomes the new mission, the driving force.

Quick side note on Jesse becoming bait: in the commentary Joss Whedon notes that this was done to answer the question that often comes up in horror movies, which is why doesn't the villain just kill this person?

Why doesn't the villain just kill Jesse?

Making him bait, having the Master have a reason for doing that, gives us a narrative reason for Jesse to survive up until the climax. So we can have that moment between Jesse and Xander. And it isn't just, oh, the Master didn't feel like killing him that day.

Now that Buffy and Xander have gotten away, we're again in the library with Giles.

He's explaining how the Harvest works. That Luke is the

vessel and the more Luke feeds the stronger the Master gets. All so the Master can break free and roam the Earth. And probably kill everybody.

So now it is about stopping that from happening. This is the one time when this particular ritual to free the Master can be performed. The group needs to figure out where this will likely happen. They decide it must be the Bronze. That's where you would have so many people that could be fed off of.

Buffy says she has to go home to get supplies, and we have her encounter with her mom.

Joyce As An Obstacle

Throughout this two-episode arc, Buffy has encountered obstacle after obstacle. Her mother now is one of the last obstacles to get where she needs to go.

Getting supplies is that sort of mechanical device that gets Buffy to the place where she has this confrontation with her mom.

What I love about the way this is done is that the supplies aren't just – Buffy doesn't just get home and we forget about them. We see her get them. And we get this nice metaphor of Buffy lifting out the top of her trunk. It has all her sort of day-to-day things, the Buffy the high school student things.

She lifts it out and underneath are all these supplies for killing vampires. This really shows very nicely Buffy's hidden life.

She takes all those supplies to the Bronze. She gives them to her friends and they do use them in the climax.

I like this so much because as writers, we all sometimes need to insert something to get our character, usually our protagonist (though maybe the antagonist), from one place to the next so that the next scene can happen.

It's that connective tissue that brings us from point A to

B. And it can feel like we shouldn't need to bring in something artificial. We shouldn't need to think up something to take the character from this point to the next.

But this shows that, yes, that is perfectly fine. As long as that device has a narrative purpose. As long as we make it pay off, and here it does.

Now we have another scene that is this wonderful conflict.

Because it could easily have been just angry mom who's mad at Buffy and grounds her. Because Joyce got a call from the principal and on her very first day Buffy has already skipped class.

That would be a legitimate conflict because it would be very real. It comes out of the story.

Buffy did skip class. Her mom doesn't know why, and it's not that unreasonable for her to get angry.

But instead we get something so much more interesting, nuanced, and layered. Joyce says she got a call from the principal that Buffy already skipped class and "we just got here."

When Buffy says she needs to go out, Joyce doesn't just say you're grounded, you're punished. She says, "No. The tapes say that I need to learn to say No."

So Joyce has been listening to parenting tapes. (Which would be audiobooks if it were being made now.) She says she's listening to these parenting tapes. She also says she's read about the dangers of over-nurturing.

We learn from this that Joyce cares about being a good parent.

She is making an effort. She's listening to tapes. She's reading. Probably she feels guilty that something about the way she was parenting caused or contributed to Buffy getting into trouble, getting kicked out of school. And she really wants to do something better or different for her daughter.

She wants to be a better mom. So this isn't just mom punishing Buffy out of anger – or even practical mom punishing Buffy to try to teach her not to do these things.

It is a parent struggling to do the right thing for her daughter. In response Buffy of course is frustrated because she needs to go save the world, and she has to deal with her mom.

Yet the dialogue, her expression, all of it tells us that Buffy's not angry at her mom for being a mom. She wants to be the daughter her mom wants, and she wants to be able to tell her mom.

Her anger and frustration comes from that dual role. It's exactly what her trunk has shown us. She has to respond to her mom. Play the part with her mom of being the daughter, the high school girl. And she can't reveal what's underneath.

Her anger and frustration are very real. But she doesn't take it out on her mom. She is struggling to find a way to explain it and she can't.

This is a real conflict. It's not something that is easily solvable. You have two people with good intentions who truly want the best for each other who have this conflict. And that I just love. The best conflict that you can have as a writer is that type of conflict.

So Buffy resolves this by sneaking out of the house. Because that's the only way she can get out.

And she is late to the Bronze, but she does get there.

Moving Toward The Climax

Now we are driving forward to our Climax. Notice something else — that from the three-quarter point to the climax the action is going very fast.

There isn't, I don't think, any more exposition in there. It's just the events going one after the other, arising out of that Three-Quarter Turn and moving toward our Climax.

Fighting Style Reflects Character

The Climax fits the theme of the show, as it is not only about Buffy. We see all our main characters engaged in this fight. And how they fight — particularly Willow and Xander — so fits with their characters.

Willow throws holy water on Darla, who is attacking Giles, and Darla runs away.

I love this for a couple reasons. One is throwing holy water fits Willow because she's not the Slayer. And she has been probably the least physical in her fighting. She's not wanting to go down into the tunnels with Buffy. I have no doubt if she had the strength or something to add, some super powers, she would be right there. But she knows that she doesn't. She goes with her strengths, which is she stays and researches with Giles and contributes that way.

So the holy water fits. It is a type of tool or weapon that we definitely believe Willow would use.

I also like it because we had this early scene with Cordelia at the water fountain. Cordelia's mean to Willow, and Willow runs away. Now we see Willow in a physical confrontation with a vampire, and Willow throws holy water, and Darla runs away.

This is such a nice bookend for Willow and showing of her character growth.

Was it deliberate on the writers' part? That there's water in both and that Willow runs away in one and Darla in the other? I have no idea, but it's really nice and I really like it.

We also see Xander, very consistent with who he is and his loyalty to Jesse.

Xander is holding a stake, but it's a defensive measure. It's not clear that if he were to try to fight Jesse that he could prevail. Xander's got the stake because he knows he should have it.

But he is trying to talk to Jesse. He's trying to reason with Jesse despite that Jesse is a vampire.

What does Xander really think he can accomplish here? Because he's trying to talk Jesse into, presumably, not killing people, and yet Jesse can't at this point choose not to be a vampire anymore. We don't have any reason to think that he can choose to not want to kill people. Or that he could do anything other than what he is going to do.

Xander on some level knows this. He's been told this. Yet, he is still trying to say Jesse, basically, "You know, don't you remember who you are? Don't you want to be a good person?"

Xander does kill Jesse, but it's by accident. Someone else runs into them. The stake gets pushed into Jesse's heart. And Jesse is dusted.

This sequence of events fits with who Xander is. Also, I feel like we don't really want to see Xander have to kill his friend. I think that there are going to be hard choices in the show and we know that there are going to be terrible losses. But at this point right now, we don't make Xander do that.

Also, if Xander and Willow were able to just slay vampires with no problem, that would really undercut the whole idea of Buffy being the one person who could do this.

The Climax Of The Pilot

Going to our climax, where Buffy fights Luke and prevails. This too so fits her character and the premise of the show.

Buffy is strong, but she doesn't win over Luke by being physically stronger. He is presented as being extremely powerful. He did overpower her the first time they encountered each other. She wins both by her Slayer strength and by who she is as a person. She is quipping. And she taunts him about sunrise and fools him by throwing something at the stage curtain. It drops down and this artificial light floods the stage. Luke, because she has said this about sunrise, cowers instinctively.

Now that he is caught off guard she is able to stake him from behind.

And I love it because it makes the show so much more interesting than if Buffy were just a super being who is super strong physically.

It is not just that she's strong. It's that she can outwit the vampires. That is something that I noticed before watching the commentary. Then in the commentary, Joss said that as well. That he wanted to show that Buffy was not just strong but also smart and that she could outwit her opponents.

He also commented that her quipping and joking around is part of what makes her not Superman. It makes her human, so we worry more for her. It also makes her more interesting to me and goes with her intelligence and her wit.

Falling Action In The Harvest

Now that Luke is defeated, we see the Master's frustration. He is not going to get out today. Buffy and her friends have prevailed in this battle. They haven't won the war because the Master still exists. But they have prevailed and stopped the Harvest.

Now we are in the Falling Action part of the story.

In that part, our protagonist reacts, absorbs the result of the climax. If the protagonist prevailed, we usually see some sort of celebration. In The Hero's Journey story structure, that is a specific part of it. The hero gets the Holy Grail, prevails in the quest, wins the battle, and celebrates.

If you are a Star Wars fan, in the original movie you'll remember there was that scene where everyone's getting awarded medals.

So we don't have anyone getting medals here, but we do

have our core four —Giles, Xander, Willow, and Buffy – at the base of the stage recognizing and feeling good about the fact that they won something.

What I did not notice, and was pointed out in the commentary, is that what we don't see are the bodies of the people that Luke drained and killed before Buffy got there. And that was a deliberate choice. Because seeing the bodies of the people that Buffy couldn't save because she couldn't get out of the house sooner would really undercut that celebration.

So while it is less realistic, I like that we have that moment where despite all the costs, despite that they didn't win everything and that Jesse is still gone, we do get a moment to acknowledge that they stopped the Harvest. They saved Sunnydale, maybe saved the world.

Also part of the Falling Action is tying up the loose ends. The things that we have put out there and the reader wants to know how each resolves.

The major one we have here is what will happen now that so many people have seen vampires and seen Buffy fighting them and winning. If that were to bring Buffy out into the open that would seriously undercut the series.

We need an explanation for how does this keep happening, and we get it from Giles.

He says people rationalize what they can and forget what they can't. This comes in the context of, I don't remember if it's Willow or Xander saying, "Oh, everything's going to be different." Giles says no, it's not, and here's why.

And then we get an example of it because we hear Cordelia doing exactly what Giles says. She seemingly has forgotten that Buffy saved her life. She rationalizes everything by saying, "Oh, there were these gang members and Buffy knew them."

What's interesting is within that there is a sort of grudging respect for Buffy. I have to think that comes out of Cordelia on some level remembering that Buffy saved her. And definitely remembering Buffy fighting even though she is now reframing it as gang members not vampires.

Why You Should Hint About The Future

We also get some hints about the future.

If you are writing an ongoing series, whether it's TV, movies with sequels, or a novel that's part of a series, it's good to have these hints about the future. They get the reader interested, or the audience interested, in coming back to the next installment.

Even if your story is self-contained, readers like to have a little hint about the future for these characters.

If you're writing a romance that has a happily ever after ending, you might give a little hint about something lovely these characters will do in the future. Or just enough to show that, yes, it will be happily ever after.

If it's suspense or mystery and the protagonist has prevailed, usually the reader wants the emotional satisfaction of knowing that there are some good things in store for our protagonist. And for whatever other characters we become engaged with. Also, maybe we want to know there's consequences for the antagonist.

So the Falling Action is where you tie up the loose ends and add a few hints about the future.

Here we have Giles commenting about what else can happen on the Hellmouth. The other kinds of monsters. And we had a little of that in the pilot's first half where he jokes about the Time-Life books, and how you can have all kinds of monsters here.

Plus we get another hint about the future – that Buffy, Xander, and Willow are going to continue to be friends. That this will be a big part of what makes Buffy's life fun. And as she deals with slaying vampires, they will probably continue to help her. These are nice hints about the future.

Story Questions The Harvest Raises

Giles' comments are also story questions. He raises a question. What will Buffy face next? The other story questions — we have a lot of them, going back to that point that we put our protagonist in emotional peril.

We have questions about:

- Buffy and school. She did cut out of school. There probably are going to be repercussions. We want to know how that's going to work.
- Buffy and her social life.
- What will happen with Buffy and Joyce.
- Cordelia and Buffy, because Cordelia is a character we come back to again and again in this two-episode arc. This suggests maybe Cordelia and Buffy will continue to interact. What will that be like?

Then there is our giant story question — the Master is still there.

Will he get out? How will he get out? What will happen?

This is something else that Joss mentioned in the commentaries, his deliberate choice to keep the Master trapped at the end of the two-episode arc. Otherwise, if he's out there in the world and you want him to be an ongoing villain you have to deal with your protagonist losing to the Master again and again throughout the season, which undercuts her.

Or you have to have all these manipulative ways of keeping Buffy and the Master from confronting each other, or come up with reasons why they don't. But by keeping him trapped he remains a threat out there. Even in our one-off episodes where he's not the focus, he still looms as this threat.

So it keeps that tension, that story question, as the series moves forward.

Why Willow Has Her Own Fan Base

A few more things from the commentary that I thought were interesting. Joss said that the network wanted Willow to be more cool and hip and more like Buffy. Thinking the audience wouldn't be very interested in Willow as this kind of brainy nerdy, as a less confident character than Buffy.

And Joss said he insisted, no, Willow needs to be as she is. That she would have this rabid fan base. Because she's someone we can know and identify with. Buffy is less so because she's that unattainable ideal.

Writing And Whedon

I am not sure if this came from the scene-by-scene commentary or was in one of the interviews that's on the DVD, but Joss said something else that I just love.

"When you're writing it's just you and the characters and it's a great place to be."

And that is so how I feel at the best moments. Sometimes I'm writing and it's a slog. I'm just getting from one scene to the next. Just getting words down on the page, and it feels like that. But other times — and this is what keeps me writing and going back to the keyboard and my characters and stories — are those moments when I just feel I'm right there in that story. In that scene, with those characters, and it feels so amazing.

When I read it all back later, most of the time what I wrote when it felt plodding and mechanical is just as good as what I wrote when it felt amazing. I don't really see a difference. I can't pick out later which scenes I really felt in the moment on.

But it just feels so much better when it's like that so I love that quote.

Spoilers

LOTS OF FORESHADOWING in this episode.

About Angel

This episode at the crypt with Buffy, there are a couple more hints that Angel is a vampire. He knows the Master, and he knows the other vampires. Again, I did not pick up on that he might be a vampire. But I have heard that some people got it at that point.

One thing that doesn't work for me in this scene in retrospect, because I know what's coming, is when Angel says he isn't going to go with Buffy into the tunnels.

He says, "I'm afraid."

Given what we find out about Angel and how his character develops later, there's no way that I believe that he's afraid to go with her. Angel is so powerful. I understand why we don't send him with her. That would undercut the whole premise of the show. It's Buffy who needs to be fighting.

It's Buffy, the one girl in all the world. If we send a powerful vampire with her in the pilot episode, that's a whole different show.

Later on, Buffy and Angel will fight together. Sometimes Buffy will save Angel. Once in a great while Angel will save Buffy. And that certainly works. There is no reason you can't have a very strong protagonist being saved by other people.

But if in your pilot you have that happen you are signaling a much different type of story.

So I understand they had to give some reason why he wasn't going to go with Buffy, but I'm not sure him being scared works. Though I think it's always interesting to look at these early episodes. You see where the characters and the plot go later and see what kind of has to be retconned in order for it to work.

Two listeners to the Buffy and the Art of Story podcast commented on that point when Angel meets Buffy in the crypt. One thought perhaps Angel said he was afraid simply because he wasn't ready to reveal yet that he was a vampire. He knew that would come out during a fight. And he felt confident Buffy would be fine. So he didn't feel that he needed to go with her. Another listener likewise thought Angel's facial expression and his tone showed he was clearly lying about being afraid. She said, "I think he just says it to get her to go on her own and realize her own strength."

I love both readings of it because they suggest Angel has a lot of confidence in Buffy. I like that my listeners had more confidence in the writers than I did at that particular moment.

Darla

Another example of what seems like retconning is Darla. In this episode, and I want to say in a couple more down the road, she is nowhere near as powerful as the backstory we eventually get shows that she is.

As Darla's character develops on Buffy and Angel, we find out just how powerful she was. How smart and how strong. And so when I go back and see these early episodes and see her much more deferential to the Master than I think she ever would be, and much more taken aback by Buffy than she would be, it really stands out in retrospect.

This is something that is explained more or less in the commentary. Joss said that initially the plan was that Willow would kill Darla. But they liked the actress so much, and the character so much, that they decided to keep her around. So that totally makes sense to me.

I think you can see that because I don't think the writers had any idea of who she would turn out to be. Or how important she was.

Character Change In TV Versus Novels

If you're writing a novel, something to keep in mind is that audience members, especially at the time Buffy was made, would definitely give the showrunners— the creators of the show — some leeway in retconning characters.

Because everyone understood that when a TV show starts nobody knows if it's going to continue or how long it's going to continue. And there's a big difference between what you might do if you're looking at one season versus three seasons or five seasons or seven seasons. So audiences are generally willing to go with a certain amount of revision later.

If you're writing a novel or a screenplay for a movie that is self-contained, most readers have a higher expectation (I know I do), that if within the world of that novel there's a character change, you justify it.

So if your character of Darla is going to be kind of in awe of the Master or a little bit intimidated — or a lot intimidated — and then three quarters into the novel you decide to give her some back story where she was super powerful and didn't take crap from anybody, that is going to be problematic. Because it is not consistent. You are not being consistent with your characters.

Characters can definitely change. You could have your character evolve into becoming more powerful, have things happen that she overcomes and so she becomes more powerful.

But if you give her a back story that doesn't fit with who she is at the beginning of the novel, that is something that readers will most likely notice and be very frustrated with.

Can Giles Fight?

There's a little bit on Giles that I likewise don't think quite fits with what we learn about Giles later.

I'm okay with not seeing him fight because he is our Watcher. He is in this space at the beginning where he is there to prepare Buffy. He's not there to be on the front lines with her.

That being said, I feel a little bit misled in that I'm pretty sure he appears as if he cannot at all fight off Darla. Or at least the way he acts to me does not fit with how we later find out Giles has this past where he raised demons. We find out he's quite a good fighter. He's very tough. He used to be called Ripper. All these things.

I would have expected to see a hint of that. Or at least to not see him doing the least fighting of everyone in this episode. I personally would have liked it better if we just didn't see Giles fighting at all.

So I feel like that's just a tiny bit of a mislead. And I've always been curious whether that was a misdirect. To kind of take the audience, with Buffy, more by surprise when we find out about Giles' past. Or if the writers just hadn't really decided yet that he would have that back story.

Foreshadowing The Season Finale

My last foreshadowing is this scene with Luke and Buffy where Luke has grabbed her from behind. And it looks like he's going to bite the back of her neck. She headbutts him and gets out of it.

Now why do I find that so compelling? Because in the

season finale we see Buffy and the Master in that same position.

Because the Master is so powerful – not just physically, but psychologically and emotionally — and Buffy is frozen in fear, or because he has this supernatural psychic power, she's not able to get out of it as she does with Luke.

Despite how strong Luke is, she did the headbutt and got away. With the Master, though, she remains frozen and he kills her. That tells us so much about the Master's power. And about Buffy's response, Buffy's fear.

It makes me wonder whether knowing the prophecy, how much did that undermine Buffy's ability to respond in that moment?

I hope I'll remember to explore that when we get to that episode. But I really like that foreshadowing of that moment, which is then escalated and comes out so differently.

Questions For Your Writing:

- **In the first chapter or installment of your story, are there story questions to keep the reader wanting to turn the page?**
- **Do any of your characters serve as foils for one another the way Cordelia and Buffy or Xander and Jesse do?**
- **With which of your characters is the reader most apt to identify? Why?**
- **Are there different types of characters that might appeal to different readers?**

Next: The Witch

NEXT WE'LL BE TALKING about Episode 3, The Witch.

That is a self-contained episode, so we can go through all the plot points in one story.

We'll also talk about how the one-off episode still advances some of our characters' storylines. That's part of what keeps the audience going through the series whether or not they like a particular one-off episode.

CHAPTER FOUR

THE WITCH

This chapter talks about Season One, Episode Three: The Witch, a standalone episode, written by Dana Reston and directed by Stephen Cragg.

In particular, we'll look at:

- **Grabbing the audience in the first scene**
- **Subplots that mirror the story's theme**
- **Misdirection and playing fair with the audience**
- **Expanding the Buffy universe beyond vampires**

Okay, let's dive into The Hellmouth.

Opening Conflict In The Witch

In the first scene, Giles gives Buffy a speech about her sacred duty and how she is now enslaving herself to this cult. We then get a shot of Buffy in a cheerleading uniform.

This is another great way to get across the exposition through conflict, which was done so well in the pilot. And it sets up, for audience members who have not seen the pilot, exactly what is going on in the show.

Remember, when this came out a lot of people might jump into a series in the middle. Or at least certainly in the first season or two. If you hadn't started a series at the beginning you could wait for reruns. But you were more likely to just start with a later episode.

So it was important to set up exactly what was going on. And that was done well here. I videotaped a lot of episodes once I got to like the show. But I don't think that I saw it in the order it aired until years later when I got the DVD sets.

Grabbing The Audience Early

This opening conflict does exactly what it should do beyond the exposition, which is to grab the audience member right away.

Our opening conflict can really be about anything. It's something to simply draw the reader in. But it's ideal if it hints at the main conflict for the story. Here we get that because our main plot will involve somebody getting cheerleaders out of the way.

It's not whether Buffy becomes a cheerleader or not. The personal conflict turns out to not be so much about that and to be more about Amy and her mother. Amy's desire to be a cheerleader — or not — and how Buffy's life echoes that.

Buffy also says she wants to do something normal. For her that is becoming a cheerleader again, which she was at her old school. At least we assume so because she already has a cheerleading uniform.

We get a hint of the main plot conflict when we see the cheerleading tryouts. This also cues us as an audience that this will be a centerpiece of the story.

We meet Amy for the first time. She says that she hates these tryouts. At the same time, she speaks about her mom with a lot of admiration and seems grateful for how much her mom coaches her, spending I think it's three hours a day, and talking about professional cheerleading coaches.

The Inciting Incident In The Witch

At about 4.5 minutes into the episode, we get the Story Spark or the Inciting Incident that sets off our episode arc. Here it is literally a spark because the cheerleader's hands burst into flames. So that is what sets off what is going to be our main plot conflict.

In a movie, often this Inciting Incident happens about 10 minutes into a 120-minute movie, so about 10% through. And that is what we see here. The episode is 43 or 44 minutes and this comes about four and a half minutes in.

Quick Wits

Buffy uses, I think it's a school banner. She grabs it off the wall and runs down the bleachers and smothers the flames.

I really like this because we have this added moment where Buffy is using her wits. Anybody could have done what Buffy did here. It didn't take any special powers other than quick thinking and the ability to run up and down the bleachers. Which perhaps not everyone could do, but it doesn't take a Slayer to do that. So I like that we start out with Buffy being quick-witted, acting fast, and being smart.

The Villain

This also sets up immediately in our third episode that we will have evil, or villains, other than vampires.

In the pilot we got a hint of that because we got Giles talking more than once about being on the Hellmouth and all these kinds of villains. But here it's explicit. This isn't about vampires.

In the interview on the DVD, Joss Whedon says this. He makes the point that this is the first episode written with a non-vampire villain. He says it was a "statement of principle." (This interview doesn't appear on the DVD that contains The Witch episode. It appears, for whatever reason, on the next DVD.)

After our Story Spark we go to opening credits. And we see Xander, Willow, Buffy, and Giles in the library in a classic scene.

I'm pretty sure this is the first time they called themselves The Slayerettes. That confirms that Willow and Xander are going to continue to help Buffy, and they have this conversation with her.

Initially everyone suspects, or at least considers, that Amber (the cheerleader whose hands burnt up) maybe did something to herself to make this happen. There's talk about spontaneous combustion. There isn't any understanding that this is necessarily about cheerleaders.

Subplot: Buffy And Joyce

Fairly quickly after that, we get a subplot for the episode. Which is the relationship between Buffy and Joyce.

Joyce is unpacking something for the gallery, which is very busy. She's doing an opening. And she's a bit distracted as Buffy is talking to her. Buffy is telling Joyce about how Amy's mom coaches her for hours every day. And Joyce is kind of half listening. Buffy's going on about this. What Buffy is really saying indirectly is: "I really wish you were that involved, were that interested in something I'm doing. Would you do that for me?"

Joyce doesn't pick up on that. Instead she's answering the literal words about Amy's mom spending three hours a day coaching. She says, "Sounds like she doesn't have enough to do."

This is such a powerful scene. Because when we write dialogue, often it is stronger if a character is speaking around their feelings or trying to get across something in an indirect way.

That indirection shows the character's vulnerability. If you feel vulnerable, if you feel afraid that the other person will reject you or not care about what you're saying, it feels safer to bring up something in a roundabout way – which is what Buffy does – or by talking about a similar situation with someone else.

In later scenes, Joyce will push Buffy to get involved in the yearbook because that's what Joyce did. Buffy is not interested in that. And they get into an argument which escalates. Buffy says, "Well, I'm not you, I'm into my own thing."

And Joyce says, "Well, your own thing got you kicked out of school and we had to move here just to find some place that would take you."

A Different Tone From Joyce

This is a very different tone than in our pilot, where Joyce kind of kiddingly said, "Buffy, try not to get kicked out of school."

Here, she is really expressing – certainly there's anger, but also worry. She is worried about Buffy. And she is very strongly criticizing Buffy, which really upsets Buffy. It's a difficult moment for the two of them.

This subplot will ultimately resolve toward the end of the episode. It's a nice example of a subplot that echoes our main plot, the conflict between Amy and her mom, this outward manifestation of it.

Amy's mom is the villain who is causing all these terrible things to happen. That is our external conflict. But the real conflict is Amy's mom wanting to control Amy's life. Or more accurately, wanting to live through Amy.

We really see this with Joyce and Buffy. Except that Joyce doesn't want to live through Buffy. She is concerned about her daughter. She's trying to get Buffy to be like her because she perceives it as something that maybe would be safer or better for Buffy. Versus Amy and her mom, where the mom's concern is not really with Amy, it's with herself.

I love this reflection between the subplot and the main plot. It's really nice when you have that kind of connection there.

Misdirection: The Red Herring

We're nearing the One-Quarter Twist in the story (which remember, about a quarter through the story spins it in a new direction, but generally comes from outside the protagonist).

Right before we get there, we have Cordelia. She's threatening Amy in the locker room after Amy makes a mistake in the tryouts that potentially could look like Cordelia's mistake. So Cordelia threatens her.

It's a creepy scene because for some reason the locker room is dark. No one else is there and momentarily we think that Cordelia could be the villain.

This turns out to be a misdirect.

It's one of those red herrings we get where we're not sure who did it.

One-Quarter Twist

In this episode our One-Quarter Twist comes around 14-15 minutes through. So it might be a tiny bit beyond the one-quarter point. It happens when Amy is the second alternate for the team and Buffy is the alternate.

Cordelia makes the squad. And we see someone, we still

don't know who, casting a spell. So we know now it's probably not Cordelia because she made the cheerleading team. This takes the story in a new direction in a couple ways.

Yeah, we know Cordelia is not the villain. But that was a very quick misdirect that we move on from. We also know that this is not personally about Amber. In the beginning it could have been something focusing on Amber, someone targeting her. Now we know based on what we see in the spell-casting that it is someone targeting cheerleaders.

And Cordelia is the next target.

Buffy Saves Cordelia

Cordelia loses her sight gradually. It takes place in a Driver's Education scene. I thought the actor who played the Driver's Ed teacher did such a good job of being irritated.

(Which personally I related to. I remember my high school Driver's Ed teacher acting so irritated that he had to actually teach me to drive, because everyone else's parents let them drive and practice before they had Driver's Ed. Anyway, total side thing that has really not much to do with Buffy other than I love this scene.)

Here, while Cordelia presumably knows how to drive, she is disoriented because she can't see very well. And the instructor is so irked that she can't find the gear shift and isn't moving fast enough. So Buffy once again saves Cordelia.

This is the second time she has saved Cordelia's life. And we see in that very creepy scene Cordelia with no pupils to her eyes.

This tells Giles that this is about witchcraft. Buffy is the one who makes the connection to cheerleading, and they make a plan to figure out who it is. So we can see that all the scenes and steps from the one-quarter point on arise out of that One-Quarter Twist that is driving the story now as the protagonist reacts to it.

The Midpoint Commitment In The Witch

All of these scenes lead us up to the Midpoint. The Midpoint is where typically either the protagonist makes a commitment (throwing caution to the wind or dedicating herself to the quest) or she suffers a significant reversal, or both.

And here we have both, which also happened in our pilot and was very powerful.

Here it's a little more understated. Buffy and Willow make this formula in their chemistry class. Buffy goes and talks to Amy and pretends to drop something so she can get a little bit of Amy's hair.

Buffy comes back after Willow makes the formula with the hair and spills this formula on Amy. Because it turns blue, we know that Amy is the one who cast a spell recently.

I see this as Buffy committing and throwing caution to the wind because she is exposing herself. This is the first time that she may come face-to-face with the villain of this piece and she becomes vulnerable by doing that.

The Midpoint Reversal

There was also a reversal here.

I didn't see it when I previously watched the episode. Partly because I wasn't watching for that, and I missed the actual moment. Even on first watch for the podcast, I was thinking there was not really a reversal. We have a spell that was cast. And another cheerleader targeted, and she now has no mouth. Which I found really disturbing.

But that's not really a reversal for our protagonist. That spell was cast before Buffy approached Amy, before she spilled the formula on her and exposed herself.

So I thought, "Okay. I don't think there's a reversal here."

But this time through I caught it. It is when Amy – and we find out later, it's Amy's mom in Amy's body – Amy steals Buffy's bracelet, which she then can use for a spell against Buffy. So there is a reversal. There's a commitment and there's an immediate reversal because that's what allows Amy to steal the bracelet.

These two things, Buffy's commitment and the reversal, now drive the story forward because Buffy and her friends are focused on getting Amy, and Amy is focused on stopping Buffy. Also, Buffy is now on the cheerleading squad. So she is an obstacle in Amy's way.

We get a scene where Amy comes home and yells at her mom to do her homework. And the mom is clearly scared of her. I try to think back to the first time I saw this and whether I suspected the mom had done a body-switching spell. I don't think that I did.

Misleading The Reader

I think that I believed that Amy was lying to everyone about her mother for some reason. She didn't want people to know that she (Amy) basically was running things at home. So I probably thought Amy was the one in charge here either way.

This is another example of dramatic irony because as the audience we now know something that the characters don't know. Although in a way this fits into leading the audience to one conclusion because we've revealed (we think) that Amy is the witch. So this sort of fits with that narrative that Amy's the one in charge, Amy's the witch.

She's controlling her mom.

Buffy Under A Spell

Buffy wakes up kind of loopy because a spell was done to her, and we get a furthering of the Joyce and Buffy subplot.

Joyce apologizes for the things she said. I like that Joyce does this, that she reflected and she is trying to show Buffy how she feels and that she's sorry. Buffy, partly because she's in this great mood as a result of the spell, is all fine with it. She says, "You know, I did get kicked out of school."

At practice she throws another cheerleader too hard. Now Amy is on the cheerleading squad and Buffy is very very sick. So notice all of this comes from that Midpoint commitment where Buffy took this action to reveal Amy as the witch.

Giles figures out it's a vengeance spell, and they need the witch's book to reverse it.

We see a nice resonance between Buffy and Amy that Buffy recognizes. Because she says this isn't Amy's fault. That it can be really hard when a parent puts so much pressure on you.

Buffy has sympathy for Amy. So we are not just seeing a villain that's not a vampire. We are seeing a Slayer who, for most of the episode, is not using her Slayer strength or Slayer powers. She's using her humanity and her sympathy and compassion for Amy. I think this is what allows her to figure things out.

Giles and Buffy go to Amy's house, thinking to confront her mother and enlist the mother's help in stopping Amy. Willow and Xander are going to keep an eye on Amy at the game that night because the cheerleading squad is cheering.

Three-Quarter Turn

Which brings us to our Three-Quarter Turn in the story. As it should, it happens three quarters of the way through the story. This is the plot turn that comes out of the Midpoint. So it grows organically from it, but yet again turns our story in a different direction.

And this happens at the house when Buffy realizes that

they are talking to who they think is Amy's mom, but that it's really Amy in her mom's body. And this is what I mean about that power of Buffy. Here is her power to understand, to empathize, and to pay attention and put things together.

Now we have to stop Amy's mom and reverse all these spells, including the one trapping Amy in her mom's body. From the three-quarter point on we drive very quickly toward the climax.

We're in the science lab.

Giles is working on the spell. As he is casting it, he's building up, he's calling on the powers and Amy – Amy's mom, but I'm just going to call her Amy – Amy is at the top of the pyramid and she stumbles. She falls and she runs out of the gym.

This, when everyone is in the same room in the science lab, brings us to the climax. And this is also interesting because at first as we lead up to it, Buffy is completely weakened. She's lying on the table. She really can't do anything. Amy raises an axe and at that moment Giles' spell finally kicks in completely and everything's reversed.

So Amy is now Amy again, and she's going to drop the axe. And Buffy is recovered and is herself so she can now fight and we are at the climax.

The Climax

While Giles is instrumental – Buffy couldn't have won without Giles – Buffy is also the one who fights the final fight. She is still our protagonist and she does resolve this conflict.

This is an example of use of a villain who can be a match for Buffy despite her mystical strength and her training. Because a physical fight against someone who casts spells, how much can Buffy do against that?

It forces her, though she is fighting physically, to also use her wits. She flips down this reflective surface. I guess it's a mirror. I've never quite figured out what that is, or why it's in the science lab. So if anyone has figured that out, please email me or tweet me and let me know.

Whatever it is, she flips it down. And the spell that Amy's mom sent her way — somewhere along the line she tells Amy, "You'll never get out of where I'm sending you, you'll never get back." That spell is reflected back and hits Amy's mom.

I should probably use her name. It's Catherine. She's Catherine the Great as a cheerleader – so, Catherine.

This is just me guessing, but I think this choice to have Buffy reflect the spell back was done for two reasons. One, it makes sense in the story because Buffy can't really physically overcome someone with the powers that Catherine has. But I also think it was just too dark, particularly at the time, for network TV. Too dark to have Buffy kill Amy's mother.

Certainly, we don't want to see Amy do it. We can't have Giles do it. It just feels wrong.

Also, Buffy is the Slayer. And we will see as the series develops, she doesn't kill humans. Even humans who are doing something terrible and who might be beyond the reach of the human justice system.

The idea of this is she is a hero.

I don't think the show wanted her to be killing anybody, but particularly someone's mom. So this is a nice way to do it because it is only reflecting back at Catherine the spell she put out there.

She is her own destruction. It's poetic justice and it feels more, it feels more okay.

If the show were done now, I don't know. There is obviously much more of a trend toward dark heroes and darkness in shows and you could do quite a bit more. I personally think or would hope that Buffy, still, the choice would be to not have her kill Amy's mom.

That's our Climax.

Falling Action In The Witch

And now we have our Falling Action. Starting with a lovely scene where Amy tells Willow about her dad being back and how they're baking brownies. And she's complaining about it, but she really thinks it's great.

Resolving The Subplot

We also see Buffy and her mom reconcile in a really nice scene that resolves the subplot between them. It also echoes or encompasses the theme of the episode.

Joyce comes to talk to Buffy. She says she's really been thinking about this and she feels like she just can't understand Buffy because Joyce is not sixteen.

And Buffy asks her mom, "Would you want to be sixteen again?"

Joyce says, "Oh, no, not even if it would help me understand you, go through all that again – forget it."

Buffy says, "I love you," and hugs Joyce.

And Joyce says, "I don't get it."

I like this because it shows that these two are doing okay despite their conflicts. That Joyce doesn't need Buffy to be a copy of her, something Buffy complained about before.

And Buffy has also seen that as much as at times she feels Joyce is too wrapped up in her work or maybe doesn't pay enough attention to Buffy, there's a downside to a mom who's so involved in her daughter's life and really doesn't have anything else.

So Buffy now is more okay with the idea that her mom is a person who is juggling a lot of things. Who is sometimes going to be absorbed in work and not able to focus on Buffy in the moment as much as Buffy might like. But we do see Joyce coming back more than once to try to make things right with Buffy.

Whether you think Joyce has the right balance, or whether she should pay more attention to Buffy, for this episode I felt they had come to a good place. One where they can both let the other person be who she is and appreciate the good about that.

We'll certainly talk about their relationship in later episodes, as I think it's one of the most interesting ones in the show.

Character Development: Cordelia

Cordelia comments on Buffy and Amy being bumped back to alternates.

I like this because we did have – I didn't talk about it much – but we did have a sense of a growing connection between Cordelia, Buffy, Willow, and Xander. Because Cordelia does talk to them in that initial tryout scene.

Which you might not necessarily expect because we know Cordelia is very popular. She views at least Xander and Willow as being way beneath her on the social scale, but she did like Buffy.

So we see Cordelia kind of chatting with them a little bit. And now at the end again, she's there to taunt Buffy and Amy about being alternates. But there is still this ongoing connection, this sense that we're probably going to keep seeing Cordelia.

Which we know because she's in the credits. But still, I like that.

Final Scene

And then we have our final scene with the cheerleading statue.

We saw that early on when Amy was telling Willow about how great her mother was. Now we see this statue or trophy of Catherine the Great in there. We realize she's in there because we see the eyes moving. And I think we hear her kind of vocalizing.

That scene still makes my throat tighten up.

More On Misdirection

There is some misdirection here with Cordelia in the locker room. The moment works as a misdirect because if we re-watch it knowing Cordelia is not the villain, it still fits because Cordelia is really set on being a cheerleader. She does not let anyone get in her way.

So I believe she would say those things to Amy even if the writers were not trying to make us think, at least for a short time, that Cordelia might be the villain.

That really is the key to whether misdirection is playing fair with the reader, or whether your reader is going to come back and feel cheated.

Deciphering The Body Switch

So let's talk about the Amy and Amy's mom switch. This is what I am not quite sure was entirely playing fair with the audience.

I don't know how much it matters. Because the heart of this episode is the emotional conflict between Amy and her mom and, to a lesser extent, Buffy and Joyce. But let's look at these scenes.

In the first scene where we meet Amy, she's saying she hates tryouts. But she also is saying good things about her mom. At least she appears to be admiring her mom both when she's talking about coaching and in the next scene when we see her admiring the trophy in the hall. So is that Amy or is that her mom?

Because at some point Amy says her mom switched months ago. And the timeline of this episode does not seem to be months-long. It seems perhaps a week or so, unless I'm missing something.

So it seems like this would have to be Amy's mom the whole time, that we never see the real Amy in the first three quarters of the episode.

Yet we really get her anxiety and her feeling that she doesn't really like cheerleading. She doesn't really want to do it. And Willow says to her, "You know, you don't have to do this just because your mom does it." Amy kind of gets mad and runs away in a way that seems like Amy, not like her mom.

There are a couple things when she's admiring that trophy. She says how her dad ran off with Miss Trailer Trash and something about how he was always no good. And the language sounds more like what her mother would say. But it also sounds like someone who grew up hearing her mom say that.

When Amy finds out she's the second alternate she says, "How much more can I do?" And at another point she says something like, "I just can't get my body to move like hers [her mom's] ...no matter how much I practice." And again this sounds more like Amy.

It's not until we get that scene where Amy goes home and yells at her mom to do her homework – or maybe the scene with Amy in the chemistry lab when Buffy figures out she's the witch – that she could be the mom.

But when she goes home and yells at who we think is her mother to do the homework, yeah, that's clearly the body switch. And after that it's pretty clear who is who.

But I just have those questions about the early scenes.

I feel like it's part of why this episode doesn't rank up there as a favorite. It's often towards the bottom of the list if people rank best Buffy episodes. That's also because it doesn't contribute to the season arc very much other than some characterization issues. And maybe because people were not quite ready in the first go-round for a villain that wasn't a vampire.

But I do think part of it is that that misdirect is a little bit shaky.

Through Lines And Character Conflicts

We do have some through lines for the season or series arc. And this won't have spoilers.

The episode sets up even more of this Willow, Xander, Buffy triangle. We've already seen Xander's attracted to Buffy. And we already have a sense that Willow is interested in Xander. It is so quickly and concisely summed up in the scene at the tryouts when Xander gives Buffy a bracelet. This happens before the credits.

Buffy says, "What's this?" And Willow looks at it, and her brow furrows, and she says, "What's that?"

Right there we've got it.

It's Xander giving Buffy this bracelet. He's attracted to her. Buffy doesn't realize it. Willow is interested in Xander, who is not paying attention to her.

Later, we get Xander talking with Willow about how he wants to ask Buffy out. He calls Willow his guy friend who knows about girl stuff, completely oblivious to how Willow feels. Then we have that reversed and come back when Buffy, under the influence of the spell, is saying how wonderful Xander is and he's not like other boys.

He's very excited about this until she says he's just like one of the girls.

So we get definitely that set up – with some humor and very quickly – that there are these feelings and this triangle set up. So that isn't really a subplot because it's going to continue. But it is a through line for the series.

Building In Character Through Lines

Character through lines are one of those things that you can build into your stories. If you have a series of novels, that is the kind of character conflict that you can set up that will bring readers back to the next book.

You can also do it if you're telling a story that goes in installments, much like this season of Buffy, where you do have a bigger story arc and you also have smaller stories within it. So if you have a five-book series and you really need to read them in order because there is an overarching five-book arc, you still may want to set up these kinds of character interactions and conflicts. Because along with the main plot, people will come back to find out what happens to these characters that they care about.

DVD Commentary And The Witch

A couple more things from the DVD interview with Joss Whedon, which I watched after I wrote up my notes for The Witch. He too made the point that the story is about mothers and daughters. Because he said they got a lot of flak from watchers about the negative portrayal of witches. And his answer basically was, "It's not really about witches. It's about mothers and daughters."

He also said it was about cheerleaders because they are the great icon of popularity. And that's why Buffy was one at her last school and wants to be one again, but she discovers it's more complicated on the Hellmouth. It's been quite some time since I was in high school, so I don't know if this is still true of cheerleaders. But certainly it was for quite a long time. And I think that's interesting that Joss specifically chose that as sort of the symbol of Buffy's being the girl that she used to be.

Spoilers

AMY AND WITCHCRAFT

Amy, Amy, Amy. I love this introduction to Amy. So maybe that's part of why I always enjoy this episode a little more than some people do. I find her such an interesting character for the series.

I suppose in a way this is Amy's backstory. But it has its own conflict and resolution. And we have the echoing of it in the Joyce-Buffy subplot. So I think that it does work very well on its own, but it's also an interesting intro to Amy.

We see her gradually get more into witchcraft in Bewitched, Bothered and Bewildered. We see her casting spells to do better in school. That is, in itself, a little unsettling because she is doing it for her own personal gain.

And one of the characters comments, "She's the last person who should be messing with witchcraft."

Maybe that's true, maybe that's not. She could use witchcraft for good. But she also was doing it for herself. Then she helps Xander cast a spell that goes terribly wrong. And we see her doing something really evil when she turns Buffy into a rat. She is under the influence of her own spell when doing that, so you could argue it's not Amy being herself.

But it is pretty key, what she does, and that Buffy could have gotten stuck that way. Of course, later in Gingerbread we will see Amy getting stuck as a rat.

Amy is also really interesting in the later seasons. In Season Six, I'm always intrigued by what seem to me to be some inconsistencies. She is so much more advanced as a witch when she becomes human again after having been a rat for so long. It's unclear how that happened.

But we'll talk about that more when we get to Gingerbread.

Giles Backstory

In this episode, Giles says that this is his first spell. He seems very nervous about it. And then in Season Two The Dark Age we find out he did a lot of spell-casting when he was young.

So that makes me think they did not yet know that backstory for Giles. And I talked about this in the pilot. I think I might have thought Dark Age was coming in Season One, but I talked about the same thing about Giles.

We see him not really being a fighter. Being very hesitant about that. And yet with his past that we learn about in The Dark Age, it seems pretty clear he also knows how to fight. And we see some of that in the Halloween episode as well.

So this is a neat glimpse into maybe originally Giles didn't have quite so many layers. I imagine they weren't planning that far ahead because they had no idea if Buffy would be picked up.

Joyce And Buffy Backstory

When Joyce apologizes to Buffy for her comments about Buffy getting in trouble, and Buffy is under the influence of the spell, she says something about being a Vampire Slayer. And Joyce says, "Are you feeling all right?"

I always wonder, did Joss have in his mind this idea that Buffy's backstory included her parents having her committed when she came home talking about fighting vampires?

Because in the Season Six episode Normal Again, Buffy will say that happened.

Here and there we see things that could fit that. In the finale of Season Two, Buffy says something like, "I am not crazy." And here we have Joyce saying, "Are you feeling all right?" At the time, on first watch, I took it as physically, like,

"Buffy, are you physically feeling all right?" As if she's thinking Buffy has a fever. Which Buffy actually kind of seems like she might have a high fever and be sort of rambling.

But after Normal Again, I think, "Oh is this Joyce worried because Buffy's talking about vampires again?" Like there's something wrong with her mentally. She's having a psychotic break. But probably Normal Again was not in anyone's mind yet. Because for one thing, if that were an issue, Joyce's reaction seems really mild.

If you had had your daughter in an institution, or in a psychiatric ward, for a few weeks just a year or so ago because she was talking about vampires, I think the reaction would be a lot stronger here.

Questions For Your Writing

- **What is your initial conflict? Does it hook the reader? Does it hint at the larger story conflict?**
- **Are there ways in which your plot reflects emotional turmoil for one of your characters?**
- **If you mislead your reader about a character, does each scene still work once the reader learns the truth?**

Next: Teacher's Pet

NEXT I'LL TALK about Teacher's Pet, another standalone episode. We will cover all the plot points. I'll talk also about the use of point of view – because a fair amount of the story is in Xander's point of view – and whether and how that works. Also about metaphor in that particular episode and in Buffy generally.

CHAPTER FIVE

TEACHER'S PET

This chapter talks about Season One, Episode Four, Teacher's Pet, written by David Greenwalt and directed by Bruce Seth Green.

In particular, we'll look at:

- **A prologue that shows Xander's inner conflict**
- **Mixing points of view**
- **A Midpoint that lacks a strong commitment or reversal**
- **Why the protagonist here is unclear**

Okay, let's dive into the Hellmouth.

Another Prologue

We start with a prologue. A woman is screaming, a

vampire's attacking, Buffy seems really nervous. Already this scene just doesn't feel right. And I love that about it. Because although all those things could be happening in Buffy, we already have a sense by Episode Four that the way Buffy is acting just doesn't feel like her.

That's confirmed when Xander says, "May I cut in?" and he slays the vampires.

So we are in Xander's fantasy. Or it could be a dream, but we find out it's a daydream. It ends with Buffy saying, "You're drooling." We cut to the science class where she is really saying, "You're drooling."

What Is A Prologue?

This is a prologue because it could be lifted out from the main plot without hurting anything. It really is giving us backstory.

But it does something key, which is to tell us that at least some of this episode will be from Xander's point of view. It's not that we haven't seen scenes before that Buffy is not in. Some scenes focus on side characters or the villain, particularly the Master. But they haven't been specifically from the emotional point of view of another key character who is on Buffy's side, at least not to this extent.

Is Xander The Protagonist?

So I can see a reason to have this prologue. It is setting up Xander's internal conflict, which was hinted at earlier. His feelings for Buffy, and his feelings that he is not quite a man.

Earlier, he linked that to not being able to fight vampires. We see that in this fantasy his feeling that impressing Buffy, being a man, is being able to fight not just as well as she does, but better.

This prologue also points to something that I struggle with in the episode. Which is: Who is the protagonist? Because next we get to what is, I think, the real Opening Conflict of the story. It's the conflict that hints at our main plot. It is certainly the Opening Conflict for Buffy, who, though I struggle with it, I believe is the protagonist in this episode.

Opening Conflict

Buffy's in science class. The teacher, Dr. Gregory, asks her questions. Willow is pantomiming the answers. Buffy does a pretty good job, but it becomes obvious what's happening.

We expect Dr. Gregory to be angry at her when he has her stay after class. Instead, he tells her she's smart. She thinks on her feet. And she should not let anyone else's negative opinions about her influence her.

He encourages her. Basically, he tells her, "Hey, imagine if you did the work, how good you could do here." She says sorry for not doing the homework. And he says, "Don't be sorry. Be smart." Buffy is very energized by this.

This is, as I think Xander will comment later, the only teacher who has really formed a positive opinion of her, or at least who has expressed one.

This is the Opening Conflict in that it is Buffy's internal conflict. Not just with living a normal life, but with how people see her. Also the way that being a Slayer interferes with her being able to truly take part in school and excel in other ways.

The Story Spark

In what is typical Joss Whedon fashion, now that something wonderful happened for one of the characters we love, it's immediately taken away. A claw grabs Dr. Gregory, and then we have credits.

Back To Xander's Point Of View

We are once again in Xander's point of view after the credits.

At the Bronze, one of the musicians on stage scoffs at Xander when Xander gives a little wave as if he knows him. This reflects that fantasy in the beginning. Part of it was Xander being a great musician and being on stage himself getting all the attention.

Blaine and another guy are bragging about women. And putting Xander on the spot. Making fun of him because they think that he's a virgin. They act like they have all this experience.

So he pretends that he does, too. He puts his arms around Buffy and Willow and wants to make it seem like they're both his girlfriends.

This further suggests this is Xander's story.

Buffy And Angel

We switch to Buffy when she sees Angel. They have a conversation. He says something cryptic about a cut that he has, and he gives Buffy his leather jacket and disappears.

This is more of Angel showing up, looking good, giving some information (usually about something ominous), and leaving.

The show kind of calls that out. Buffy refers to him later to Giles as "Cryptic Guy." Also, she calls – I forget how Angel describes the vampire that attacked him – but Buffy calls him "Fork Guy."

I like this for a couple of reasons. It does call out that this is all that Angel is really doing to this point. It's also a nice use of the language of the show.

On Writing Dialogue

One of the things Buffy is known for, as I'm sure all of you know because you're Buffy fans, is the characters' language and the dialogue. It's very specific to the world of Buffy. Which – side note – is a good way to create dialogue if you're trying to capture a certain age or a certain community. Create your own dialogue.

When Buffy came out, Joss Whedon used to get a lot of questions about how he captured so well how teenagers talk. He said he didn't, he just created his own – their own – slang.

And I guess that's more what I'm getting at. Slang is difficult to use in fiction because it quickly becomes dated. For the most part the language in Buffy doesn't become dated, because Joss made it up.

Now and then I find it a little clunky. In the pilot episode, we see a few times Buffy or other people saying, "What's the sitch?" instead of "What's the situation?" That doesn't survive, I think with good reason.

But this idea of Cryptic Guy, Fork Guy, we will see that type of language throughout this series.

Xander And Angel Meet

This is also the first time that Willow and Xander see Angel. Xander comments on him being very attractive.

I like that there are a couple possible layers there. One is the jealousy of Angel. Xander apparently hadn't realized this guy Buffy was talking about was good looking. But I also like that you get the feeling Xander really just appreciates that Angel is a very attractive man.

Building From The Story Spark

At school, Dr. Gregory is missing. Mid-sentence Xander stops talking about that, and loses the ability to speak coherently, when he sees Ms. French, the very attractive substitute teacher. Xander is unable to explain to her where the classroom is. Blaine swoops in, takes her to class.

So we are building from our Opening Conflict and our Story Spark or Inciting Incident, which was that claw grabbing Dr. Gregory.

The fact that Dr. Gregory has something terrible happen

to him moves us toward the one-quarter point in the story. On the way Buffy notices that Dr. Gregory's glasses are on the floor and cracked. She questions why, if he's just taking the day off, would his glasses be here?

And we have Ms. French talking about the praying mantis and its mating habits. Which is a little foreshadowing and also something Buffy draws on later.

The One-Quarter Twist

Fourteen minutes through the episode, Cordelia finds Dr. Gregory in the refrigerator. Minus his head.

She's going there to get her medically-approved lunch. I thought when I saw this scene that the special lunch was just Cordelia's way of not having to eat the terrible food in the lunchroom. Which I think it is partly that. But we later find out it's a specific eating plan or diet that she is on, trying to lose weight.

This Turn, as it should, spins the story in a new direction.

And it comes from outside our protagonist, who as I said, I think is Buffy here. Because she is the one who is ultimately going to figure out and defeat our villain. It spins the story to finding out who killed Dr. Gregory – who or what – because the missing head points to something evil. I guess more evil than killing alone, so potentially not human.

Buffy Disagrees With Giles

In the library, Giles mentions the Master as the possible killer, so we get a nod to our overarching season plot and villain.

Buffy mentions Fork Guy. Because Angel warned her about him, she's thinking he is the one behind this.

It's really sort of that we don't have a lead, so let's check out this guy. Giles thinks it's too dangerous. He doesn't want her to go back and look for him.

Buffy goes to the park, despite Giles' warning. She

fights Fork Guy, and the police scare him off. Which is one of the rare times that we see the police in Sunnydale this season.

It's sort of interesting that they scare the vampire off. But maybe it was also Buffy's fighting. Maybe he doesn't want to fight her anymore.

She runs after Fork Guy and sees Ms. French frighten him.

Plot Structure: Alternate One-Quarter Twist

This could also be a One-Quarter Twist in the story. Because it really does take us in a new direction to focus on Ms. French. It's late for the One-Quarter Twist, though, so I do still see that as the finding of Dr. Gregory.

The reason I'm commenting on the turn when Fork Guy encounters Ms. French is that I don't find a clear Midpoint in this episode.

There is literal a midpoint. By definition, the midpoint of the story is halfway through the episode. But I don't see a clear commitment or much of a reversal there. I feel like this is part of why this episode falters.

(If you love this episode, please tell me why. My contact information is in the Appendix.)

I'm okay with Teacher's Pet. I pretty much enjoy all Buffy episodes (with maybe one exception). They're all fun. But this one overall doesn't work for me. And I think that's one of the reasons. Unlike most episodes, the structure is just not that clear.

Principal Flutie Creates An Obstacle

We have a cameo with Principal Flutie, which I enjoy. I always like seeing him. He's insisting that Buffy see the grief counselor or trauma counselor.

This is a nice example of how you should always have obstacles in your protagonist's way. Sometimes they can be fun obstacles like Principal Flutie. And they can be ones that you really want the protagonist to power past.

Buffy does still have to be a student here. She can't get kicked out again. So she does what Principal Flutie says.

We overhear Cordelia joking with the counselor about the upside of Dr. Gregory being dead is that she lost a little weight. Because she couldn't eat, so maybe that's good. And then saying, "Oh, I'm not saying we should kill teachers so I can lose weight."

A Midpoint Reversal?

At the midpoint of the story in terms of timing, about 22 minutes in, Buffy looks through the classroom window and sees the "Full-on Exorcist Twist" as she calls it.

She's late to class. From the hallway, she peers through the small window in the closed door. Ms. French turns her head completely – 180 degrees – and looks at Buffy. She has twisted her neck in a way that humans cannot do.

Maybe this is a Midpoint Reversal because Ms. French reveals herself to Buffy. Which puts Buffy in danger. And perhaps she did that because she sensed that Buffy was a predator or an enemy because Buffy already has fastened on Ms. French.

So we could argue Buffy in a way reveals herself and so commits in full to the quest. And that it's a reversal because Ms. French sees her. But all she really is doing is looking through the window.

An earlier point that could be Buffy throwing all in, throwing caution to the wind, could be when she goes to the park against Giles' warning. But, first, it happens before the Midpoint. And second, it just doesn't seem like that big a deal.

In fact, she even says to Giles, "Yes, I didn't listen to you. Get over it." It doesn't seem big enough.

Buffy seeing Ms. French twist her head around does change the story and drive it forward because Buffy learns for certain there's something wrong with Ms. French. And Buffy draws on what she learned in science class and by researching in books. She figures out that Ms. French is like a giant insect.

Giles puts it into the terms of shape shifting. That Ms. French can shift into an insect.

Midpoint: Xander's Point Of View

We also have this continuing plot about Xander. Ms. French invites different boys to meet her on different days after school and help construct papier-mache egg sacks.

She chooses Blaine the first day. We don't immediately see what happens to him, but we do find out later that he's missing.

Xander goes after school and Ms. French has, of course, left her things at home. She invites him to come to her house that night instead. When Buffy tries to tell Xander about Ms. French and warn him, it's after Xander met with Ms. French at school. He thinks Buffy's jealous.

So here is where we see it mostly from Buffy's point of view, but it is key for Xander as well. Because he first is saying, "Oh, I get it." That of course Buffy's jealous because now someone else wants him.

Then we see the shift where he realizes, no, Buffy really isn't jealous.

And then he's mad because he says, "Fine. You know, you just can't believe this woman's interested in me when you're not."

Dramatic Irony, Danger, And Ms. French

From Buffy's point of view, this interaction is key because it convinces her that Xander's okay. He's already gone to see

Ms. French and he's still alive. So Buffy and Willow aren't too worried about Xander at first.

This is dramatic irony. Because we know something Buffy doesn't, that Xander is still in danger.

Now we see a lot from Xander's point of view. He's at Ms. French's home. She is seducing him. She drugs him. We hear someone yelling in the basement.

The whole scene is mostly played for laughs. We do see Xander flashing back to his daydream about Buffy. So we know that though he is so attracted to Ms. French, he is also still thinking he really wants to be with Buffy.

Xander wakes up in a cage next to Blaine.

We then have Giles reveal that Ms. French will only prey on boys or men who are virgins. And there was a funny line from Buffy when Giles goes on about the history and the details.

Buffy says "Giles, while we're young!" I really like that line.

The Three-Quarter Turn

So now we are roughly at the three-quarter point of the story, which is about 34 minutes. And again, I'm having a little bit of trouble figuring out what the plot turn specifically is here. Things are happening and changing, but I'm not sure anything really spins the story in a new way.

It could be that reveal that Ms. French only preys on virgins.

That doesn't really change anything that happens, though. She's already captured Xander and Blaine. They've already figured out she's a shape shifter. It's not as if Buffy's not going to go after her regardless whom she preys on.

So it doesn't really change anything.

Buffy finds out she can kill Ms. French by dismembering

her. That doesn't change that much. Okay, so she can't just use a stake.

Xander's Plot Turns

If we go back to Xander's story, there is a significant plot turn. Which is the switch from him believing Ms. French is trying to seduce him to her drugging him and throwing him in a cage.

So that is a plot turn.

And I feel like this is part of why it's fuzzy here. Who is the protagonist? Is it Buffy or is it Xander?

Because we could argue here that Xander threw caution to the wind by agreeing to meet Ms. French at her home. So his story has more clear structure to it than the story about Buffy.

Fork Guy Becomes Less Scary

Now Buffy has to find Ms. French. We should be racing from the Three-Quarter Turn to the Climax.

Since Buffy doesn't know where Ms. French is, we have her going to the address that is in the school records. But she learns the woman who lives there is a retired substitute teacher named Ms. French. The shapeshifter has stolen her identity.

Buffy goes back to find Fork Guy because she thinks he can probably track Ms. French. This also feels like a bit of a let-down because he has been built up to be very dangerous. He fought Angel and survived. He fought Buffy and survived. (Granted, he ran away when the police came, but still we don't usually see vampires get away from Buffy.)

So we think that he's pretty powerful. Yet she subdues him seemingly pretty easily and gets him to take her to Ms. French's house.

Now perhaps it's because Xander's in trouble, making her extra-motivated. But we don't really see that. So we just have this supposedly super dangerous vampire that Buffy is able to control.

We do see Xander prying a bar out of the cage so he can fight Ms. French, so he is certainly being active.

The Climax

Buffy breaks into Ms. French's house.

And then is probably my favorite thing in this episode. Buffy figured out that bat sonar will affect Ms. French's nervous system and partially disable her. So she sent Giles off to record it. She's got this little mini recorder with her. She goes to play the bat sonar very dramatically. But it's a lecture, or talk, that Giles gave. The tape is on the wrong side.

(For those of you haven't seen them, there used to be these little mini tapes. People would dictate, sometimes at work, something onto them. Then a secretary would type it.)

Buffy flips the tape. She fights Ms. French. Eventually she gets that sonar to work, disables Ms. French, and chops her up and kills her.

So that is our Climax between Buffy and the villain.

Falling Action

Now we're in the Falling Action. Xander admits that he was an idiot. He should've listened to Buffy.

Willow comments on how terrible it is that Ms. French preyed only on virgins. Xander and Blaine are very embarrassed. Giles confirms it. And Blaine says, "My dad's a lawyer, no one better say anything about this."

And Xander, seemingly out of anger over the virgin aspect, though maybe he was going to do this anyway, now destroys all these eggs in these egg sacks.

So that could be the Climax of Xander's story, but it happens after our actual Climax. So it's kind of the definition of anticlimactic.

We also have Angel and Buffy flirting a little bit in the Bronze.

And there's a new science teacher, who is kind of generic, in class. Buffy is bored.

We see her find Dr. Gregory's glasses and tuck them into the lab coat hanging on the door. So we get that feeling of Buffy still remembering Dr. Gregory. And we hope that she will take with her the encouragement he gave her and what he told her he saw in her.

Challenges With Plot Structure

Let's go to the big picture on this episode.

I've already commented that the plot structure here isn't all that clear. You can certainly argue that there's no reason a writer has to use the plot structure that I like to follow. But I will say you see it in almost every movie and book, certainly any genre book. But even literary fiction, I will see these plot points. Maybe it's because I like well-structured stories, so that's what I gravitate toward. But generally, if you have a very powerful story, it follows that structure.

At the very least, your protagonist should be clear. Here, it's not.

Maybe there's just too much of a split between Buffy as the protagonist and Xander's own story arc and plot.

You can certainly have stories for more than one character, but I think this is an example of where maybe the balance didn't quite work as well as it could have.

Generally, your protagonist should be your main point of view character, have a goal, actively pursue that goal, and have the most at stake.

Point Of View And Character Growth

Here, we have a point of view split.

I like getting Xander's point of view. Yet I feel like that's part of what is not quite working here.

We get a lot of Xander, but he doesn't really grow as a character. Yes, he says to Buffy, "I was an idiot." Essentially says, "I should've listened to you."

But he still is super embarrassed that it's revealed that he's a virgin.

He's kind of in that same place that he was in the beginning, other than now he knows Blaine also is a virgin. So he has learned that he's feeling inadequate compared to what people like Blaine *say* about their lives. And their lives may be just like his, but he doesn't know it.

We don't really get a sense that he has some character growth. While he fights, he's not the one who defeats Ms. French.

Also, his goal is unclear. First, it's to be with Buffy. But then it's to be with Ms. French. Is he actively pursuing either? Not really. Because Ms. French in a way casts a spell on him. He for the most part forgets Buffy and is drawn into her orbit. But he doesn't really make a choice about that. He's under Ms. French's power.

Buffy's POV, Character Arc, And Motivation

When we go to Buffy's story, she certainly is the protagonist of our external conflict. Her goal is to find out what happened to Dr. Gregory and stop it from happening to anyone else, which she does.

Her emotional story, which I think could be really engaging, is that she finally has a teacher who doesn't see her as a delinquent. Who doesn't care about her past. And who sees her as smart and capable, wants her to excel, and believes that she can.

This gives her a great reason to want to find out what happened to Dr. Gregory.

But the story pretty much drops that. Yes, it certainly gives Buffy an extra reason to care. But it's not like she wasn't going to try to find out what happened, even if this was a teacher who didn't like her.

If any teacher ended up beheaded in a locker, she would be looking into it.

And because we spent a lot of time on Xander's story, we don't really get that much on how key this is to Buffy. It is there, because we have her tucking the glasses in at the end. But even that moment doesn't have quite the resonance it could if we had followed more of Buffy's emotional journey.

So I'm not saying the writers had to do that, or it should have been written differently. But I feel like there is tension here between these two stories, neither of which is really fully developed.

For an episode that goes into Xander's point of view and still has another story, check out the spoiler section. I'll talk a little bit about that.

Challenges With Tone

There're two other things I find a little challenging in this episode. One is the tone.

Buffy crosses drama and humor. It was made to do that. It's one of the first shows that did it so very well, and it really was groundbreaking. Its success is partly responsible for how much humor you now see within dramas and action movies and TV shows.

Here, though, somehow it undercuts the danger. The fact that so much of Ms. French and Xander's interaction (including the seduction scene) is played for laughs makes the threat less real.

We also get Ms. French as a praying mantis, looking fairly comical. Especially when she does this eeny-meeny-miney-mo thing to choose between Xander and Blaine. Those kinds of things usually work great for me in Buffy. For whatever reason, in this episode, to me it comes off as too silly.

An Episode-Long Joke?

Plus, the whole episode more or less seems like forty-five minutes of the joke that Blaine's a virgin despite how much he's pretending otherwise.

There's also this implication Dr. Gregory was a virgin. And I think well, does that matter? Why is that there?

I don't know. Which leads me to the idea that maybe what I'm struggling with is less the tone and more the metaphor.

Metaphors

For me, Buffy is strongest when the metaphor works. The big-picture metaphor of our seasons in high school is "High school is hell." And that makes it so emotionally compelling.

Here, what is the metaphor we're working with?

It could be a metaphor for a teacher inappropriately preying on her high school students sexually.

And the difficulty with that, I think, is that it's played for laughs. So we don't have the fear factor there. Some of this is because the dynamic is a woman teacher and boy students. Decades ago, there was a view among a lot of people something like, "Oh, if a male teacher preys on girl students, that is problematic, that is dangerous. But an attractive young-ish female teacher preying on her boy students is a gift to them."

In today's world, we're more concerned about all students in this scenario.

So maybe I'm doing that thing that I generally don't like doing, which is trying to critique Buffy from twenty-plus years later and looking at it in the context of today.

But even if you set aside that now we might be more concerned about a woman teacher pursuing her male students, because it's played mainly for the joke we still don't get that sense of menace.

So I feel like the metaphor falls apart. Because we even

textually have Buffy and Willow joking about boys being too dumb to see what's happening when older women are coming on to them.

And Xander, as I mentioned, destroys these egg sacks after learning about the virgin aspect of it. Suggesting that that's what's driving it, his embarrassment, not anger or fear over this teacher assaulting him.

Overall Series Tone

Probably overall the issue is that the show as a whole hadn't quite found its tone yet. It could have done this as a very dark metaphor, and maybe initially that was the thought. Or maybe that was an option on the table and it veered campier instead.

Normally the camp in Buffy works pretty well. But this one just didn't work for me.

Maybe it worked better for other viewers, or perhaps it worked better at the time. It's hard for me to recall my first viewing of it.

Spoilers

THE ONLY REAL spoiler here is the Season Three episode in Xander's point of view. That is the episode that includes Faith, who I always enjoy, and is where there are zombies. I guess not exactly zombies. The gang that killed themselves and come back to life. (I guess that does make them zombies. But they're pretty intelligent.) And Xander gets mixed up with them.

So while there's another plot going on with Buffy saving the world (yet again from an apocalypse), we have Xander trying to save himself and stop a plot to detonate a bomb.

A Clearer Point of View

There, I feel like the Xander point of view works much better. Or I should say I am more engaged by it. And there is a clear protagonist: it is clearly Xander's episode. Another plot involving Buffy is still there, but we get pieces of it mainly from Xander's point of view.

So I feel like that is a really good example. Perhaps it's not what they were trying to do in Teacher's Pet. But maybe they were experimenting with using another character's point of view for an episode and then nailed it later on.

So if you haven't watched that one and you want to juxtapose the two, you could watch the Season Three episode (The Zeppo).

Questions For Your Writing

- **Who is your main point of view character?**
- **Is that character also the protagonist? If not, what other aspects of the story make that character the protagonist?**
- **What tone are you aiming for with your story?**

Next: Never Kill A Boy On The First Date

NEXT I'LL TALK about Never Kill A Boy On The First Date,

when Buffy tries to go out with Owen. (Who, in Xander's words, "has a certain Owenocity.")

It also picks up our Master storyline again. I will talk once more about two intertwined plots. Or maybe it's more intertwining of plot and theme, which I think was done really well in that episode. And I'll also talk a little bit about the difference between game changers and cliffhangers.

CHAPTER SIX

NEVER KILL A BOY ON THE FIRST DATE

THIS CHAPTER TALKS about Season One, Episode Five, Never Kill A Boy On The First Date, written by David Greenwalt and directed by David Semel.

In particular, we'll look at:

- **All the major plot points**
- **Two plots that merge**
- **Characters' inner conflicts**
- **The difference between a game changer and a cliffhanger**

Okay, let's dive into the Hellmouth.

OPENING Conflict

We start in the graveyard. Buffy slays. Giles critiques. This interaction sets up the roles of our two characters for anyone who's new in the audience. Giles finds a ring on the ground and says he'll consult his books. And we get a cut to a dusty book slamming down on a table. It's not Giles though, it's the Master.

The Master hints at one of our plot conflicts, which is the Anointed One. He quotes a prophecy about the Anointed One and says, "The Slayer will not know him. He will lead her into hell." Also that the Anointed One will rise from the ashes of five who die.

Story Spark And Intertwining Plots

Right about 10% in, at 4 minutes, 30 seconds of a roughly 43-minute episode, we get our Story Spark or Inciting Incident. Usually this is right about when we will see this happen in the episode.

Buffy figures out that the ring relates to the Order of Aurelius. She sees this in a book in the library when Giles is saying he can't find anything. And we get this nice line that shows the developing playful relationship between the two.

She says, "Two points for the Slayer, while the Watcher has yet to score."

Owen comes into the library. Now this is our real conflict and our Story Spark.

Two Plots Merge

We basically have two plots here that merge into one in a way. We have the main plot with Buffy. She's trying to have a normal life – specifically, to date a boy that she is very interested in – while also fulfilling her Slayer duties. The other plot is Buffy trying to stop the Anointed One from rising. Or killing him if he does rise.

I'll talk a little more later about why the Owen-Buffy conflict is the main plot.

In the DVD interview Joss Whedon says, "This episode is so important because it is about Buffy maintaining a normal life, and it juxtaposes her vampire slaying directly with a date with a cute boy." So this is the most on target that we have addressed this issue for Buffy. In the other episodes to date, it's been more of an ongoing subplot or a side issue. An additional internal conflict for Buffy.

Owen

We see how much Buffy likes Owen because she gets flustered when she talks to him. She follows him upstairs in the library. She's happy that he's even thought about what she's like. And she has a hard time paying attention to Giles later when he tells her about this Order of Aurelius.

On the way from 10% through to our first major plot turn, we see Buffy clashing with Cordelia in the cafeteria. And they literally crash. Cordelia purposely crashes into Buffy near Owen's table. But Owen is not distracted. He and Buffy make a plan to meet at the Bronze at eight.

The conflict escalates when Giles tells Buffy about the prophecy he found. He says the Anointed One will rise from the death of five and that it is going to be tonight. And Buffy argues about missing her date, but eventually she agrees because she's going to do what she needs to do.

Giles warns her about the hazards of getting involved with anyone or revealing her identity and how it could put people close to her in danger.

Next we see Buffy and Giles on the roof waiting, sitting. Clearly, nothing's been happening. And he finally says, well, maybe he made a mistake.

The One-Quarter Twist

Now we're at the first major plot point. Usually this happens about one quarter of the way through the story. Here, it is almost exactly on target: 11 minutes and 23 seconds of a roughly 43 to 44 minute episode.

We see the bus. First, we see this little kid, who I think is playing with a paper airplane. And then we see this scary sort of guy we learn later is a murderer. He also gets turned into a vampire. He's talking to everyone about how "you will be judged." The scene on the bus escalates as the scary guy preaches to the bus driver, and the bus driver is telling him to sit.

There's someone in the road. We see it's a vampire. I don't know that the bus driver picks up on that, but he swerves and crashes.

All of this is inter-cut with Buffy at the Bronze. She gets there. Owen is dancing with Cordelia and Buffy leaves disappointed.

Too Long?

This bus scene has always felt a bit drawn out to me, even though I overall like this episode. I'm curious if anyone else feels that way. I've also wondered whether they ran short on this episode and perhaps kept in more of that scene than they really needed. It ends when we see the vampire killing people.

We cut to Buffy at school the next day, and she's complaining about how she has no life. Then Owen comes up to her at her locker. He's flirting with her, and it turns out he does still want to see her.

So while we had that One-Quarter Twist in our plot about the Master and the Anointed One, we also get a bit of a One-Quarter Twist here in that Owen changes things by revealing he's not really interested in Cordelia. He still wants to see Buffy.

We also get this moment where Buffy and Owen are flirting and he gives Buffy what looks like an antique pocket watch. The joke is so she'll know what time to meet him. Xander, who is jealous, glances at his Tweety Bird watch. His expression is just so clear.

Before Owen came back, or actually later in the episode, Xander will say to Buffy something like, "What you need is someone who already knows your darkest secrets."

Character Through Line: Xander

I found it interesting that in the DVD interview, Joss Whedon commented that Xander has a terrible crush and, "What happens is sort of typical to what happens to Xander in his life."

The reason I found that interesting is because for the most part, unlike Teacher's Pet, this story is not about Xander. We already have two plots with the Anointed One and the Master, and then Buffy and Owen.

Xander's interest in Buffy for this episode isn't really even a subplot. There's a little bit of a story happening here, but it's really more of a character through line for the season. So I found it interesting that Joss seemed to be saying that was what the episode is about in a way.

But he also said that it's about Buffy struggling to have a normal life. And I think what this points to is part of why the show works so well and why any good ensemble show works so well.

There are many different ways to come into the world of the story. Many different characters that audience members can identify with. So one person might really identify with Xander, and that brings that person into the story in a way that they might not have engaged with it if Xander were not there.

The Main Story Arc

We also see the Master telling a vampire that, when this work is done with the Anointed One he'll be one step closer to freeing himself from his underground prison. So this does a couple of things.

It is a reference to our season story arc about the Master

trying to get free and take over the world. It also is why I say the main plot is Buffy and Owen and Buffy trying to have this normal life. Not Buffy trying to stop the Master. Because this makes it clear that if the Anointed One rises and comes to the Master, it'll be a step forward for him.

It will help him, but it isn't going to win the day.

Side note: There's also this moment when the Master tells the vampires to give their lives, if necessary, to bring the Anointed One back to him and to kill the Slayer. I have always wondered why vampires would give their immortal lives for another vampire's cause. That's done a few times in the series and it's never really explained why they would do that.

Great Dialogue: Buffy And Giles

There is more great dialogue when Giles tells Buffy the day after the missed date that he miscalculated. Tonight is when the Anointed One will rise. She says it can't be that night because she has this date.

And he says, "Oh, well, I'll just jump in my time machine, travel to the Twelfth Century, and tell the vampires to push their prophecy back a few days so you can take in dinner and a show."

Buffy says, "At this point, you're abusing sarcasm."

I enjoy so much this developing relationship between them where they can have this kind of conversation.

That Buffy dropped everything the first time and missed her date does a couple of things. One, from an audience perspective, it helps us be on her side here because she did do the right thing the first time around. And it's not unreasonable for her to feel that if Giles made a mistake before, he may have made a mistake now. It also gives Giles a reason to capitulate when she points this out.

And he concedes that point when he shows up at her

house with this article showing that five people died in this bus accident and there was a murderer on the bus. Also, as Buffy points out, a bus crash isn't exactly the type of thing that they usually are used to dealing with.

Buffy Commits At The Midpoint

So now we are at the Midpoint. Because Giles is confronting her with these new facts about the bus crash, despite everything I just said the cautious thing would be for Buffy to be vigilant and skip her date.

But remember, our protagonist at the midpoint in a well-structured story typically commits all in, throws caution to the wind, and goes ahead with her quest. Here Buffy's quest is to have a normal life and to go out with a boy she really likes. She throws caution to the wind and says, "If the Apocalypse comes, beep me."

And she goes out with Owen.

(For those of you who haven't seen them, in the time before cell phones you could call someone's beeper from a landline. They would get a message, which looked like a text, with just your phone number. And you would know to call them.)

Often at the Midpoint, we see the protagonist suffer a reversal. Sometimes we see both the commitment and reversal. But here we just have Buffy throwing caution to the wind. And I think that it works really well. Buffy's action at the Midpoint propels the story toward the next major plot turn.

The Intertwined Plots

What we have now are scenes intercut with one another, just as Buffy's life is split between her desire to have a normal life and her Slayer duties.

So we get Giles going to the funeral home. Vampires surround him and chase him. He barricades himself in a room. Xander and Willow see this. They're going to go get Buffy because they aren't able to get Giles out.

In between all of that we see Buffy at the Bronze. She is talking with Owen, happy to be there, and yet checking her beeper. She looks worried when there is no message, but she dances with Owen anyway. He comments on feeling like she's two different people.

Cordelia tries to separate them.

I don't quite think Cordelia would be as over-the-top as she is. But it is fun because this is basically the high school fantasy of everyone who wasn't Cordelia, and perhaps even people who were. That this person that you are so interested in will return your feelings over, or instead of, somebody else who is more popular or better looking. And that wonderful feeling Buffy gets to experience that, yes, Owen does want to be with her and not Cordelia.

It's especially nice because Cordelia has been mean to her. So we see Buffy getting not just normal life, but a little bit of the high school fantasy.

We also have some fun when Cordelia sees Angel for the first time. She says, "Hello, Salty Goodness," and then just cannot believe it when he, too, talks to Buffy.

Conflict When Angel And Owen Meet

We have nice conflict when Angel and Owen meet. Angel is so surprised by the date. And Buffy has trouble explaining how she knows Angel.

She's also offended that Angel is surprised – she's reading him as surprised rather than jealous. I think he is both.

I get why she sees surprise though. She's been feeling like she has no life. She's tired of people like Giles or Xander and Willow – well, not Willow – but Xander and now Angel, saying in one way or another that she's not allowed to have a social life. That she should just be vampire slaying all the time.

Xander and Willow appear. They pretend they're double dating and get across to her that Giles is in trouble. Buffy tells Owen he can't go with to the funeral home.

And there's a nice shot with Buffy and Owen talking, and Angel is in the background between the two of them. I don't remember if I noticed that when I just watched the episode for fun or watched it the first time.

It's clearly very symbolic. I think it's subtle enough that it doesn't bang you over the head. But it was very noticeable now as I looked at this whole episode for how Buffy's two lives clash.

The Three-Quarter Turn

This takes us up to the next plot turn. Typically, that happens around three quarters through the episode. So we have a couple of things right around there at about 32 minutes in.

Owen follows Buffy to the funeral home. I think that is the turn in the Owen-Buffy plot because clearly had he not followed her, we wouldn't have the rest of the storyline between them. It would end very differently.

Buffy gets rid of Owen, sort of. She finds what she thinks will be a safe room, leaves him there, and finds Giles. Then about almost 35 minutes in, we get the turn or twist in the plot over the Anointed One. Because Owen's looking at this dead body. And he says he's read about them a lot. (We've heard that he is very fascinated by poems about death.) But now he is seeing an actual dead body.

Owen says, "I've never seen one before. Do they usually move?"

And the murderer sits up, and we realize he's a vampire. He says, "I have been judged."

The Anointed One

So this is a pretty significant turn in our story because now we know who the Anointed One is. Or at least we think that we do.

I was a little bit confused in previous viewings. I had thought the murderer was a vampire all along, from the moment we saw him on the bus. I don't think I caught the first few times that the guy in the road whom the driver swerves to avoid was the vampire. For a long time, I thought this murderer was a vampire the whole time.

But watching it carefully, I realized that when he sits up, he's saying "I have been judged" because he was human and he died. He was an evil human, but he was a human. And now he is undead. He feels this is a judgment on him and his worthiness apparently.

Later he says something like, "They told me while I was sleeping." So he sees some great significance to all of this. And that adds to our perception that this vampire is the Anointed One.

The Climax

So now from the Three-Quarter Turn to the Climax the story moves very fast.

Everything comes from that Three-Quarter Turn. With the Owen-Buffy story, it's Buffy trying to keep Owen safe and to still hide her identity from him. While she also, in the Anointed One plot, is trying to kill this vampire and protect Giles.

Giles gets knocked out. There's a lot of fighting. At one point Buffy is out for a moment. She wakes and thinks that Owen is dead. It looks like the vampire killed him.

Buffy fights the vampire. She's really angry. With Giles' help, she sends the vampire into the incinerator.

That fight is our Climax of the Anointed One plot. After

it, Owen is confused. He leaves, and he doesn't want Buffy to walk him home.

The Falling Action And Climax

Now we get to the Falling Action from the Anointed One plot.

Xander, Willow, and Buffy walk down the stairs. This is when Xander says, "You need someone who knows your darkest secret and still likes you." And he says, "someone like…"

And Buffy says, "Owen?" because Owen appears. He still wants to see her. But it's because of all the danger. He found it invigorating. He felt alive and excited. And he thinks she's amazing.

I think this is the Climax of the Owen-Buffy arc because this is the moment where everything comes together and Buffy says she doesn't want to see him again. Saying No is her last act protecting Owen.

And then there is Falling Action in that plot because Giles comes over to talk to her. He gives her credit for making this choice. And tells her about learning at the age of ten that his destiny was to be a Watcher. And how unhappy he was and the sacrifices that he needed to make.

Buffy says that Giles and Willow and Xander understand the score. They know to be careful. But Owen would get killed in a day in her world, and she can't risk that.

Buffy's Choice About Owen

I also think (though Buffy doesn't say it) there has to be an element there of wanting Owen to want to keep seeing her for who she is as a person. Aside from being the Slayer. And while I think he does – I think he likes that part of Buffy, too – I don't think she wants someone who mainly wants her for that reason.

We will deal with the different parts of who Buffy is in a

relationship quite a ways down the road. But I can't help thinking there's a little of that, too. But I'm guessing. Buffy's dialogue suggests it is mainly that she needs to protect Owen.

Character Development: Buffy And Giles

Buffy feels deep regret that she didn't listen to Giles in the first place. Well, I guess in the second place. She listened to him the first time. But when he showed her that article, she is afraid that Giles could have gotten killed because she was off trying to have a date.

But he reassures her. Which I so love about Giles. He says, "We're figuring it out as we go." And she's doing pretty good, and at least they stopped the Anointed One.

I like this about Giles so much because it would be easy to write a one-note sort of Giles who is always scolding Buffy. Who would shake his finger and say, "Yes, I could have gotten killed. See what happens when you try to be social."

But Giles is so much more nuanced than that. And it's partly because of knowing Buffy and recognizing that she is a whole person. In the beginning, I don't know that he was ever one-note, but he was much more about the dire warnings. He, too, has already grown and Buffy has grown.

It's such a great relationship. And there is plenty of conflict there already without having him behaving like a punitive parent.

Cliffhangers Versus Game Changers

Now we get the Game Changer.

A Cliffhanger is where we end something without resolving the conflict. The good guy plunges over the cliff, literally, and we think the he's going to die, and cut. You need to come back for the next episode to find out how our protagonist gets out of that situation.

So the story does not wrap up.

If the story was about our protagonist having to catch the

bad guy, we're left with, "Can the good guy survive and still get the bad guy or not?" Unless you're writing a really dark story and the good guy just dies at the end. But if we don't see that he dies, you still have a cliffhanger. You need to come back for the resolution.

That is different than a game changer.

Here, we find out the Master is with the little kid from the bus. And the Master repeats his prophecy about the Anointed One. So we know that murderer vampire was not the Anointed One after all. This child is.

Buffy actually failed to stop the Anointed One from rising. So our Anointed One plot resolved. Buffy doesn't know how it resolved. She thinks she prevailed, and she actually lost. But the plot resolved, and as the audience we find out how. So we're not stopping short of the Climax or of the resolution.

But we do change everything. Now going forward we have a new threat. We have an Anointed One, and we have a threat Buffy is completely unaware of.

That's a game changer.

Endings And Installments

A game changer is a great way to end when you're writing something that's in installments. You resolve the plot but change the game to bring the reader back.

But it can be a struggle to figure out the difference between a cliffhanger and game changer. It's not always such a clear distinction. That can be tricky because if they don't realize it's an installment style story, readers do not like to be left with a cliffhanger.

In my Awakening supernatural thriller series, I did have what I saw as a game changer at the end of the second book. It's a four-book series, so it ended at the middle of the series. I thought that was a good place to have a game changer.

But some readers felt like it was a cliffhanger. And I did get a few comments about that, about not liking that. Especially at first when I didn't have all four books released yet. (Once they were all out people didn't seem to mind so much. They could just go right on to the next one.)

So it's something to really think about when you're ending your story.

Here, I think it's really well done. Because we do wrap the plot, and obviously we know this is a series. It's a nice hook for us to come back and see what happened.

Commentary On Creating Characters

A couple of more things from the DVD interview. These were not specific to Never Kill A Boy On A First Date, although it all kind of relates.

Joss Whedon said there is a little bit of him in each character, which I think is true for any writer. But he specifically commented that Xander is very much like he was in high school. So perhaps that's why we get his comment about what happens to Xander in this episode, even though it is really not a Xander-centric episode.

He also said something I'd forgotten about, though I'm sure I must have watched this interview way back when I got the DVDs. Joss said that he went to an English boarding school, so some of Giles comes from that, from his experience.

And he said Giles is the classic British guy in the horror movie who says, "The vampires are coming, the vampires are coming," and consults his dusty books. (As I talked about, I love that about Giles. And I love that we do get more nuance from him.)

Spoilers

ONE QUICK THING. I love that after Cordelia sees Angel and says the salty goodness line, she says something like, "Call 911. That boy will need oxygen when I'm done with him."

And I just find that fun given that we are going to find out in another, I think two episodes, that Angel is a vampire. He doesn't need oxygen at all.

The other spoiler occurred to me only as I was recording the podcast episode. My comment about Buffy wanting Owen to like her for her might have come from my having watched the Buffy-Riley relationship.

Remember the episode The Replacement? It's the one in Season Five where the demon splits Xander into two people. And Buffy and Riley have this conversation. She asks if Riley would like her to split out those two parts of her, the Slayer Buffy and Buffy Buffy (the person).

Because that's what that demon Toth was trying to do in the first place and missed and hit Xander.

What's interesting to me about that is in that episode, Buffy is struggling with feeling like Riley would prefer her to *not* be the Slayer.

He denies it. He says he wants the whole package, and he's in love with the whole package. Yet there is a lot that happens that suggests that maybe he's not okay with it. Or he just hasn't found a way to come to terms with it.

But there she is feeling like she wants Riley to want the whole package. By that time, I think she feels more integrated with who she is than she does when she's dealing with Owen.

We'll see what I think when we get to that season. I'm excited about getting to that point so we can talk more about that Buffy-Riley relationship. And of course soon we'll get to talk about the Buffy-Angel relationship.

Questions For Your Writing

- **Is there an inner conflict that the plot of your story forces the protagonist to confront? If so, how do the plot points force the issue?**
- **Does your protagonist need to make a tough choice at the end of the story? If no, would that be appropriate in your story? If yes, can you make it harder for the protagonist?**
- **Have you used a game changer or a cliffhanger at the end of one of your stories? Did you get any feedback about that from readers?**

Next: The Pack

NEXT WE'LL TALK about The Pack. As with Never Kill a Boy on the First Date, The Pack is a standalone episode. I'll talk about all the major plot points and subplots. We'll also talk about building up feelings for the victim and misdirecting the audience. We talked in The Witch about misdirection as to the villain, but this time there's a bit of a misdirect as to the victim.

CHAPTER SEVEN

THE PACK

THIS CHAPTER TALKS about Season One, Episode Six: The Pack, a standalone episode, written by Matt Kiene and Joe Reinkemeyer and directed by Bruce Seth Green.

In particular, we'll look at:

- **Interweaving the main plot and a character-based subplot**
- **Using dramatic irony to increase tension**
- **Building the character of the victim to make the loss greater, or more serious, for the audience**
- **Misdirection regarding the victim**

Okay, let's dive into the Hellmouth.

OPENING Conflict With Obvious Exposition

We start with Buffy at the zoo alone. A group of four mean kids teases her. One of them says, "Were you this popular at your old school before you got kicked out?" This particular line feels to me like a backfill for the audience. Not the, "were you this popular at your old school?" I feel like that works.

But the "before you got kicked out." It seems like something thrown in there to remind the audience – or inform a new audience member – that Buffy was kicked out of her old school. I say that because these four kids don't seem like ones who would mock Buffy for being kicked out. They appear to always be on the edge of being kicked out themselves. It seems more like they might think she was cool for that.

It's one of the rare times, or I guess first time so far, that I felt like the opening dialogue was a little bit obvious in being there to fill in the blanks.

However, I do like that these kids are teasing Buffy. We see that she feels bad that she doesn't have the social network or the friends or the standing that she had in her old school.

We then see the mean kids picking on Lance. I noticed as I watched this time that he's in a red shirt. Which I think is kind of fun. It might or might not be a reference to the red shirts in Star Trek who always end up getting killed.

This scene is part of what initially makes us think that Lance is going to be the real victim here. Certainly these students do victimize him. But he survives the episode, which I did not expect.

The first time I watched it, and even this time, my initial thought when they reach the hyenas was, "Oh yeah, they're going to throw him in to the hyenas and kill him." Which doesn't happen.

For now, they steal his notebook.

Principal Flutie

Lance, though, doesn't rat the mean kids out when Principal Flutie intervenes. This interaction between Flutie and these kids builds Principal Flutie up as someone we like.

In the pilot I liked him a lot because we saw how much he cared about the students and about Buffy. Also how he was dealing with an internal struggle to both be supportive for her and yet protect the other students from this newcomer who burnt down the gym at her old school.

Here, there's this nice interaction where Flutie shows some self awareness.

One of the mean kids starts to talk. Flutie says, "Did I ask you to speak?"

And then he realizes he did just ask the kid what happened. And Flutie says, "Okay, I guess I did."

So we get a little humor and a little awareness on his part of conflicting directives he's sending. I like that because often we see authority figures never acknowledging that they either are wrong or that they are being confusing, and that it's not fair to yell at someone after that. We also see that Flutie wants to protect the weaker student.

We ought to expect that from school authorities, but it doesn't always happen.

Story Spark In The Pack

So we've talked before (and I'll continue to talk) about our Story Spark or Inciting Incident that usually comes about 10% into a movie, book, or TV episode.

In Buffy, so far it's nearly always been right about at that 10% mark, about 4 minutes, 30 seconds into a roughly 43-44 minute episode. (That runtime includes credits.)

Here it comes a tiny bit later, at 5 minutes, 8 seconds.

The kids grab Lance as if they're going to throw him over the bars to the hyenas. Xander followed these kids in to try to help Lance. He told Buffy he'd go because this doesn't require actual slaying. So far Willow and Xander both say these kids are mean, but not physically dangerous. Although Willow kind of second guesses herself on that.

The hyenas' eyes flash when the kids threaten to throw Lance in. And then the kids' eyes flash, including Xander's, and they all turn on Lance. He runs away.

So this is where, in my memory, I'm always thinking they actually threw Lance in and he died. But he does get away and we go to the credits.

Dramatic Irony At The Bronze

Now we're at the Bronze. That moment with Xander's eyes flashing in the previous scene is another example of dramatic irony. That's where the audience knows something that the protagonist or other characters do not.

And here it's that Xander was affected by whatever happened in the hyena pit.

At the Bronze, he acts strangely. He sniffs Buffy's hair, he grabs Buffy's food, and he laughs when the mean kids make fun of another student who is overweight. When Buffy and Willow stare at him, Xander shrugs and says, "Ah, the kid's fat."

More Character Development: Principal Flutie

Our next scene starts in the point of view of this little pig. I think his name is Herbert. And he is running through the hall. And I just kind of enjoy that perspective.

Then we get to Principal Flutie. He is trying to catch this pig. Buffy grabs the pig for him. And again we, at least I, like Principal Flutie. He's so excited about this pig and he has put this little razorback on it. Tried to make it look fierce.

He's insistent about that. When Buffy says the pig is cute,

Flutie says, "No, he's fierce. He's a Razorback. He's our mascot."

And we also get that he's a little afraid of the pig. Buffy tries to hand it to him, and he backs off and tells her to take Herbert.

So Buffy carries him into the room and puts him a cage. It's this nice moment of vulnerability for Principal Flutie. That's another reason that we like him. He shows a little bit of fear. Shows his human side.

And he starts talking to her about the old days and school spirit and how things were better back then. Again, we get this self-awareness on his part. He says, yes, when he was young there were old guys telling him how things were much better in their times. So that is also very nice.

We get a little bit of a hint of the later conflict and of what Xander is. Because the pig squeals when Xander walks by.

This is a hint to Buffy. She doesn't know it at the time, but it adds to her feeling of strange things around Xander.

The One-Quarter Twist

All of this is building up to our first major plot turn. That turn usually happens around a quarter way through an episode or a story. It turns the story in a new direction and comes from outside of our protagonist. So here we should see it roughly 11 minutes into the episode. It's often been slightly later than that, though.

Here, we've got a few things that could be that One-Quarter Twist. Right at 11-12 minutes is that pig squealing. So we could see that as a bit of a turn, but I don't think that it's enough. It doesn't really change anything. It just adds to Buffy's awareness of weirdness around Xander.

So where I see this turn is about 14 minutes in. Two things happen.

We have a dodgeball game in gym class. Xander throws really hard at Willow to get her out. You can tell how hurt she feels. Yes, it's a game. But, one, he didn't have to throw it at Willow. There are plenty of people on both teams. He could avoid throwing the ball at her. Two, even if their deal (because we don't know) is, "Hey, yeah, if we're playing a game, we're both going to try to win," he doesn't have to throw so hard at her.

This really is a turn in the emotional arc or subplot between Xander and Willow. She sees this, as we'll discover in a moment, as perhaps part of his feelings for Buffy. That he doesn't really want Willow around anymore.

The story also turns for the hyena kids. Buffy is the only one left on the other side. All they have to do to win is hit her with the ball. With that many of them, they probably could, though it might take a while.

But instead they turn on Lance, who is on their side. They throw all the dodgeballs at him even after he falls to the floor. This attack happens 14 minutes, 43 seconds in. I feel like this is the plot turn because this is what truly tells Buffy, our protagonist, that something is seriously wrong. Both with Xander and even with these kids.

Because we've been told and seen that they're mean kids. But this seems a little over the top. Because you would think they probably would want to win the game.

And maybe more telling – they don't know Buffy's the Slayer. All they know is she played dodgeball pretty well. So it doesn't make sense that they would turn on the person on their own team instead of her.

Moving Toward The Midpoint

From there, everything escalates as we move toward the Midpoint. We have this scene with Xander and Willow in the hallway. He is so mean to her, telling her he doesn't need her anymore because he's dropping geometry.

We later see Xander with the mean kids (who I'll call the pack from now on). They're stealing food. And about 18 minutes in, we see that the pack is going to eat this pig. That is off screen, but it's clear what's happening.

Xander is not with them because we find out he is — actually, I'm not sure on the timing on that, why he's not with them. He does later confront Buffy, but that's not happening yet. But for whatever reason, he is not with the pack when they eat the pig.

Buffy goes to Giles and says Xander is acting in this terrible way. Giles really downplays it. He says Xander's a teenage boy, that's what's wrong with him, and what is Giles supposed to do about it? Buffy says, "Get your books, look stuff up."

She also remembers that the pig was scared of Xander. Giles says, "Well, boys prey on the weak."

Right around here, Buffy remembers the zookeeper talking about hyenas preying on the weak.

The Midpoint Of The Pack

So this is roughly our Midpoint in the episode. There isn't really, for Buffy, that strong moment at the Midpoint that we typically see. One with our protagonist fully committing to the quest, throwing caution to the wind, or suffering a major reversal.

We do have a sort of caution to the wind for the pack eating this pig. That is definitely committing that they are hyenas now.

Protagonist Issues

The problem with that from a storytelling perspective is they are not the protagonists here. This is a little bit like the issues with Teacher's Pet, where we had a very Xander-centric-Xander point of view episode. Yet he wasn't exactly the protagonist.

That's even more of an issue here. Because we don't know the pack. They aren't drawn in a way that we care about them.

We care about Xander, and this episode is about Xander to a large extent. But he isn't our protagonist. He is entirely carried along by events. Yes, he makes choices, but it is while he is possessed. So it's not really Xander.

And it's not Xander's actions that get him out of that. It is mainly Buffy's actions and those of Willow, Buffy, and Giles combined. Also, if we use the moment of the pig as that point of no return, Xander also wasn't part of that.

Midpoint Issues

The Midpoint here, in my mind, is a little bit weak, though we definitely have things changing. We do have a new direction. It comes out of Buffy's realization when she puts together Giles saying "preying on the weak" with the zookeeper's comments. Buffy's realization drives the story forward to the next major plot turn and then the Climax.

So Buffy is an active protagonist, and we do have a Midpoint here. But it isn't super clear or compelling.

Right after this, Willow comes in and says, that Herbert, the pig, is dead. And he was eaten. Willow asks Giles what he's going to do.

In a really nice repetition of Buffy's line, but with a different inflection, Giles says, "Get my books, look stuff up."

So he is acknowledging that he was wrong.

The End Of Flutie

Our next series of scenes intercuts between the room where the pig was kept in the cage and Principal Flutie interacting with the rest of the pack.

Buffy goes to that room to look around. And that is where

Xander creeps up behind her, and she doesn't hear him. Which is significant because we know Buffy has Slayer senses, heightened senses, and she doesn't hear Xander creep up behind her.

He tries to sexually assault her. You could argue to some extent he succeeds because he does pin her and I think that he licks her face. I wasn't overly worried for Buffy because she is holding back. She doesn't want to hurt him, but eventually she will because she has to stop him.

Flutie And The Hyena Kids

We cut back and forth to Principal Flutie. He finds the rest of the pack and takes them to his office. And we see this interaction which is really tense. They are a physical threat to him. But also I feel like this scene embodies the fear of any authority figure, which is that their authority will be ignored.

To a lesser extent, I imagine any principal or teacher feels this way. What if the students decide to just not listen to you? There is a limited amount you can do if the student doesn't care about sanctions, like going to the principal's office or being suspended. Or having their grade dropped.

The control that the authority figure has is dependent on the student being invested in that system.

And here we get students who, though Principal Flutie doesn't know it, are no longer students. They have become hyenas. They toy with him and then attack him. And he is so shocked. I feel like his initial shock as they're approaching is less that he really fears physical violence and more that he just doesn't know what to do with them flouting his authority.

But then it becomes clear that they are going to attack him. We get that cut to his picture and we hear him screaming.

Surprise And A Shift

We don't see this awful act, just like we didn't see the pig being eaten. But we know what's happening. And there is some playing for — I guess I would say for the comedy here — because throughout Principal Flutie's voice has become higher. It becomes squealing. He's clearly being likened to Herbert the pig.

I was probably surprised the first time around by this. At some moment in the scene, before Principal Flutie realizes it, we realize they're going to attack him. Because we know they're the ones who ate the pig. Well, I guess he knows that too. But we know they've become hyenas, while he is still thinking they're just dangerous students. Or unbalanced students, however you want to put it. He doesn't know they're possessed.

Until that really started to shift, I didn't necessarily expect them to attack him. Because Lance had been set up as the one who was not going to survive here. Also because I like Principal Flutie. From the pilot on we see him as this continuing character we're expecting will be part of the series for a while.

This is about 27 minutes in and this, even more than eating the pig, is the moment the pack throws caution to the wind. They have now killed and eaten a human.

Buffy, Xander, And Giles

Buffy drags Xander into the library. She says he tried to commit felony sexual assault. She also says she hit him with a desk.

So we didn't see that happening, but we know she's subdued Xander. I think that's a deliberate choice by the writers because we don't want to see Buffy hitting her friend with a desk, no matter that he's possessed or behaved terribly. These days, if the show were made, perhaps we would see that.

Giles comes in and tells them that the pack ate Principal

Flutie. And Buffy says maybe the zookeeper can help. She comments that perhaps he didn't quarantine the hyenas because they were ill.

Three-Quarter Turn

Though Buffy connected the idea of what the zookeeper said before with the hyenas, this is the first time she suggests he can help them, that perhaps he knew something was wrong with the hyenas.

Willow says she will stay and watch Xander.

So we have some really nice turns in the story here, and we are right around the three-quarter point in the episode, about 33-ish minutes in. The major plot turn at this moment in the story should grow from the Midpoint, and it should spin the story in a new direction. Unlike the One-Quarter Twist, it's not coming from outside the protagonist. It's growing organically from our Midpoint and spinning the story yet again.

Two things do that here.

Turn In Xander And Willow Subplot

In our Willow and Xander story, around 32 minutes 45 seconds, he tries to trick her into coming close enough so that he can take the key to the cage from her. And she, likewise (though he doesn't realize it), is testing him. She is well aware of what he is doing. He lunges for the key after saying all the things Willow would want to hear. How he cares about her, how maybe this is all — I guess she wouldn't want to hear this — but he's saying, it's really Buffy that's the problem. Their lives didn't need saving before she came to Sunnydale, and so forth.

Basically, he is saying how much he values his friendship with Willow.

This is what Willow would hope Xander would say. But she recognizes that he may be manipulating her. He asks her why she stayed to watch him if she's so suspicious of him. As he lunges for the key she says, "I wanted to see if you're still yourself."

After he grabs for the key and she jerks away, she says, "Now I know."

So that is right around our three-quarter point. It's a turn where now Willow is certain that the hyena took over Xander. I feel like she makes a distinction. She believed that perhaps Xander would be mean to her. There's that point where she says to Buffy, "Maybe three isn't company anymore." That maybe he just doesn't want Willow around, which is an awful thought for her. But she can believe that might be Xander.

It's Buffy who is convinced that this is not Xander. And I feel that's because Willow has that vulnerability over how she feels for Xander.

Here, though, she knows that even if he were being a little bit mean and swept up in his feelings for Buffy, he would not physically try to hurt her or attack her. Here he shows that's what he's willing to do. So she knows it's the hyena.

I love that too, because it's this very mixed thing for Willow. On the one hand, it shows that Xander, her friend, still cares about her. That it wasn't his choice to be so mean to her. But on the other it puts him and everyone in terrible danger.

Main Storyline Three-Quarter Turn

We also have a major turn in our main plot of Buffy trying to stop these hyenas and save Xander. About 32 minutes 52 seconds in the zookeeper tells Buffy and Giles about the hyenas being vicious. And there being rituals.

Right then Giles mentions the predatory act part of the

ritual. And the zookeeper is surprised and asks how Giles found that out.

Buffy cuts off this discussion. Not because she realizes right then that the zookeeper is the perpetrator, but because she's annoyed they're just talking about books when there are important things to do.

I love that the story has just spun in a new direction, but Buffy doesn't realize it. Also, I don't think I caught the zookeeper perking up at Giles' predatory act comment until I rewatched knowing what was coming.

But this definitely takes the story to a new place. Now the zookeeper knows how to make this ritual work, and he did not know that before. The focus will be on him trying to take over this power as Buffy is trying to stop him. So she has a more formidable foe that she is not aware of yet.

Danger And De-Possession

During the first watch, what looks like the key plot turn is when the zookeeper says the pack will find its missing member. We all realize Willow is in great danger because the pack is going to go after Xander. There is a shift right there. In addition to this plan to try to de-possess everyone, Buffy and Giles also need to save Willow.

At the library, we hear one of the hyenas calling Willow's name. She thinks it's Xander and tells him to shut up. Right then is a cut for the commercial break.

So we talked about cliffhangers last time. This is a little cliffhanger right before the commercial break.

On return, the pack frees Xander, they go after Willow, and she hides.

Xander is there when she comes out from under the desk. But Buffy and Giles arrive in time to help save her.

Buffy tries to lure the pack away, while Giles and Willow head toward the zoo.

Moving Towards The Climax

All of this is moving very fast toward the Climax. Eventually we get to the zoo and the zookeeper is there in ceremonial paint and garb. Giles sees a design on the floor and catches on right as the zookeeper knocks him out.

(Once again, I think Giles has been knocked out in two-thirds of these episodes so far. And he will continue to get knocked out. He would probably have some really serious brain injuries from all of this. Happily, in the Buffyverse that isn't a problem.)

Willow comes in, she doesn't know where Giles is. But she lets the zookeeper tie her up because she thinks this is part of the plan. We then get to our Climax.

The Climax Of The Pack

Willow has a knife to her throat. She says to the zookeeper, "Oh, now you're going to pretend to do a predatory act?" And he says, "Something like that." She yells out that it's a trap.

The zookeeper becomes possessed by the hyenas. Xander tackles him to save Willow. This is a nice Climax to the Willow-Xander relationship arc, that Xander does this. Because immediately when the hyena leaves him, he goes to save Willow.

Then we have the Climax of the plot itself.

Buffy is continuing to fight. The zookeeper runs at her. She's in front of the railing walling off the hyenas. He goes over and they kill him.

The Villain's Death

As in The Witch, we see that Buffy doesn't kill a human being. Despite that he is doing evil things, things beyond the reach of the human justice system, she still doesn't kill him, although she is instrumental in his death.

But it is again a sort of poetic justice. He wanted to have

this power of the hyenas, and now the hyenas are killing him. So yet again, we have this theme of he is his own undoing. Therefore, I think in the show's moral compass or moral universe what happens to him is okay. But we're not seeing Buffy kill somebody.

The Predatory Act

Something I found interesting as I watched this time, I was thinking about the predatory act aspect. And I thought, "Does the zookeeper really commit a predatory act?" Because while he has the knife at Willow's throat, he doesn't actually kill her. Clearly, we don't want Willow to be killed.

So is that really a predatory act?

But I remembered that with Lance the predatory act was the mean kid pushing him up to the guard rail and threatening to throw him over. That was enough of an act to trigger possession. So here, the zookeeper threatening Willow likewise triggers the possession.

Falling Action In The Pack

Now we have our Falling Action. There is a conversation about Principal Flutie and when he'll be replaced. Xander pretends he doesn't know what he did. Nobody tells him that he tried to assault Buffy or anything else. He does say no one messes with his Willow. So that's a nice part of the Falling Action for the Willow and Xander arc.

Giles tells Xander when he's alone that he couldn't find anything about memory loss with possession. Xander asks if Giles told Willow and Buffy that. Giles assures him his secret is safe.

One of the things that is not tied up in the Falling Action is what happens to the rest of the pack.

We know that Xander has these memories. The pack therefore also must have them. And they ate a pig and then killed and ate Principal Flutie. Which no matter what kind of people they are would just be horribly traumatic.

And we just leave that, we don't deal with it at all.

I understand that it isn't their story. But I feel like that is part of what is unsatisfying for me about this episode. It's just left hanging.

We also don't deal at all with the fact that they too are victims of the zookeeper's scheme. It's as if the show is saying, "Well, because they're mean kids, who cares what happens to them." I don't think that was the writers' intent. I think they were just focused on the story they were telling. But it does leave this open space here.

The Big Picture

This isn't one of my very favorite episodes. Like a lot of Season One episodes it doesn't contribute to the season arc. I don't mind that so much. I really enjoy some of the one-off episodes. But it also, for me, just doesn't have the same emotional resonance as other episodes do.

The possession is not so much of a metaphor for anything, and maybe that's it. As I said before, I like Buffy best when the metaphor works And here, I'm not sure. We have this metaphor of mean kids being like hyenas. But the possession isn't their choice. Yes, they do this predatory act that sets it off. So you can argue that's partly their choice, but I don't know if that works that well.

I will take back something though. It does contribute to the story arc in the sense of Principal Flutie being gone now. His absence opens a space for someone new to come in.

Spoilers

About Angel

There is maybe a tiny bit of foreshadowing here when Xander, as he is trying to assault Buffy, says Buffy only likes men, I think he says, "who are dangerous and mean, and guess who just got mean?" He's referring to Angel, which is interesting, because we have not seen Angel being dangerous to Buffy or mean. But I guess he has an air of danger. He's always coming to warn Buffy about terrible things.

Next week we'll find out that he's a vampire ,and she will keep seeing him despite the danger there. So I guess this is a little bit of a hint of that. It also foreshadows Season Two where Angel does become a threat to Buffy and everyone else.

A Philosophical Question

Which raises a philosophical question. (I know I'm far from the first one to contemplate this.) Why does Xander get a pass for everything he does while possessed by the hyena, but Angel's whole arc in Buffy and Angel is to make up for what he did as Angelus, when he was a vampire? In fact, throughout Buffy, we mostly feel that people are not at fault for what they do if they are possessed.

One reason might be, as we'll see later, that Angel makes a choice in a way to become a vampire. It's unclear to me if he knows what it is he's choosing, though, when Darla turns him. We'll have to look at it more closely when we get that flashback. Right now it's been a while since I saw it and I don't recall how aware he is. He's definitely portrayed as willing to go along with Darla, but I'm not sure you can argue he knows what he is going to become.

We do get perhaps some answer to this in Amends. That's where The First appears as Jenny Calendar and shows Angel the kind of man he was. Which echoes this idea with the mean kids. They were behaving terribly, and so this episode is not concerned about the fallout to them and what happens to them. So maybe there is a parallel there. Maybe that is a principle or philosophy of the show or a theme. We'll talk about that more as we learn more of Angel's story.

The New Principal

There is that little foreshadowing here, going back to Principal Flutie. As in who will the principal's replacement be? Much as I miss Flutie, it is really fun to see Principal Snyder.

Questions For Your Writing

- **In your latest novel or story, did you tie up all the loose ends? If not, how do you plan to do so?**
- **Does your story include a subplot? How does it fit with the main plot?**
- **What can you do to build up the victim, or any other key character in your story, so that the reader feels more invested in and concerned about that character?**

Next: Angel

ANGEL IS one of my favorites. It comes exactly at the Midpoint of Season One and definitely turns our season-long story arc in a new direction.

CHAPTER EIGHT

ANGEL

THIS CHAPTER TALKS about Season One, Episode Seven: Angel, written by David Greenwalt and directed by Scott Brazil.

In particular, we'll look at:

- **The way the writers weave the main plot and two separate subplots together**
- **What your protagonist needs**
- **Turning the season antagonist into the protagonist for the main plot**
- **Buffy's Season One Midpoint Reversal and Commitment**

Okay, let's dive into the Hellmouth.

A MAIN PLOT And Two Subplots

As I sat down to analyze the plot points in this episode, I struggled to figure out exactly where they were. Which seems strange because I love this episode, and I think it is very well structured.

After a while I realized it's because we have a main plot and two subplots.

The main plot is really the Master's plot to kill Buffy and win Angel back. The Master is our protagonist in this episode, though he acts through Darla, and though he normally is our antagonist during this season.

Our other plot — which you could see as the main plot since Buffy is our traditional protagonist and it's her show – is Buffy wanting to be with Angel. Falling for Angel. Which is really part of Buffy's overall series struggle to try to have a normal life, a personal life, while being the Slayer..

We also have a subplot of Angel wanting to be with Buffy. Angel is the protagonist of this plot.

I'll talk as I go along about why I don't see the Buffy-Angel subplots as one cohesive subplot. All three plots are woven together so well, though, that it did take me a while to see them separately.

The Opening Conflict

We start with our opening conflict. Remember, that conflict is what draws the reader in and gets the reader intrigued, and it might or might not relate to the main plot.

Here, it does – if we see the Master's plot to kill Buffy and win Angel back as the main plot.

The Master starts out by saying, "Zachary did not return from the hunt." And there is a conversation between the Master, Colin (the little boy Anointed One One from the last episode), and Darla.

They are all blaming Buffy. The Master asks Colin what he would do. Colin says "I would annihilate her." The

Master says something like, "From the mouths of babes." Darla wants to be the one to kill Buffy. But the Master says no, Darla has a personal interest. He'll send "The Three."

We don't know who The Three are. But the tone tells us that this is something serious and ominous and not good for Buffy.

Party At The Bronze

The next scene is at the Bronze. It is the fumigation party before they fumigate the Bronze and get rid of the cockroaches. Everyone gets a free drink if they bring up a cockroach that they killed.

Willow is explaining this to Buffy, which also obviously tells the audience about what is going on here. But Buffy is really not paying attention. And Willow says, "What's it like where you are?"

This is when they get into a conversation about Angel and how Buffy is thinking about him, but she can't really see how she'd have a relationship with him.

She says, "How would that be? Every time he turns up it's, 'Hi, honey you're in great danger.'" I've talked before about getting exposition in through conflict. These are two exposition issues: the fumigation party and the Buffy-Angel relationship.

The conversation is very quick, but it brings viewers up to speed with what's happening. And it does it through conflict because Willow's explaining something and Buffy is not paying attention. They are good friends, so Willow doesn't take it personally. But there is a little conflict there and that helps keep us interested even as both characters are really telling us things that we need to know.

We also see Cordelia and Xander exchange some insults on the dance floor.

Story Spark

We now move to our Story Spark or Inciting Incident which typically comes about 10% into any story. And here we see that Story Spark right on target at 4 minutes and 10 seconds.

The Three, these very powerful vampires, attack Buffy. There's a fight. Two of them end up holding her, one is advancing toward her. She looks nervous, and there is a cut.

So this is the Story Spark for our plot that is driven by the Master, who wants to kill Buffy.

Two More Story Sparks

We have the credits. Then Angel, who was lurking in the shadows, joins the fight. He pulls one of the vampires off Buffy. For the moment he saves her. The fight continues. Buffy then saves Angel and they race to her house. She says something like, "Get in, come on in," which allows him to enter. Though at that point we don't know that invitation is necessary for him to come in.

I see this moment as the Story Spark for both the Buffy subplot and the Angel subplot. It gets their personal relationship rolling. That relationship will move to another level in this episode, as both of them will discover (in less than direct ways) how the other one feels.

Main Plot And Subplots

So why am I seeing Buffy's plot, Angel's plot, and the Master's plot as three separate plots? And, particularly, why are the Buffy and Angel stories not just one subplot? I think it's because I see a different protagonist for each one.

In her podcast How Story Works, story expert Lani Diane Rich gives a great definition of a protagonist: "A protagonist does three things. The protagonist is the viewpoint character, that's the first one. The protagonist must have an active goal and propel the story forward. Also, the protagonist has the most at stake."

Those three things are key to how I separate these plots.

Main Plot: The Master

In the main plot, the Master is the one who moves that story forward. He is our viewpoint character, either personally or through Darla, for that story of trying to kill Buffy and trying to turn Angel. And he has the active goal. His choices and decisions move the story forward. Buffy in that story is not the one with the active goal. She reacts to the Master's plot. She is defending and pushing back against it.

In the Master's plot, he has the most at stake because getting rid of Buffy is key to his strategy of getting out from his underground prison. Getting Angel back is important to him for that reason, and also because he wants this group of vampires around him, including Angel and Darla.

Subplot: Buffy

When we get to Buffy's and Angel's relationship, Buffy is the protagonist of her side of the story. We see much of it from her viewpoint — including how she feels when she thinks Angel read her diary. When they kiss and he vamps out, all of this is told from her point of view. Both as to how she feels about it and what she chooses to do at different points in the story.

So there she has the active goal which is to resolve her feelings about Angel. And first that takes the form of moving the relationship forward or finding out if he feels the same way.

It later becomes dealing with the turn, the reversal, that he is a vampire, and then deciding to trust him. But the relationship, how she feels about him, is her story. In that story she has the most at stake (no pun intended).

Subplot: Angel

When we look at the Angel-Buffy relationship from Angel's perspective, we see scenes where Buffy is not there.

He is the viewpoint character. We see him struggling with his past. Who he is: not human, not vampire, something in between, and his struggle with how to live with that. Darla brings that to the forefront, symbolizes that, and he ultimately must make a choice.

He has an active goal: he wants not just to be with Buffy, but to find a way to make up for the past, to change and be a hero. So that is his active goal. In that story he has the most at stake because he is at a true crossroads.

So that's why I'm seeing these as three different stories. When I started looking at it that way it was easier for me to see how the plots moved in those stories and intertwined.

Misdirection

Back to Buffy and Angel in Buffy's house. Angel tells her that now they are okay, they're safe inside the house because vampires can't come in unless they're invited. She says she heard that before, but she never tested it. That quick conversation in the heat of the moment gives the audience yet another rule about vampires.

Also, we talked before about misdirection. Soon we'll see that there was maybe not so much misdirection about Angel, but key information the show held back— that Angel is a vampire.

If we go back and watch the episode, knowing that he is a vampire, this rule about inviting vampires in works. Buffy did in fact invite him into her home. This rule also becomes key later when Joyce invites Darla in.

So the show played fair with the audience. If we look back at all the episodes to date, we don't see Angel doing anything that is inconsistent with being a vampire.

Buffy And Angel Grow Closer

Angel is injured. He takes off his shirt, and we see his

tattoo. Buffy helps bandage him and they have a moment. But Joyce comes home, cutting off any romantic interplay.

Buffy tries to stall her mom, hoping, I think, that Angel will get out of the house. Or not out of the house, as The Three are out there and she doesn't know that Angel's a vampire. But she's obviously trying to stall for time, and Joyce is a little bit suspicious.

Then Angel comes out of the kitchen. And I really like that about Angel, that he wants to be as upfront as he can. He doesn't want to hide in the kitchen and not let Joyce know he's there. Buffy claims he's a student at community college, and he's helping her with history.

I really like Joyce in this moment because she clearly knows there's something more going on. But she doesn't give Buffy a really hard time about having this guy over when she's not there. She just says, kind of pointedly, "It's late." And Buffy says yes, she'll say goodnight as well. She pretends, after Joyce goes upstairs, to say good night to Angel. Instead, she takes him up to her room.

Willingly Suspending Disbelief

In fiction, there's the concept of suspension of disbelief. Usually we mean the story is so good it lures us in, and we suspend our disbelief in things that otherwise we would not believe in. Like vampires. Because we love the story and it's convinced us.

There's also what I think of as a willing suspension of disbelief. That's where as a reader or audience member we aren't quite persuaded by something, but we go with it because we enjoy the story. We make a more active choice.

Here, I feel like I willingly suspend my disbelief about Buffy taking Angel up the stairs into her room without Joyce knowing. Buffy and Angel have this conversation. The house I don't think is that big. So I'm sure that Joyce would hear them. But I'm willing to just go with it because I want to have this scene and these moments between Buffy and Angel.

Buffy wants Angel to stay the night so that he'll be safe. She personally likes him being there, but she really doesn't want him out there on his own.

One-Quarter Twists In The Subplots

They have what I'm pretty sure is their first truly personal conversation. Buffy asks what Angel's family thinks of his career choice. Angel says they're dead. It was vampires, and it happened a long time ago. This raises a brief story question that's going to be answered at the end. It makes us intrigued about Angel's past.

Also, as with the need to invite vampires in, it plays fair with the audience. Because it is something that is consistent both with Angel not telling Buffy he's a vampire, and with Angel telling the truth. He is trying to be as honest as he can with Buffy. Before they go to sleep, Buffy says, "So this is a vengeance thing for you?"

When he lays down on the floor and she's lying in bed she asks, does he snore? He says, "It's been a long time since anyone was in a position to tell me." It's a very intimate moment. They're sleeping in the same room. He is telling her he hasn't slept with anybody else in a long time.

I see this as the One-Quarter Twist for both the Buffy subplot and the Angel subplot. That major plot turn generally comes from outside the characters and spins the story in a new direction. And while this isn't totally outside the characters, because they are making a choice to have this conversation, they were thrust into the situation by The Three. Otherwise it's hard to imagine, given what has happened in the series so far, that Buffy and Angel would ever end up in Buffy's bedroom at night, going to sleep, having this conversation.

Back To The Main Plot

Our next scene is at the library. We get Xander feeling outraged that Angel stayed overnight. Maybe not outraged, but he's feeling jealous. And when Buffy is talking about how wonderful Angel was, he says, "Oh, that's the oldest trick in the book."

Buffy says, "What, saving my life? Getting slashed in the ribs?" And Xander says something like: "Oh yeah, guys do that kind of thing all the time."

Now I think we get to the One-Quarter Twist in the main plot of the Master trying to kill Buffy. Giles says that Buffy must be hurting the Master if he sent The Three. She has to step up her training. But The Three failed and so will offer their lives in penance. We then transition to the Master. So really what Giles has offered – in the context of conflict because everyone is worried about Buffy – is the exposition that The Three are finished.

The next scene is really that turn.

One-Quarter Twist: Main Plot

About 13 minutes in, the Master lets Darla in fact kill The Three. And that turns the Master's plot, which is our main plot. Note that it did come from outside the Master. While he's the one who has Darla kill The Three, it is apparently lore or tradition (or some code of honor that The Three have) that because they failed, they forfeit their lives. Buffy and Angel defeated The Three in the sense of getting away. Now they forfeit their lives. So something outside the Master turns the story.

As a One-Quarter Twist should do, the twist here triggers a new direction and propels the plot toward the Midpoint. The Master must find a new way to get to Buffy. That is what is going to move us toward the Master's Midpoint commitment.

Buffy Prepares

We next see Buffy preparing to deal with whatever the Master throws at her next. She is in the library training with Giles. She wants to use the crossbow. Giles says she's not ready yet. He wants her to use these long poles (I forgot the name for them).

She makes a joke about "What, am I going to fight with Friar Tuck?" She beats him so quickly, and then she gets to have the crossbow.

The Midpoint: Buffy Subplot

At night Buffy brings Angel food. He has been hiding out in her bedroom all day. They have this mix up about her thinking that he read her diary. She tries to backpedal around the things she wrote about him and claim she was writing about someone else.

At the same time, he is saying he can't be around her. He's older than her, but he thinks about kissing her whenever he's with her. They kiss, and he vamps out. Buffy screams. Angel dives out the window.

Though it's a little bit early – about 17 minutes in, not quite at our Midpoint of the episode – I see this as our Midpoint reversal for Buffy in her personal plot to resolve her feelings about Angel. To have this relationship move forward.

Midpoint Of The Series

In the pilot episode, we saw two things at the Midpoint. Generally one or the other or both will happen in well-structured story: (1) a major reversal for our protagonist or (2) a commitment by the protagonist. She fully commits to the quest and throws caution to the wind.

Here, this is a significant reversal for Buffy, no question. This person that she has fallen in love with turns out to not be a person. It is typical of what Joss Whedon will do in his shows. The character has a wonderful moment, exactly what she has wanted. Angel feels the same about her, kisses her. And then immediately that is yanked away in the most awful way that Buffy could probably ever imagine.

This Midpoint Reversal propels the story forward. Everything Buffy does from this point on is driven by this reversal at the Midpoint.

Next we see Xander, Buffy, Willow, and Giles talking. Xander says Buffy has to kill Angel. There's a little bit of comic relief with Cordelia, who overhears Xander say Buffy's dating a vampire. And Xander pretends that he's talking about an umpire, not a vampire, and "everybody hates them."

Darla And Angel

We then see Darla going to Angel. She reminds him of their past together. They have a conversation that is antagonistic but there is a lot of chemistry between them. As they revisit their past sexual and romantic relationship, she baits him. Scorns him. She says, "You're living like them, you're fighting us like them. But guess what, you're not one of them."

As she says that she opens his blinds. He has to cower away from the light. So it is a very visual and visceral argument that she makes to him. Not just using words but actions. She says, "Go ahead, talk to Buffy, tell her about the curse. Maybe she'll come around. And if she doesn't, you know where I'll be."

So this is the Master, through Darla, propelling the story forward. I guess at this point she is both acting for the Master and for herself. You could see Darla as having yet another subplot that is part of the Master's plot. Because she isn't only doing this for the Master, she's doing it for herself. She wants Angel back.

So I can definitely see an argument for her own subplot. Or even maybe that she is the one driving our main plot here.

That's getting really complicated to go into four plots. But

I think it works so well because these character storylines are all so well integrated that it all weaves together into one story. A story that has very strong character work and plot turns.

I can't help pointing out the exposition here, which again, we get through conflict. This is the first time that we hear about this curse, and it's in this very heated discussion between Angel and Darla. That's a great way to throw in that little teaser hinting at something about Angel that we don't yet know.

The Midpoint: Main Plot

We are nearing the Midpoint of the episode – around 22-23 minutes in. In the library, Giles finds references to Angelus in a diary. He tells us about Angelus being a vicious vampire, then coming to America, shunning other vampires, and staying out of – I was going to say out of the history books – out of the Watcher diaries. But Giles does say that Angel was the most violent and vicious animal.

This moment also could be the Midpoint for Buffy's plot. In a way it's part of her major reversal, but I still see that as happening when Angel vamps out. That's so much more personal.

What we get immediately after that is what I see as the Midpoint of our main plot. The Master and Darla are talking. Darla's saying, "You gotta let me take care of it. Take care of Buffy and Angel. We'll get Angel to kill Buffy and bring him back into the fold."

Here's why I see the Master, not Darla, as the protagonist of this plot. It is up to the Master to say yes. The fact that Darla is presenting this idea but waiting for the Master to greenlight it means that he is the one in control. He makes this commitment. Throws caution to the wind and fully commits. Now he isn't just going to try to kill Buffy, but to get Angel to do it and bring Angel back to them.

Because for a hundred years Angel has stayed away from vampires.

Note that although Buffy normally would be our protagonist, she is not the one driving the action in this plot. The Master is driving the action.

From the Midpoint to the end, it should be the protagonist's choice or commitment, or what happened at the reversal, that propels the story forward. Here, the Master does that by making a commitment.

Moving Toward The Three-Quarter Turn

Buffy and Willow are in the library. Buffy says she needs to get over Angel so she can kill him, but she can't. "He's never done anything to hurt me." So she is moving forward from her reversal, trying to process that information. To deal with it and figure out what she needs to do.

Darla is listening to this conversation and forming her plan. She learns a lot. Both about Buffy's life, so that she can weasel her way into Buffy's home, and about what is it that Buffy needs to be willing to kill Angel. Because the only way Angel will kill Buffy is if Buffy is trying to kill him.

We switch to Joyce, who is home alone. Darla rings the bell and pretends to be a schoolgirl in her schoolgirl outfit. She says she's there to help Buffy study. And she seems to know so much (although some of that information Joyce also gives her). She knows that Buffy and Willow are at the library studying about the Civil War. She really seems to know Buffy and talks about helping her with another aspect of history.

Joyce is persuaded that Darla is a friend.

And after all, just last night Buffy had another friend, a guy, there that Joyce had not met yet. Who supposedly was helping her study. So it doesn't seem strange that this girl shows up that Joyce never met before.

Inviting Evil In

Joyce invites her in, and we get a nice moment where Darla says, "Thank you for inviting me into your home."

In the kitchen, she attacks Joyce. Angel comes to the house. He sees this, comes in, and tries to stop Darla. Darla thrusts Joyce at him and disappears after encouraging him to go ahead and give in to what he needs.

He's holding Joyce. Presumably this is the first time, or at least the first time in a long time, that Angel has been in this position where he is holding a human who is bleeding. We can see it's difficult for him. He does not want to bite her, to drink her blood. At least in his mind he doesn't want to. It's not who he wants to be. But he has this very visceral reaction, much as he did when he kissed Buffy, being so close to a human. You figure this moment must be even more difficult for him because there is blood there.

Three-Quarter Turn: Buffy Subplot

Buffy enters and sees this. It looks very damning for Angel because he's holding Joyce, he's vamped out, and Joyce is bleeding.

So this I see as Buffy's Three-Quarter Turn for her personal plot. From the Midpoint reversal to here she was still struggling with what to do. She didn't want to kill Angel. She was trying to figure out how to get herself to do it. But we saw that she was not there yet. If she could've found a reason, a way, to make it work, to not kill him, certainly that's what she would've done. Because she does talk about how he's never hurt her and asked why he didn't attack her before and so forth.

But now she sees Joyce, and she is ready to kill Angel because of this.

This moment does arise from Buffy's reversal because it's why all of this is happening. If Angel hadn't vamped out, if she hadn't discovered he was a vampire, none of this would have happened. For one thing, he probably wouldn't have been back at Buffy's house. Darla's plot wouldn't have worked on him.

And because it's TV we go from that moment to a commercial break. Great way to hook the audience and keep them watching through the end of the episode.

Throwing Angel Out

Buffy throws Angel out and says if he comes back she'll kill him. It's clear she is done.

At the hospital, Joyce is recovering. She's going to be okay. And she says, "Your friend came over." Buffy, of course, given what she has seen, assumes that it was Angel.

Joyce also comments about Giles being there and how the teachers at the school really do care about the students. Which is kind of nice. It tells us how she sees Giles being there. Which, looking back, it would be really strange that the high school librarian shows up at the hospital. But I think because Giles is just so appropriate about everything that we don't have a sense that Joyce should find it odd that he is around.

The Three-Quarter Point Turn: Main Plot

Buffy now says she will go after Angel. She was stupid before, and she knows she has to kill him. She knows he lives near the Bronze, and she brings her crossbow.

Darla now goes to Angel and says Buffy is hunting him. And she says something like, "You've had a hundred years with no peace because you won't accept who you are." She keeps pushing him on this, asking what he's going to do, what he wants.

About 31-32 minutes in he says, "I want it finished." This is the Three-Quarter Turn in the Master's plot line, so our main plot. It grew from that Midpoint commitment by the

Master to get to Angel through Darla. The Master set it up so that Buffy is hunting Angel.

Angel has to make a choice. And his choice is "I'm going to finish this." It looks like he's done. He's done trying to straddle this line. He is going to embrace being a vampire again.

The Midpoint: Angel

At the same time, I see this moment as the Midpoint commitment for Angel's subplot. Angel is throwing caution to the wind and saying, "Okay, I'm done. I'm going to embrace that I am in fact a vampire. I'm not going to let Buffy kill me. I'm going to kill her because I cannot be a human being. I've tried and I can't and it's too painful and it's too difficult."

The fact that these two storylines come together here shows something that I feel is generally true in stories. Subplots usually roughly follow the same plot structure as a main plot. But often those points come at different parts of the narrative. So you might have that first major plot turn from outside the protagonist in a subplot, but it might not come one-quarter way through the story or the episode.

And the Midpoint commitment for the subplot is not necessarily at the halfway mark of the overall story. But it is a turning point, and either a commitment or a major reversal in that subplot. And it generally comes in the middle of the story for that subplot's protagonist.

So we see that here. Our main plot roughly follows the timing that we're used to in a structured story. And the Angel subplot kind of weaves in and out of it, as does Buffy's subplot.

The Climax: Buffy Subplot

We're back at the hospital. Giles and Joyce talk. It becomes clear to Giles that it was Darla who attacked Joyce, not Angel. It is too late to catch Buffy. She's already on her way to the Bronze. But Giles, Willow, and Xander head there to try to meet her and let her know.

Now we move into our Climax scene for Buffy's subplot about her personal feelings about Angel. She and Angel confront each other.

She attacks first. She shoots him with the crossbow and misses. Now does she miss on purpose? Hard to say. She comes very close, and we have set up that this is a new weapon for her, so it might be an accidental miss.

As other podcasters and other bloggers have mentioned, I wonder what is the deal with the crossbow? It makes no sense to me. It does not seem like a terribly useful weapon for one-on-one fighting. If I think ahead to the series, the crossbow is used at times for a long distance shot at a vampire. But it doesn't make a huge amount of sense that she is relying on it so much when she can use a stake so well.

But maybe it would be too hard for her to actually stake Angel. Maybe having that distance, she can deal with trying to kill him.

And I'm completely reading that in after the fact. I have no idea if that was the goal of the writers or if it was just that they wanted a weapon where Buffy could conceivably miss. Because I don't think we buy at this time that she would miss if she tried stake Angel.

He might fight her off, but we wouldn't get her just missing him. And he makes the comment that she was a little off in her aim. His comment opens up the space for them to have a conversation instead of just fighting and not talking.

Angel And Buffy Talk

She asks him why he didn't attack her before. Was it a game making her feel for him? And she says she's killed vampires before, but it's the first time she hated one.

He tells her he killed his family, friends, other people and children for a hundred years. Then he stopped for a hundred years, didn't hurt anyone, didn't kill anyone.

So she's saying, "What happened, why did you start with my mom?"

He tells her about a Gypsy curse, and his soul being restored. So again, we're getting his back story in a very dramatic way in the middle of conflict. Also, this is not this character giving exposition to another character who already knows it. Buffy does not know the story, and she does need to know it to understand what happened.

The key thing Angel says is, "I can walk like a man but I'm not a man. I wanted to kill you tonight." That tells us that when he said that line to Darla earlier, "I want it finished," he meant it. He was saying, "I'm going to kill her." That's part of why I see that moment with Darla as his Midpoint commitment. He, at that time, committed to doing something drastic that otherwise he was not going to do. It is him throwing caution to the wind, throwing away a hundred years of not killing anyone.

Three-Quarter Turn: Angel Subplot

Buffy offers him her neck. I think she puts down the crossbow, offers him her neck, and says, "It's not so easy is it?"

It's about 37 minutes in, and Darla says, "Sure it is!"

Before that, Angel did not know Darla was there. Buffy didn't know that. And this I see as the Three-Quarter Turn for Angel's subplot. It grows from his commitment, which he made to Darla. That brings the plot to this point because Darla has come expecting that he is going to kill Buffy.

It also turns the story in a new direction because Angel does not attack Buffy. He chooses to let Buffy live, and to embrace instead his humanity.

Darla coming in at that moment will now turn Angel's

story. And she could not do that if he had not given her that hope. She might not even be there if he had not given her that hope that he was going to go forward and kill Buffy.

Character Development And Vulnerability

Darla says, "The saddest thing in the world is to love someone who no longer loves you." And I love this because we are getting vulnerability from Darla. Yes, she's the villain. We don't want her to win. But I like that this is personal for her. It is not about just doing what the Master wants or freeing the Master. It's because she still loves Angel, still wants to be with him. She created him as a vampire and now he doesn't want to be with her.

She says to Angel, "You had a chance to come home. You threw it away. You love someone who hates us. You're sick, you'll always be sick."

When she says, "You love someone who hates us," this is the true climax of the Buffy subplot. Buffy realizes that Angel is in love with her. Someone else has told her that, but she realizes it.

I find this a really interesting reflection because in our pivotal scene between Buffy and Angel in her bedroom, Buffy tells Angel how she feels. But it's also in a very indirect way. She blurts it out because she thinks he's already read her diary. So he finds out in a roundabout way for sure how she feels. And now she finds out through Darla, not by him saying it directly, how he feels.

This gives both of those moments more power. Because it seems more certain and true when something like that comes out in that roundabout way. And the fact that Darla, who loves Angel and hates that he loves Buffy, is the one who says it, makes the moment Buffy learns Angel loves her so strong.

Guns In The Buffyverse

Now Darla pulls out guns, which seems really weird to

me. We don't see, I don't think it's too much of a spoiler to say, we don't see guns a lot in the Buffyverse. And though the show has not been going that long, it already seems kind of jarring.

Darla says something like, "You don't think I came alone, do you?" I always wondered about her use of the guns, and maybe it was just that the writers hadn't quite figured out yet how they were going to handle the fact that guns and weapons exist. Or maybe this was their opening effort to show that guns don't work in the Buffyverse.

(However – I was talking recently to a friend who loved the Dirty Harry movies. And I don't remember which one this came from, but there was a line where Clint Eastwood said something like "I didn't come alone" and pulled out his guns. I believe Joss Whedon's about my age, and he may very well have watched those Dirty Harry movies. I watched them in black-and-white in reruns on Channel 9, which is also the station that played Buffy in Chicago. I can't help thinking this moment was somewhat of a purposeful call back to that Dirty Harry movie.)

Anyway, we do get a little bit of a comic, sort of campy scene. Giles flips on a strobe light to confuse things. (Xander, Willow, and Giles previously came into the Bronze and yelled down to Buffy what she already knew. That it wasn't Angel, it was Darla, who tried to kill Joyce.)

Buffy ducks behind this counter. And she's running back and forth, and it looks very much like a shooting gallery scene. Which is kind of funny and adds some lightness.

Climax for Main Plot And Angel Subplot

The Climax of the Angel subplot is also the Climax of the Master's main plot, which is that Angel kills Darla. This is such a strong Climax for the main plot. It ends the Master's efforts to get Angel back and also deprives him of his favorite, Darla.

But it is an even stronger Climax for the Angel subplot because when he kills Darla, he is also essentially killing his past as Angelus. Or I guess he can't kill that, but he's severing his ties. Darla represents Angel's life as a vampire. She sired him. He was with her all his time as a vampire until this curse. Also as he struggled to deal with the curse, because she knows something about that and about who he became when his soul was restored to him.

This is his point of no return. He is killing part of his own life. It may be a part that he doesn't want to embrace anymore. But it was such a huge part of who he was, and he had this deep connection with Darla.

Falling Action

We now shift to the Falling Action about 40 minutes in. We have 2-3 minutes left. We need to tie up the loose ends and see the fallout from the climaxes of our different plots.

In our main plot, the Master is destroying things. He says Darla was his favorite. He mourns the loss of Angel. And Colin says, "Darla was weak. We don't need her. I'll bring the Slayer to you and when you rise you'll kill them all." Which makes the Master feel so much better.

We then get the Falling Action for both the Buffy and Angel subplots.

At the post-fumigation party at the Bronze, Buffy and Willow are again talking about Angel. It's a nice bookend to the beginning of Buffy's story when she talks with Willow. Buffy says she feels like Angel is still watching her. Willow points out that's because he is, and he's right across the room.

Buffy goes over. They talk about how this relationship can't happen between them, how hard it is, and they kiss anyway. Her cross is burning him when they kiss. But she doesn't know it, and we only see that as she walks away. And that is the end of the episode.

This Falling Action also does another thing we want, which is to draw the audience back in on two fronts. In the main plot it raised the importance of Colin and hinted at things to come. And here, of course, we want to know what will happen with Buffy and Angel.

DVD Commentary On Angel

Angel the episode wasn't written by Joss Whedon but by David Greenwalt. That kind of surprised me because I just assumed Joss would've written this episode himself. David Greenwalt went on to become the co-creator of Angel. So I looked him up to see what he had to say about Angel.

I didn't find a commentary specifically on this episode. But I did find a lot about the show, Angel, on the BBC UK homepage.

Here's just one of his quotes about Angel:

He's been around for 251 years and he's done every horrible thing you can imagine, and then was cursed with a soul a little over 100 years ago. It's a metaphor for being cursed with a conscience, for being cursed with 'Oh my god I remember all the terrible things I've done.' So he's on a road to redemption, he really wants to make up for his horrible past. He'd have to live 500 years to really do it, so it's a one-day-at-a-time thing.

I like this quote because I feel like it really encapsulates the struggle that Angel has. That he does remember every horrible thing that he has ever done. He's on this road to redemption, but it is hard. He was very tempted to embrace what could be seen as the easier path. To basically, I think, try to kill his conscience by killing Buffy.

Instead, he embraced his humanity by loving Buffy.

Spoilers

Cordelia And Xander

There is no way I would've guessed that Cordelia and Xander would eventually become a couple. We get this trading of insults both at the Bronze and then outside when Buffy is talking about being in love with Angel and the vampire-umpire thing.

You definitely get that they have this insult trading that could easily become banter. Also the fact that they keep doing that, it's a little bit of a hint. Initially, though, I saw it just as comic relief. Now knowing what happens with them, I can sort of see it.

Buffy And Angel

We also get foreshadowing of Buffy eventually needing to kill Angel. The first time she finds out he's a vampire, it is set up that her duty is to kill him.

I think that the writers had to deal with that in this episode. So it wouldn't necessarily mean she eventually will face that choice in a more devastating way. But it does set us up for that so it fits when we reach Season Two.

Season One Arc

On a larger scale, as to the season arc, I find it significant that Angel aired in the middle of the season. It is the Midpoint of the Season One story arc.

If we see the season arc being more about Buffy dealing with trying to live a normal life and be the Slayer, this episode is a reversal. Because this is when she realizes the man she's falling for, who has been helping her fight, is a vampire. He is absolutely the wrong person for her. The worst person for her in the sense that he is not a person at all.

It is also a commitment for her, a throwing of caution to the wind. Even when she doesn't know about the curse, all she knows is he's a vampire, she is not willing to kill him. She resists killing him. And she only does it when she is pushed to it by believing that he attacked her mother.

Before that she commits in that sense of saying, in essence, that her feelings matter more.

Her feelings don't matter more to her once she sees, or thinks she sees, Angel actively trying to kill people. But when the evidence is that he's a vampire, but she doesn't see him as a danger right now, she commits to instead following her heart and how she feels. And to her instinct to trust him.

Likewise, when she offers him her neck, she doesn't know yet what he'll do. He might still try to kill her. And he tells her, "I came here to kill you."

So this is a commitment on her part to be more than just the Slayer. Certainly, the Slayer Handbook – we're going to hear about that much later in the series in a sort of funny way – I think it would definitely say, "Yeah, hey, he's a vampire kill him." In fact, Kendra makes that argument when she comes into the show.

So this is also commitment. And I feel something of a statement of the series. Which is that generally Buffy is not going to kill vampires or demons that she has reason to believe are not actively trying to hurt anyone or kill anyone. The most major example of that is Spike much later down the road.

Season Arc And The Master

Back to the season arc. The Master commits at the Midpoint by calling in The Three. This is the first time he has gone outside of his small group of vampires to bring in the big guns.

But more so at the end we see a shift to Colin, as the Anointed One, being more active. Saying, "I will bring her to you and you'll rise and you will kill them all." In our Season One finale, it is Colin who brings Buffy to the Master. So that is both a Midpoint in our story arc and a bit of foreshadowing. It tells us that Colin will be pivotal and sets us up for that.

Questions For Your Writing

- **Does your story require the reader to suspend disbelief? If so, what parts of the story will persuade the reader to do it or not notice it's necessary?**
- **Can you identify the major plot points of the subplots in your story?**
- **Think about a character whom you want readers to like or empathize with but it's not quite working. Is there a way to show the character's vulnerability?**

Next: I, Robot… You, Jane

Next we'll be talking about I, Robot… You, Jane. And it is probably, like Teacher's Pet, not a huge favorite episode of a lot of fans. I think that it holds together better than Teacher's Pet. Or at least I always like it better when I come back and watch it. Maybe just because it's a Willow-centric episode, and I find it really fun.

CHAPTER NINE

I, ROBOT... YOU, JANE

THIS CHAPTER TALKS ABOUT I, Robot... You, Jane, Season One, Episode Eight, written by Ashley Gable & Thomas A. Swyden and directed by Stephen L. Posey.

In particular, we'll look at:

- **Using a prologue to raise the stakes**
- **Chapter endings that hook a reader**
- **Quickly weaving in information or action you don't have the time to show**
- **What makes an antagonist interesting – or not**

Okay, let's dive into the Hellmouth.

I, Robot... You, Jane Begins

I was a little bit surprised when I re-watched this episode

for the podcast. I always remember it as one that I'm not that excited about. The Internet demon who turns into a robot is what sticks in my mind. While I didn't think that villain was terrible, I didn't find it that intriguing.

But there was so much more fun in here than I remembered. Also, some really interesting things about technology, looking at it from a perspective of twenty years later. In addition, the episode foreshadowed a little more than I remembered. I'll talk about that in the spoiler section. There are some great storytelling things in here, too.

Another Prologue

We start once again with the prologue. I also had forgotten how often we get prologues in Buffy. So this could challenge that idea that I mentioned that many writers, viewers, and readers are not too fond of prologues. But maybe not, as this is one I didn't find super compelling. I feel like it's part of why this episode sticks in my memory as one that I don't particularly like, though it turns out I kind of do.

I don't know if the first part of the prologue is necessary. We're in Italy in 1418. (The characters are speaking Italian but we get subtitles.) The demon Moloch is with his follower, who is dressed in a robe. So perhaps he's some type of monk. Moloch asks if the follower loves him. Though the follower professes his love, Moloch snaps his neck.

Then we switch to a group of monks saying Moloch walks again and that people are falling under his power. They need to form a circle and bind him.

Back to Moloch. He senses this is happening. He's weakening, and he disintegrates into tiny little pieces that are captured in a book. The book is then slammed shut and put into a box.

Raising The Stakes

There are things the prologue does well. Initially, I was

thinking it raises the stakes. But I guess what it does is *show us* the stakes. We see that people fall under the sway of Moloch. He claims to only want their love, but even when they give him what he wants he kills them anyway.

So later on, as we get into Willow and what's happening with her, we're aware from the outset that if this is Moloch, she's doomed. He may claim to be devoted to her, but devotion is not what he does. What he does is kill people. The prologue also tells us how to capture Moloch and the danger this old book poses.

These are all things that I think we would have gotten from the context of the rest of the episode. All of that is woven into the story in a really effective way. So I don't know that the prologue was necessary.

Perhaps though, the show wanted to signal (especially in these early episodes) what kind of episode each was going to be. The prologue gives a clue that this is a monster–of–the-week episode. It isn't going to be focused on the Master.

Opening Conflict

The other thing the Prologue does is give us our Opening Conflict. Opening Conflict can relate to the main plot, and this Prologue does. But it also could show an entirely separate conflict relating to our protagonist. The idea is just that we need some sort of conflict to draw the reader into the story before we get to that Inciting Incident (what I think of as the Story Spark) that gets our main plot moving.

So here we do get that Opening Conflict with Moloch. But it didn't draw me in all that much. We also have a first scene of our present-day story, which has some initial conflict that draws me in. It is not about a monster of the week. It is between Giles and the high school computer teacher, Jenny Calendar.

Meet Jenny Calendar

This is the first time that we meet Ms. Calendar, as the students call her, and as Giles calls her. I love that she calls him Rupert. I think she's the only one to call him by his first name so far in the show. Which makes sense because we see him mainly interacting with the students. He does interact with Joyce, but she knows him as the high school librarian and calls him Mr. Giles. She doesn't know him that well yet, so she's not calling him Rupert.

This makes a nice dividing line and sets up that perhaps there is going to be a little more of a relationship between Jenny and Giles. (I'm going to keep calling him Giles because that's how I think of him.) It also draws a nice line between the teachers and the students. Because of course the teachers don't call each other Mr. and Ms., at least once they know each other. They might in front of the students, though, as Giles does call her Ms. Calendar.

That she calls him Rupert also gives us a sense that she is a little more informal, a little more relaxed. He's using Ms. Calendar, the very formal approach. She is coded as more current, or more fun. We will see some other hints of that later.

Interestingly, while this opening scene with Jenny and Giles isn't specifically about the monster in the sense of being about Moloch, it is about technology. When I really think about it, technology, in a sense, is the antagonist here. The villain. Especially if we see this from Giles' eyes. He several times mentions feeling afraid of computers, of technology, and of these changes.

Scene Cuts

We have a nice cut between these opening scenes. At the end of the 1418 scenes in Italy, we get the monks putting the book in a box and saying, "May this accursed book never be read again."

Cut.

Then we're in the library, Buffy opens the box and says, "Oh, great, a book."

We have lots of these kinds of cuts in Buffy, where one character is saying one thing or something is happening. Then you get a cut, and the other character either is saying something very similar that perhaps relates to a different situation, or is actually handling a book when we've just mentioned a dusty old book. And here it is the very same book years later. So we have that connection.

You can use this in your novels as well. It can be a really nice way to draw the reader from one scene to the next and create connections between characters, even if they are in very separate scenes or situations.

In her podcast Still Pretty, Lani Diane Rich says she gets tired of this type of cut. She calls it an "irony smash." I can see that if it really stands out to you, it might start to bother you. I personally love it every time that it's done. (So quite possibly I do it too often in my writing. I'll have to look back at that and see.)

Buffy taking the book out starts the scene with Giles and Ms. Calendar. The reason Jenny is there is that they are apparently scanning books into some sort of repository on the computer for the school. Giles confuses the word Scan with Skim, which is kind of fun. Obviously today even someone who was not particularly computer savvy would know the difference. But I really enjoy that Giles does not.

Technology As Antagonist

These computers at the time this episode was made were big and boxy. The monitor here is quite large. I definitely remember having one of those. So it really fits when Giles calls it the Idiot Box. Ms. Calendar tells him, "That's the TV." Not sure if anyone calls the TV the Idiot Box anymore, either. TVs also generally are not boxy. So all around, it's kind of a fun recollection of what technology was like then.

This whole scene is a great example of a separate smaller conflict that draws the reader or the viewer into the story before you get to the Inciting Incident. There's tension between Jenny and Giles. They are not at each other's throats, but they're coming from very different perspectives.

We also meet a couple new students. Dave, who is helping out and seems fairly nice and kind of quiet. And Fritz, who goes into a rant about the only reality is virtual reality. Jenny comments on that, something like, "Thanks for making us all look crazy." We get this distinction of yes, Jenny is very into technology, but Fritz represents the extreme.

So we get a little hint about Fritz maybe being a little bit out there.

Jenny makes the point to Giles that more email than regular mail was sent the year before. Giles says that is a fact he regards with genuine horror. Jenny teases him about being in the middle ages. So we've definitely drawn lines about views about technology.

(I also had forgotten about when email was not so common. The idea now that you would get more regular mail than email seems so strange when we all have In Boxes full of unwanted email.)

The Story Spark

We're coming up to our Story Spark, which sets off the main plot. It happens here slightly past 10%. But not much – right around 5 minutes into the roughly 43-minute episode.

Willow is in the library late, by herself, scanning books. She scans in the Moloch book and the characters disappear as she does that. (I couldn't tell what type of alphabet it was.) She does not notice. Then right at 5 minutes we see the screen and the words "Where am I?" So right away we know something very serious is up. And we go to the credits.

That idea of Moloch awakening in the computer keeps the viewer coming back after the credits.

On return, we see Willow and Buffy in the hall. Willow looks very happy. She says she met a boy. Buffy asks when, and Willow says a week ago, right after the scanning project. We might make the connection to that "Where am I?" in the computer, but maybe not because it takes a while for it to come out that Willow met this boy online.

Technology At The Time

Meeting online was not so common then. So we get this joke when they are in the computer lab and Willow says, "I met him online." Buffy says, "On line for what?" Again, very fun, because no one would say that now. (I'll also note that the joke would work best somewhere where people say they stand "on line." In Chicago, where I'm based, we stand "in line.")

It does give us an idea that meeting people online was very new then, because Buffy is serious when she says that. It takes her a second to catch up and realize what Willow's talking about. She already expresses a little bit of concern about Willow not actually having met this boy in person.

Willow just wants to be happy and excited about this boy. So there is a little bit of tension.

Characterization: Jenny Calendar

We have a moment with Jenny that shows nice characterization. She says, "Buffy, are you supposed to be somewhere?" Buffy says she has a free period. And Jenny says, "Cool, but we have lab, so make it a short visit."

This is a quick way to show Jenny has a good relationship with her students, and she is relaxed about rules. You have to think many other teachers would tell Buffy to leave. Also, seemingly the students more or less listen and respect her because while Buffy does sit down, and she and Willow do talk, they aren't disruptive about it. We don't get a sense that it's a problem.

We have some more old technology here because Willow is typing in messages back and forth with Malcolm. (No one has cell phones, so there isn't texting on a phone.) We hear this computer voice reading his messages. And we have Willow speaking as she's typing.

Most of this is a device for the viewers. It would be very boring to just watch people type back-and-forth. But it is fairly true to the technology. You certainly could do it that way if you wanted to. (Generally speaking, you didn't have a computer voice read emails or messages to you or chats to you. But I'm pretty sure that at that time my computer could do that. And that is definitely how the voice sounded when it read, very mechanical. Also, I admit to sometimes talking to my computer, even now. But that's usually when I'm swearing at it because it's not doing what I want.)

Buffy questions Willow more strongly, saying, "What do you really know about this Malcolm?" And this camera sitting next to the computer focuses on Buffy. It kind of moves and focuses. That is not something I recall most people having, a separate camera, but I suppose you might have it in a computer lab.

Now we see a different computer bringing up information about Buffy. I stopped the DVD to see what it tells us about Buffy. One thing is that her GPA is 2.8. Another is it says, "Athletics: none,." Which tells us a bit about Buffy right there. She is so capable and strong and clearly athletic, but she obviously doesn't have the time to be involved. And her GPA is not that great though we have seen that Buffy is very smart.

So if you caught this, it's a nice thumbnail of what Buffy's school life is like and how slaying affects her. I love it because it's such a small thing, and I would never have seen it if I weren't stopping it because I am talking about the episode. Yet somebody thought about it and figured out what that would say.

We see Fritz looking at the screen. "Watch her" appears. So if we didn't get the Malcolm-Moloch connection before, we understand now that Buffy's question about Malcolm put her in the sights of our villain.

Creating An Interesting Antagonist

This is a good moment to talk about villains. Usually the most intriguing villain or antagonist is one whose motives we understand and perhaps at least in part empathize with. A well-developed villain should be as layered and nuanced as our protagonist. Here what we have, both in Moloch and in Fritz, is the trope of the mustache-twirling villain from the cartoons who is just evil for evil's sake.

What is Moloch's goal? He says he wants his followers' love. But even when he gets it, he kills them. We get the impression – well, we find out through the episode – that he just creates chaos everywhere. Chaos, pain. For example, later he comments about how great it is that somebody is plotting to murder his wife. So he just loves evil for evil's sake.

Likewise, Fritz, we don't know anything about him other than he expressed these extreme views about virtual reality. That it's the only reality and if not jacked in you're not alive. We don't get any real sense of who Fritz is. Or why he so quickly goes along with what Moloch wants.

That I think is part of why, as a whole, this episode doesn't stick in my mind as one that I really enjoy. Our villain, our antagonist, is not that interesting.

Which also goes to the point that the antagonist does not

need to be a villain. In Buffy, generally, the antagonist will be a villain because that's the show it is. It's horror and it's meant to be partly scary. So we are going to have a monster or some evil being as the villain.

But in any story, the antagonist can be simply someone who has a goal that is opposed to the protagonist. (The antagonist and the protagonist should have mutually exclusive goals. That creates the most conflict.)

Jenny comments that Fritz and Dave are logging a lot of computer time. Fritz says it's a new project. She asks if she'll be excited about it, and he says, "You'll die...." in a very creepy voice. I guess this is here just to heighten the tension. But we already know that Moloch kills people, so this is one of these moments that to me doesn't really add anything.

Moving Toward The One-Quarter Twist

We are moving, as each of these scenes builds, to our One-Quarter Twist. That is the plot turn, usually a quarter of the way through the overall story, that spins the story in a new direction and usually comes from outside the protagonist. Generally, it does not make things easier for our protagonist. It adds something to the story for the protagonist to deal with or to look into.

Coming up on this point, we see Willow and Xander together. Xander wants to know if she wants to go to the Bronze. Willow brushes Xander off. She's going to go home and talk to Malcolm. And Buffy comes up later, and she can't go to the Bronze, either, because she has slaying. Xander is feeling a little bit left alone, and a little bit jealous, which Buffy calls him out on.

He says, "No, I don't feel that way about Willow," but Buffy says, "You were used to being the belle of the ball."

I feel like those are very real sentiments. Xander doesn't

want to date Willow, and I believe he wants her to be happy. He wouldn't say, "Oh, I don't want her to date anyone." But he is used to being first in Willow's life. They have been friends for a long time. She has these feelings for him. He's used to being the belle of the ball, the one that she cares about most.

The One-Quarter Twist

Around eleven minutes in, which starts out our One-Quarter Twist, Xander says he is concerned because he could say he's anybody online. There's a joke about how he could say he's an elderly Dutch woman, and who's to say different if he's in the elderly Dutch woman chat room? Buffy at first sees his point and they both get a little spooked. But then Buffy says they're overreacting.

While Buffy dismisses Xander's concerns in the moment, I see this as the One-Quarter Twist, because Buffy had these concerns earlier. She was raising them with Willow: "What do you really know about this boy?" Now Xander has pointed out that Malcolm might not even be a boy. I feel like before that Buffy was more just picturing a boy who might not be good for Willow. Or she had some general concerns. But now it's a lot more specific.

Despite dismissing Xander in the moment, Buffy does start asking some pointed questions. She asks Willow more questions. She goes to Dave to ask if she can figure out who is sending Willow these messages. So all of this comes from Xander. He really prompts Buffy to take this very seriously. Buffy doing that causes Malcolm to accelerate his relationship with Willow and to focus even more on Buffy.

There are some other things that happen just slightly past this one-quarter point that really go with that new direction of the story. At 12 minutes, we see Fritz carving on his arm. We also see, at almost 13 minutes in, that Willow comes to school late. She says she overslept and Buffy says, "To the fifth period?"

Buffy says, "This isn't like you," and Willow says, "What's not like me?" She says boys don't normally chase her, and she thought Buffy would be happy for her.

Buffy wants to be happy but she urges Willow to meet Malcolm face-to-face. Somewhere safe. Willow says so what if she blew off a few classes. That worries Buffy even more. Willow says, "Malcolm said you wouldn't understand." And Buffy says, "Malcolm was right."

Very nice example of conflict and tension between two good people. Both of whom we like, and whose points of view we understand and care about.

This is where Buffy asks Dave how to find out who is sending an "E-letter," which I love. When Buffy mentions Malcolm, Dave immediately says, "Leave Willow alone." Buffy thinks maybe he is Malcolm.

Buffy now goes to Giles. He says he doesn't know what to tell her, computers frighten him. So again, we get his fear of technology. Being a little bit sarcastic, he says, "What am I going to do, suggest that you tail Dave?" and Buffy says, "What, in a trench coat and dark glasses?"

The next scene, of course, we see her in the dark glasses. Not quite a trench coat, but something with a bit of that styling. She's being quite obvious and is seen by a camera at the warehouse where she follows Dave. And I love this because I don't think it's too much of a spoiler to say that we will find out Buffy pretty much is never good at undercover.

Dave is talking to a guy in a lab coat. Lots of things are being loaded into the warehouse. Buffy can't tell what those things are.

Back at the library, Xander says that this company closed down. It was a computer research company. His uncle worked there as a janitor and got let go. Buffy and Xander make plans to break in. Giles is trying to plausibly deny that he had any knowledge of it. Jenny comes in, and she makes a comment on how often Buffy and Xander are in the library. (It is kind of odd that these students are always hanging out in the library.)

Malcolm and Willow are communicating. She's telling him she never felt this way about anyone and Buffy doesn't understand. Here, Malcolm makes a mistake. He says, "Buffy is trouble. That's why she was kicked out of her old school." This makes Willow pause because she knows she never said that to Malcolm. She cuts off their chat.

Building Towards The Midpoint

Notice how the last scene grows out of the One-Quarter Twist. Everything from that point on should come out of that plot turn and build toward the Midpoint. The Willow-Malcom scene grows out of the One-Quarter Twist because Buffy's further efforts to figure out what's happening got her in Moloch's crosshairs. As a result, he's been checking Buffy out so much that he slips and just says this thing about her being kicked out of school, without realizing that he and Willow never had that conversation.

It builds toward the Midpoint because it adds to Moloch's view of Buffy as the enemy, because Willow stops talking to him. Probably for the first time, she doesn't want to talk anymore.

We have a little more of Jenny and Giles talking about technology. They both make some really good points. Jenny accuses Giles of being a snob. Says he wants to hoard knowledge in books, have it locked up somewhere for a bunch of old white guys. But Giles says, "Just because something is new doesn't mean it's better." She says, "Computers aren't a fad, we're creating a new society."

And Giles says, "Where human interaction is all but obsolete? Where people can be completely manipulated by technology? I'll pass."

Another great example of two people with opposing views, who both have really good points. (See the Appendix for thoughts on whether this conflict predicted technology issues today.) And to ratchet that up, it is hard for them to come to the same place, because they're both devoted. Giles loves his books. He is a librarian. Jenny is a computer teacher. So it's also about their professions.

(One caveat on that. Even back when Buffy was airing originally, some librarians critiqued it because they said Giles would have to know about computers. There would be more computers in the library, and Giles does everything on paper. That completely fits the show, though. As I mentioned in an earlier chapter, Joss said that Giles is meant to be that guy with the dusty books, who says "The vampires are coming!")

In the world of the show, Giles and Jenny are completely opposed.

Jenny points out that this book doesn't have anything to say, it's blank, and asks if it's a diary. Giles looks at it and recognizes Moloch. He doesn't want to let on to Jenny what this is about. So he agrees it must be a diary and then says, "It's been so nice talking to you." Jenny says, "We were fighting," and Giles says, "Must do it again sometime."

A fun way to end that scene and move our story because now Giles realizes this is Moloch.

Weaving In Action

We have a very quick flash where we see one of the problems that Moloch is causing. A nurse says, "There was nothing in the files about a penicillin allergy." This gets in that Moloch is already causing chaos by being in the Internet. It's an example of a very quick way to let your reader or viewer know of something that is going on that you don't want to stop the whole plot to explain. Whatever happened with the allergy is not the key part of our protagonist's story. But it's important, so we quickly see it.

At 21 minutes in, Dave tells Buffy that Willow is looking for her in the locker room. Buffy goes to the locker room. The shower's running. She goes in thinking she might find Willow, but it's just a shower running. Nobody there. She goes to shut it off, and Malcolm has set this up so that she will be electrocuted. But Dave warns her away. At the last second he had an attack of conscience, and he warns her away.

The Midpoint

This is our Midpoint in the story. It's a little after 21 minutes in a 42-43 minute story, and here what we have is a reversal for Buffy. Rather than saving or protecting Willow, she is almost killed.

What's interesting is we have some pretty big commitments by other characters.

Dave first makes a commitment to his quest or his cause by sending Buffy to the locker room. So he is going to set her up to die. But he then throws caution to the wind by following his conscience and warning her, which is going to lead to his death. Pretty big reversal. So he commits, commits in a different direction, and has a reversal roughly all around this time. Fritz, too, very shortly will fully commit to Moloch's cause by killing Dave. So that is definitely going all-in on the quest, throwing caution to the wind.

These are all very big things that are happening around the Midpoint. And Moloch – in a way he, too, does that because now he kills a student (Dave). That is something that Buffy cannot miss. It's part of what leads her to the conclusion she reaches about Moloch and Malcolm and so forth.

All these things that happen at or near the Midpoint drive the story forward.

Our next scene is in the library. Buffy hasn't yet found Dave's body, so we don't know that Dave is dead. She says, "I don't know what would make Dave do that," referring to the attempt to kill her. Giles says maybe he knows and explains about Moloch the Corrupter.

Based on that, Buffy figures out that Moloch is in the Internet and is first to grasp how dangerous that could be. She tries to delete the file. But Malcolm's image pops up. And he says, "Stay away from Willow." This is our first time that Buffy and Moloch come face-to-face. Buffy now understands that Moloch is the enemy, Moloch is the one doing all these things.

And we cut to the commercial.

Writing Strong Chapter Endings

The last scene ending is a great hook to keep viewers coming back after the commercial. I think of these types of hooks when I'm creating chapter endings.

The end of the chapter is a natural point for a reader to stop reading. How often have you said to yourself when reading, "Okay, I'll read just one more chapter?"

If you can write a chapter ending like many of the Buffy pre-commercial scene endings, it makes the reader want to keep going to the next page or, if the reader has to stop, keep thinking about wanting to get back to your book.

So watching where shows break, if you are watching a network show that has commercials, is a great way to study how to keep readers engaged and going on from scene to scene.

The Protagonist: Buffy

Buffy now says they need to find Willow. But in the computer lab, she instead finds Dave's dead body. She realizes it was set up. Dave didn't commit suicide. Buffy tells Giles to get Ms. Calendar to help him and figure out how to get Moloch out of the Internet. Giles argues a little bit. He doesn't know how he is going to explain this. She tells him to figure something out and leaves.

Note how Buffy, our protagonist, is the one who figured out that Moloch was in Internet and that Ms. Calendar can help.

Willow is at home. She gets the "You've got mail" message from Malcolm. He says he wants to see her. She tries to ignore it, and the computer turns itself on again. Then the doorbell rings. She thinks it's her dad who's forgotten his keys. But it's Fritz. He drugs Willow and hauls her away.

In our next scene we see Giles. He's listening to the radio. Again we have this very quick take on the chaos that's happening. The news is reporting all these problems that are occurring, clearly from things Moloch is doing through the Internet. Jenny comes in and interrupts that. Giles stutters through this explanation of what's happening. Jenny says, "I know."

The Three-Quarter Turn

This brings us up to our three-quarter plot turn. This turns the story yet again, but it grows out of the Midpoint reversal or out of the protagonist's actions at the Midpoint. Here, right around 31- 32 minutes, we have a series of scenes that turn the story.

Buffy and Xander discover Willow is not home. They decide to go to that warehouse. That decision is going to take us to a whole new venue. Also, they have a new aim. They're still trying to destroy Moloch and get him out of the Internet, which has been the goal since our Midpoint. And they still want to protect Willow. But the goal is new because now it's not convincing Willow that Malcolm is Moloch and he's dangerous. It's ensuring Willow is not physically in danger because she's been kidnapped by Moloch. So now they have to both get Willow somewhere safe and defeat Moloch.

Jenny tells Giles she's been seeing portents for days. When he mentions Moloch, she says, "Moloch the Corrupter?" Giles is very suspicious. He says, "You don't seem surprised. Who are you?" She explains that just because she is the computer teacher and is into technology doesn't mean she doesn't know about magic. That technology and magic are not mutually exclusive. Also, she says she's not a witch. She doesn't have that kind of power. But she calls herself a techno-pagan.

All of this seems to reassure Giles, and she is clearly the one who can help. As it should, the story is moving very quickly now from that Three-Quarter Turn toward the Climax.

The Antagonist: Moloch

Buffy calls using a payphone. (Remember those? Maybe?) She tells Giles what they're doing. We then see another part of this turn, which is that Moloch has a robot body. He is both in the Internet and controlling this body. In front of Willow, he kills Fritz.

Seeing this part, I again thought, "Why do people keep supporting these demons?" So in addition to Moloch being this sort of mustache-twirling villain who is just evil for evil's sake, we also have that people support this kind of demon apparently just for evil's sake. Moloch kills Fritz. So Dave's been killed for not doing what Moloch wanted, but Fritz gets killed just because he's there, because he's a follower.

So I know we were told in the beginning that Moloch preys upon those who are weak of mind. Also, he's the Corrupter, and he has this way over people. So it is probably unfair to say that they are choosing to follow this demon. But it feels a bit like weak storytelling to me. It is less interesting to have a demon who just has this magic power of making people follow him rather than the followers having some reason. Some deep need the demon is filling, something that makes us understand why they would devote themselves to this demon.

Willow's Turn

Willow, too, has her own sort of turn in her personal story. Moloch is saying he wants to give her the world, he wants to repay her for freeing him, and she knows now that he's evil. But she is so angry because she's been deceived that when he says this about repaying her, she says, "What, by pretending to be a person?! Pretending to love me?!" The turn is not just that Willow expresses this anger, but that we're worried for her because nothing good can come out of this.

The reality, though, is loving Moloch or rejecting him leads to death. Either way, she probably figures she's going to die. So she's saying what she has to say. She's probably not even thinking it through, she's just expressing how she feels.

A Surprise Climax

Buffy and Xander get trapped by the security system in the warehouse hall. It looks like there is some sort of gas that is going to knock them out. We switch back and forth between them, Willow yelling at Moloch that she'll never be his, and Giles chanting while Jenny types into the computer and connects with a coven online.

Giles raises his voice to cast out Moloch.

Moloch puts his hand on Willow. He's about to kill her, and the chanting apparently works. Moloch is weakened. His robot body sags. He's out of the Internet. It looks like Willow is safe and Giles and Jenny have prevailed. (This still is a victory for Buffy, our protagonist, because she is the one who figured things out, set this in motion, and told Giles to go to Jenny.)

This could be a very satisfying conclusion, but we get the surprise ending. It's the real climax. Moloch is out of the Internet, but he's not back in the book. He's in the robot body.

Moloch is not a threat to the whole world anymore. But he's definitely a threat to our main characters. So we have this ultimate fight. Willow gets her chance to contribute because at a key moment she uses a fire extinguisher and is hitting Moloch with it, giving Buffy a moment to figure out what to do. Buffy goads Moloch into punching her at just the right moment and just the right place. Because she ducks, he hits an electrical panel, and it electrocutes him.

Note that once again, though Buffy's strength is important, her wits win the day. She is not stronger than the robot, but she outwits Moloch. Kind of ironically, she does it by using technology. Using the electrical panel and subverting his robot body, which is vulnerable in a way that the demon might not have been.

Falling Action

Now we have our Falling Action. Giles goes to the computer lab. It's apparently the first time he's been there. Jenny teases him about being afraid of computers. She points out that a book started all the trouble and asks what he doesn't like about computers.

This, too, is such an interesting back-and-forth because he says, "the smell." And she says, "They don't smell." Giles says, "That's it. Smell is our most powerful memory trigger."

That's something that's good to remember when you're writing fiction. A smell can evoke so much. It's directly linked to memory. So putting in a smell that evokes feelings for the reader – a scene for the reader – can do so much more than a visual description. Many of us, especially now that there is so much good long-form storytelling available on TV or streaming, watch much more than we used to. I still read a lot, but not as much as I used to. The downside of that is it's easy to fall into visual-only storytelling, or perhaps visual and sound, because that's what we can get through the screen. But the sense of smell is so powerful. A key smell, like the one Giles identifies when he says that "books smell musty and rich," can bring me right back into that local library I loved so and spent so much time in as a kid.

Giles And Jenny Story Arc

Giles and Jenny don't really reach an agreement. But I would say they agree to disagree. Jenny says he's old-fashioned, but we get the sense she likes him. There's a little bit more flirting, and this raises a good story question to carry viewers through more of the season. What will happen between Jenny and Giles?

I really like seeing Giles in a relationship with an adult. We only get to see him interacting with the kids. He is very important to their story and to Buffy as a father figure, but I like that Giles can also have a personal life.

This romantic tension between Giles and Jenny also does a little bit to obscure the question Giles asked her and his suspicions. He wondered why Jenny knew so much. Why did she know Moloch? Why was she watching what was happening? So he asked, "Who are you?"

By the end of the episode we've kind of forgotten about that. Or at least I did the first time I watched. Initially, Jenny seemed a little bit suspicious when she came in and she already knew all these things. But now I'm not worried about it because she and Giles seem to really be getting along and clicking. And she helped defeat the villain. So it sort of distracts us from that question that Giles asked.

Another Story Question On Love

Now we have the rest of our Falling Action. Buffy, Xander, and Willow sit outside the school. Willow's very sad. This is the first boy who liked her, and he's a demon. She says, "What does that say about me?" Buffy and Xander are reassuring her. Buffy says, "We're on the Hellmouth," pointing out this isn't about Willow. Buffy jokes about how she fell for someone and he turned out to be a vampire. And Xander says, "Yeah, and the teacher I had a crush on was a giant praying mantis." They all laugh, and then they get very somber when they realize that's pretty depressing.

And that too, raises a little bit of a story question: Will love ever work out for any of them being on the Hellmouth?

Spoilers

BEFORE REWATCHING FOR THE PODCAST, I had completely forgotten both that this was the episode where we met Jenny and that question that Giles asks her: "Who are you?"

As I mentioned, the episode does a great job of seeming to answer that question. It all seems good. Jenny chides Giles for thinking technology and magic can't mix. We think that's all that suspicion was about. That Giles was being a little snobby, or at least stuck in his own viewpoint, not realizing that, yes, Jenny could be tech savvy and still know about magic. So we think that's all there is to it.

In Season Two, of course, we'll find out that she is from this Gypsy clan – and I apologize for the use of the word Gypsy, that really isn't one that a lot of people consider appropriate anymore. It is how the show characterizes the curse for Angel. That he was cursed by Gypsies. Which is probably how Angel would have described that clan back when this happened to him. And the show continues to use the word.

Jenny is from the people that Angel hurt. We find out that she is there to watch Buffy and Angel. When that comes up in Season Two, I likewise wondered whether it was something that the writers decided on later because they liked Jenny. Or whether it had always been planned.

Now, watching this episode from that perspective, I think it probably was planned. Or at least they had an idea that perhaps there would be something with Jenny later that was questionable, or that she might have a dark side. Whether it was specifically about watching Angel or not, this was a nice way to start out with Jenny. And I'm happy to see that initially Giles was somewhat suspicious of her.

Questions For Your Writing

- **Does your main conflict reflect any larger issues, the way this story reflects tension over technology? If so, can you bring it out through characters with opposing views who are still both good people?**
- **Can your climax include a surprise where the antagonist appears defeated but rallies and attacks again? Or where your protagonist seems to have lost but then prevails?**
- **If you have a twist about a character later in your story, can you weave in a**

hint of suspicion now, and then show it seemingly resolved?

Next: The Puppet Show

NEXT WE'LL TALK about The Puppet Show. In that episode we get to meet another new character, Principal Snyder, who himself is very ominous. And perhaps is our villain. We'll find out.

CHAPTER TEN

THE PUPPET SHOW

THIS CHAPTER TALKS about Season One, Episode Nine, The Puppet Show, written by Rob Des Hotel and Dean Batali and directed by Ellen S. Pressman.

In particular, we'll look at:

- **Why and how characters on the protagonist's side still push against her, creating conflict**
- **Including hints and red herrings while still playing fair with the audience**
- **Quickly signaling a new character's worldview and personality through conflict**
- **Replacing one character with another who plays the same role**

Okay, let's dive into the Hellmouth.

Opening Conflict

There's no prologue. Instead we have a voiceover that says, "I will be whole. I will be new." And we see students rehearsing for the talent show. Cordelia sings The Greatest Love of All, and she's terrible. We see Giles looking horrified. Then we get a tuba player struggling through his number.

Buffy, Xander, and Willow come into the auditorium to make fun of Giles, who got roped into heading the talent show. He says, "Our new Fuhrer, Mr. Snyder," insisted he do this. That line of dialogue is such a great way to give a one-sentence summing up of the new principal before we see him.

Giles also says if Buffy had any shred of decency she would participate or at least help. But Buffy says, "I'll take your traditional role and watch." A very nice way of quickly setting up some of the dynamic between these two characters for any audience member who isn't yet familiar with them.

Character Development: Principal Snyder

Principal Snyder comes in. Because the three (Willow, Xander, and Buffy) are mocking Giles, he tells them they must participate in the talent show. He also says he's been watching them. He knows they left campus early the day before, and they're always in one scrape or another.

So right away we have Principal Snyder at odds with our three characters. And we see the contrast between him and Principal Flutie. In that first interaction with Buffy, Principal Flutie tried so hard to be on Buffy's side while still taking care of his other students. In case we weren't sure about that contrast, we now have the three begging Snyder not to make them participate in the talent show. Xander extols the merits of detention. And Snyder says right out, "My predecessor,

Mr. Flutie, may have gone in for all that touchy-feely relating nonsense, but he was eaten. You're in my world now."

At about 4 minutes in we have yet another student practicing. It's Morgan with his ventriloquist dummy. And Buffy says right away that dummies give her the wig, ever since she was little.

Morgan's act is really bad at the start. He moves his lips. He's not funny. But Sid, the dummy, says, "All right, time-out!" and he takes over, making fun of Morgan. His jokes are a little racy. Everyone claps. And the students and Giles don't know that it is truly Sid talking at this point. Being the audience members and knowing what kind of show that we're watching we right away suspect something.

On the DVD, Joss Whedon commented that he knew early on he wanted to do a classic evil ventriloquist dummy story, but he wanted to put a spin on it, which he definitely does.

The Story Spark

We have now reached our Story Spark, also known as the Inciting Incident. It's what kicks off our main story arc. Usually it comes right about 10% into any story. So any movie – if it's 120 minutes long – look for it about 12 minutes in.

Here, it is slightly later than 10% unless we consider it as the moment that Sid first starts talking. But I think it actually comes a little later. Because we could have a ventriloquist dummy that talks by itself, and that might not be a story arc here.

What we have is some creepy music and a girl in the dimly lit locker room (nobody ever seems to replace light bulbs in the locker room in Sunnydale). At 6 minutes, 10 seconds we hear again the slow creepy voice. Now it's a voice-over that says, "I will be flesh."

This line is a great hook. We cut to the credits and a commercial. And we of course are wondering what will happen. We know it's nothing good.

We don't actually see the Story Spark here. But we find out later that one of the dancers was killed in the locker room. That sets our main plot in motion because Buffy decides to investigate. When we come back from the credits and commercial, rather than finding out immediately what happened in the locker room, though, we are back with the students, who are all inept.

Another thing Joss Whedon said in the DVD commentary is that he had fun with this because the students are forced to do a talent show, and what we discover is all the students are talentless. That includes a magician who can't find the rabbit for his hat, which has apparently jumped away. And we get several other students similarly struggling throughout this episode.

Buffy, Xander, and Willow talk about how a dramatic scene is the easiest way to get through the talent show. And Willow says to Buffy, "You must have other talents." Buffy says, "What am I going to do? Slay vampires on stage?" And Willow says, "Maybe in a funny way." That is a little bit of foreshadowing for our Climax because that is almost what happens.

Afterwards, we see Morgan and Sid (the ventriloquist dummy). Sid comes on to Buffy. Buffy says, "Horny dummy, ha-ha," but threatens that if he doesn't find a new schtick he'll become a Duraflame log. This is part of why this sort of gross humor works in this episode. The show recognizes it's not appropriate and Buffy calls it out each time one way or another. So the show is not saying that these kinds of jokes are okay.

Character Development: Snyder

We also get throughout the beginning of this episode back and forth dialogue between Giles and Snyder. One thing I like about the way this is done is that it is broken up. So we don't have one long scene with the two of them talking. Instead, we get it interspersed with other action and with the tryouts.

Principal Snyder says, "Schools have no discipline these days. Flutie would say kids need understanding. Kids are human beings." Giles tries to argue with him, but Snyder says, "Sunnydale High has quite a reputation: suicide, spontaneous combustions." So we find out that, yes, the authorities are very aware of what is going on here. They may not know what's causing it, but they know that evil things are happening.

Snyder claims he thinks the problem is Buffy, Willow, and Xander. He says he has to keep an eye on those three. This escalates our conflict. Initially we have Snyder and Buffy and her friends clashing. But now we know specifically that he sees them as perhaps the cause of these incidents. Or maybe he's evil and that's why he's keeping his eye on them.

He says he "runs a tight ship: clean and quiet."

So of course we hear a scream. This is about 9 minutes in. It's where we find out that the dancer was killed. We see everyone filing out of the locker room. And there's a twist here, because maybe this wasn't a demon, according to Giles. A large knife was found, suggesting it was a human because demons don't need knives. They have nails and claws.

The One-Quarter Twist

This is our One-Quarter Twist that spins the story in a new direction. Because everyone thinks this is really a human. Not something that is really in Buffy's mandate to investigate. They all agree she should check into it, though, just in case. Buffy is the only one who really thinks that this was, in fact, a demon. Maybe she just doesn't want to believe that a human being could do it.

We then get our core characters talking to other students to find out what happened. Giles talks to the magician. He's practicing a card trick and he's terrible at that too. He actually tells Giles which card to pick. Xander interviews Cordelia. We get some humor because she's saying, "This is such a tragedy for me! Emma was like my best friend!" And Xander says, "Emily," which was dancer's actual name.

When the four regroup, they discover that almost everyone they have talked to mentioned Morgan and his ventriloquist dummy, who of course we already were a bit suspicious of.

In the auditorium, we see Sid alone on stage. He says he and Morgan have to be on the lookout and figure out who's going to be next. Buffy walks in and hears this, and Morgan comes out and claims he was rehearsing. Buffy asks some questions about Emily. Morgan is rubbing his head, seeming distressed. Sid tells her to get lost. Buffy apologizes, assuming that it is Morgan talking through Sid. She says she doesn't want to make Morgan mad.

Morgan says, "It's him! He's…" and then he trails off.

In the next scene once again – and even more so – everybody thinks that Morgan is behind this. Except for Buffy. She says all they know is he's weird, not that he's a murderer. This is something we will see throughout the episode. Buffy has one idea and her friends – although they remain her allies – overall push back against her, including Giles.

Creating Conflict

This pushback is a great example of how if you write a mystery you need multiple people, or forces, pushing back against your protagonist. Not just the antagonist. Because usually we don't know who the antagonist is in the bulk of the episode. So we need multiple sources of conflict. If we follow the antagonist all the time and show the antagonist all the time, that would give away who it is.

Also, usually we see mysteries primarily through the point of view of the sleuth who is trying to solve them. And while Buffy is not solely a mystery show, that is a strong element of certain episodes. Including this one where we don't know who the villain is.

Because of this need for conflict, often the protagonist's friends and allies must oppose her. That works best when those friends have really good reasons. We don't want them to be unsupportive just because they are difficult people. If that's the case, as an audience member or reader, I don't really want to hang around them. So we want to like the friends for the most part, but understand why they are disagreeing.

Here we've got that. Everybody has mentioned Morgan, and he is acting strangely. So there are reasons to suspect him. Also, Buffy is mainly responding based on her instincts and feelings. While usually that would mean a lot for a Slayer, in the very beginning she admitted she had this general fear of ventriloquist dummies. They have always spooked her. So it's understandable that her friends think that she might be influenced by that.

Giles, who might be digging into this more for her, is hampered because he has to oversee the talent show. Buffy argues with him a bit on this because a murder is more important. But Giles makes a really good point. He has to stick with the talent show because Snyder is watching all of them.

So that was a very nice set up in the beginning between Giles and Snyder. Not only do we see the conflict between Snyder and our core group, but it is a driving force in keeping

Giles occupied so that he can't be as much help as he normally is.

He does tell Buffy to check Morgan's locker. Morgan and Sid see her breaking into it, and Snyder catches her. She acts very innocent. He says he knows there's something going on with her. We also hear Sid say to Morgan, "She's the one. The last. And I'll be free."

Moving Toward The Midpoint

Next, we have a scene with Joyce and Buffy. Joyce wants to know if everything's okay? Buffy definitely does not want her mom to come to the talent show. Joyce tells her to get some sleep, she'll feel better. And we see Sid out the window when Buffy shuts the lights off. This is another great hook and we cut to a commercial.

(As I mentioned in a previous chapter, these cuts for commercial breaks are very much like chapter endings. I love to watch network television to see how that is done so purposefully.)

Sid attacks Buffy in her room. She screams. Joyce comes in and sees nothing, but she notices the window is open. Buffy is sure she closed it.

At 20 minutes in, we have the magician again with a trick, struggling with his assistant, who is in a box. But she doesn't disappear. We also see Cordelia and Giles arguing about when Cordelia will sing. He pretends there's something wrong with her hair to distract her, something that Xander told him about. We're approaching our Midpoint, where typically our main character suffers a major reversal or makes a commitment to her quest, or both.

The Midpoint

Here we have a pretty strong reversal for Buffy. At 21 minutes, 16 seconds in, so halfway through this 43-minute episode, nobody believes Buffy that Sid was in her room.

I see this as a major reversal because normally if Buffy relates something that happened to her, everyone is going to believe her and be right there to fight with her. But this time they don't. They double down on the idea that she is nervous about ventriloquist dummies and afraid of them.

Xander keeps pointing out how much what Buffy is saying sounds like a cat getting in the window. And if we hadn't seen it, he's not wrong. Even Giles says, "You know, it could be a dream," because she has been thinking about dummies. When Buffy says she's the Slayer, why won't they listen to her, Xander says, "The Dummy Slayer?" So this is very frustrating for Buffy.

It does not deter her, though, so in that sense she does make a commitment because she believes in herself.

We also see, almost at that Midpoint, what looks like a commitment by the antagonist, who we think must be Sid. It's a commitment for him, a going-all-in, when he goes in to Buffy's room. He risks exposing himself and getting chopped to pieces. He doesn't know yet she's the Slayer, but he is still revealing himself to her. Now it's clear that Sid can move around on his own, although it's possible Morgan is controlling him.

Giles does say there could be a demon, not a human, behind this. And he tells us there's a demon that each seven years needs a brain and heart to retain its humanity. The group considers Morgan for this. But Giles is less sure about Morgan now because a demon is strong and Morgan seems to be weak. And when we later find out that Morgan has brain cancer, part of why that doesn't come completely from left field is that Giles made that observation. Also, we saw Morgan rubbing his head earlier. So it is one of those twists that surprises us a bit and yet it fits.

Buffy has another encounter with Sid in class when he

spins his head around to stare at her. Sid is also causing conflict for Morgan by making jokes and talking back to the teacher. She of course assumes it is Morgan doing it. After class she shows a lot of compassion for Morgan, asking if he's okay, saying she's worried about him. So again, we get that sense that something is wrong with him. But it could be that he's evil, we don't know yet. Eventually we will find out that is not so.

He's upset and impatient, and he wants Sid back. When Sid is not in the cabinet, Morgan is clearly very worried. He's saying, "Where could he have gone? He knew to wait for me." This underscores for the audience that Morgan probably isn't a demon and isn't going after Buffy, because he is worried about what Sid is doing. He's telling us Sid has moved independently of Morgan.

However, at the moment, Sid is not doing anything nefarious. He is in the library because Xander swiped him. I like this moment of a small surprise. We're thinking that Sid is out stalking somebody, and instead Xander is having a bit of fun with him. Xander teases Buffy about her fear of Sid. But Buffy says to keep an eye on Sid while she goes to talk to Morgan. So Xander did have a purpose here, not just to plague Buffy. He knew Buffy wanted to talk to Morgan alone.

Notice that all of this is coming out of that reversal at the Midpoint. Everything is focusing on Sid, despite that the others aren't quite convinced by Buffy. Buffy goes looking for Morgan in the auditorium which, like the locker room, is very dark.

More Snyder – As A Suspect

Buffy encounters Snyder. They have a conversation that sounds ominous and makes us wonder whether Snyder could be the demon. He's already been set up as an opposing force to Buffy and her friends. Now he says he's not sure how safe it is for a girl like her to be there alone. She tells him she can take care of herself.

The other reason we suspect Snyder is he is the only new character. We don't know if he's going to be continuing on the show. That is yet another reason to suspect him from an audience-member perspective. And even from Buffy's perspective. It's logical to think that it could be somebody new to the school.

However, about 29 minutes in, Willow finds a reference in a book about man-made objects that can become human by harvesting organs. So we have this switching suspicion. On the one hand, there's Sid the dummy, who maybe needs organs to become flesh, and we heard in the very beginning, "I will be flesh." On the other, there's a potential demon, who could be Mr. Snyder, who needs that brain and that heart.

Moving Toward The Three-Quarter Turn

We're moving toward that Three-Quarter Turn in the story, which will again spin the story in a new direction. But, unlike the One-Quarter Twist, it should come from the protagonist's actions and grow out of the Midpoint.

As we're leading up to that, Xander realizes that Sid the dummy is gone. Buffy is still backstage. When we hear creaking, we are nervous for her. She finds Morgan's body, but we don't quite see it. The chandelier above falls on her and, once again, we break for commercial.

When we're back, we're deep in Buffy's point of view, looking through her eyes. Everything looks fuzzy and out of whack, and we think she might have a head injury. She's struggling to get the chandelier off of her. This is a really nice way to immobilize Buffy. Normally we'd figure she could lift that chandelier right off of her. But because she seems to have hit her head, and not be seeing right, and be weakened, it makes sense that she's pinned.

In the interview on the DVD, Joss commented that they had to have something like the chandelier because you need a fair fight between Buffy and the dummy. So 32 minutes in, Sid attacks her, they fight to a standoff, and they taunt each other.

The Three-Quarter Turn

And here is where we get to the Three-Quarter Turn. Sid says something like, "You win, you can take your heart and brain move on," and Buffy is saying, "Those would've been great trophies for you. You lost, you'll never be human." Sid says, "Neither will you." And then they both say, "What?" Because they've mostly been focusing on what they're saying and not listening. And suddenly it hits them both that they are both hunting for this demon.

So this takes the story in an entirely new direction. We no longer think Sid is the villain. Buffy no longer thinks he's the villain. He explains that he was a demon hunter and was cursed, so he became a dummy or was trapped inside this dummy. He's been hunting the last of seven demons. If he kills the last one, he will be free.

And he confirms what Giles found: that this demon needs a heart and brain every seven years to stay human. Everybody figures this human-demon will move on now because it has its heart and its brain. They assume whoever is missing from the talent show line up that night will be the one who was the demon. They're certain it's someone in the talent show because of where the murders occurred.

Sid and Buffy watch from up above while Giles gathers the cast and everyone together. Sid says he's surprised she's a Slayer and explains that the curse being lifted means that he will die. His original body is long gone, and there's nowhere for his spirit to return to.

They're both surprised when no one is missing from the talent show cast. Buffy jumps down to talk to Giles and Sid disappears. When Buffy goes backstage, there's something dripping. Morgan's brain falls into her hands, which completely grosses Buffy out. She washes her hands many times.

Once again everyone thinks, or at least Willow and Xander think, that it's Sid. They're once again pushing against Buffy because she disagrees. But she had that conversation with Sid. She feels sure he really is a demon hunter. So we figure it is probably Mr. Snyder.

The puzzle of the brain is solved when they figure out, by Willow looking into school records, that Morgan had brain cancer. The demon rejected his brain. Xander, Buffy, and Willow assume that the demon will be looking for a good brain, a smart person. They're a little worried about Willow, because she is one of the smartest people there.

We cut from that to Giles. He's talking to the magician. I'm pretty sure this is the first time that we get the magician's name, which is Mark. Giles is talking about calibration and calculations for this guillotine that Mark is using in his act, which he's demonstrating by chopping a cantaloupe in half. Mark says his assistant is sick. He needs Giles to help. As it hits us what's going on, Xander, Willow, and Buffy realize that Giles could be the target because of how smart he is. They run for the auditorium.

Giles is already lying in the guillotine. Mark locks him in. Giles asks how the trick works, and Mark admits there is no trick. He will get Giles' brain. Now, I like to think Giles was a little slow on the uptake here because he was so distracted by the presence of Mr. Snyder, and what that is going to mean for Buffy and for him. And by the need to run the talent show, while also helping Buffy. Because I'd like to think he might've figured it out before Mark locks him into that guillotine otherwise.

The Climax

This brings us to our Climax. From the Three-Quarter Turn to the Climax the story is generally fast-moving, with not much exposition. There was a little bit of an exception here, though, when Sid and Buffy talked. But I feel like that worked and didn't slow the story because we still had that tension of waiting to see who the villain was. And because we needed that moment for Buffy to be convinced that Sid was not the villain, even when he disappeared on her.

Other than that, we've been driving towards the Climax with almost all action and people figuring things out and moving forward. Once we hit the Climax, it is very quick. We have moment after moment after moment, and each one escalates the conflict further.

We have Mark using a small hand axe to hack at the rope that's holding the blade up. So we have literally Giles' life hanging by a thread. Buffy tackles Mark and they fight. The problem is that rope is so frayed that it snaps. Buffy can't be fighting Mark and stop the rope, so Xander catches it and holds onto it.

But they need the key to the lock to free Giles. It's really hard for Xander to hang onto the rope. Mark has the key and he is fighting Buffy. There's no way Xander or Willow are going to be able to get that key. So Xander kicks the axe to Willow. He's still hanging onto the rope. She's chopping at the lock. And Buffy forces Mark into the box that he used earlier for his assistant.

But it still gets worse, because Mark turns into a demon. He's now super strong and is fighting his way out. We saw as he was locking up Giles that the demon flesh was starting to come through Mark's skin. So he has become a full-on demon again.

Just in time, Giles is freed. Willow gets the lock open, and Buffy and Sid, who has joined the fight, wrestle the demon onto the guillotine in place of Giles and chop off its brain. So we have that moment that is almost our Climax.

But Sid tells Buffy he needs to stab the demon to end this or the demon will come back. This is needed to truly end this story arc. Buffy offers to do this, but Sid says he will. He stabs the demon and falls onto its body, just a wooden dummy again. So his spirit is gone. Buffy holds the ventriloquist dummy in her arms and says "It's over."

Falling Action

Now we have the Falling Action, which is going to wrap up our plot with the talent show and Giles and Snyder. The curtain goes up. We see Buffy holding, cradling, this wooden dummy in her arms. We have this demon lying on the guillotine, its brain chopped off. Willow, Xander, Giles, and Buffy are all just frozen in shock, with Willow holding the axe, and complete silence. It looks so much like a staged scene.

And Snyder, in the audience, says, "I don't get it. What is it? Avant garde?" and we click to the credits.

Now we have one of the most fun scenes in all of Buffy. For the credits there is just one quick screen and then we get a post-credit sequence. I believe this is the only one in Buffy. You may never have seen it. On the DVD commentary, Joss said he only got to run it once. I'm assuming that was because it added to the run time, so it wasn't ever shown in reruns.

It is Xander, Willow, and Buffy doing their dramatic scene for the talent show. They are so awful. Buffy is completely wooden in how she delivers the lines. She looks bored and irritated. When she has to move from one part of the stage to the other, she just kind of stomps around Xander. Xander is trying to be dramatic, but he forgets his lines. Willow freezes and then runs off stage. All of this is intercut with Snyder and Giles sitting next to each other in the audience. Giles looks very pained at watching this.

Joss said that this scene took longer than any other one to film because no one could stop laughing. That by itself is worth ordering the Season One DVD set, in my opinion.

Playing Fair: Red Herrings And Hints

One of the things I mentioned in the beginning of this chapter is the use of red herrings and hints while still playing fair with the reader. Now that I've gone through the whole episode I want to highlight a few things there.

First off, we have Mark the Magician. I like the way he's brought in. Although we don't have a reason to suspect his motives, he is very much in the episode. We don't get his name right away, but he is the first student we see when we come back from the opening credits. Eventually we know that the villain is somebody involved in the talent show. But we discount him because every time we see him he is very inept. He loses his rabbit, he's no good at the card tricks, his assistant doesn't disappear. So we don't suspect him.

At the same time, we don't really notice that he is the one student that we keep seeing. Yes, we see Cordelia, but she's a regular on the show, so we know she's not it. Otherwise, we see various different students throughout, whose names we don't learn, and who don't return. So he is the one new character, other than Mr. Snyder, who we see again, and again, and again.

Now I will say, if Buffy were a sleuth or follow-the-clues type of mystery, I feel like you would need a little bit more with Mark. You would need some sort of hint that he was up to something so that there would be a reason an audience member might look at him. But because Buffy is more overall thriller and horror than straight out solve-the-mystery, I think that Mark works very well here. While we're a little surprised to learn he's the villain, it's not a complete surprise because we have seen him quite a bit on screen.

Sid is a fantastic red herring.

It starts out with Buffy being creeped out by him. Which focuses us on him, and yet she immediately tells us she's just always been creeped out by dummies. So we get a double message there. Yes, he's the first creepy thing we really see. And yet we know that there's a reason why Buffy feels weird about him that might have nothing to do with him being evil.

Sid's storyline is also so good because it plays fair with the audience. If you rewatch, every conversation, everything Sid says, fits with either him being the demon or him being the demon hunter. When he is sitting there in the library while Giles, Willow, and Xander are researching, if you listen to their dialogue, there's nothing in it (and nothing Buffy says before she leaves) that would tell Sid that Buffy is the Slayer, that she's on the side of the forces of good. That she could be an ally. He still has every reason to think that she is the demon working against him.

So this is what I mean by playing fair. Yes, we are surprised by the twist that Sid is not the villain but a demon hunter. But it has been set up so that it works both ways. If we go back and watch, there is nothing that is out-and-out lying to us or that wouldn't make sense given what we now know.

Snyder works great as a red hearing for the same reason. Everything he says that's menacing or disturbing fits with the actual reason that he gave: that he knows there are a lot of strange things in Sunnydale. He's noticed that Buffy, Xander, and Willow are always getting into what he calls "scrapes."

And he says they left early the day before, which I have no doubt they did.

He is suspicious of them. Everything he says fits that and also fits his general view of students, which he expresses to Giles. He doesn't like students. He thinks they're disorderly, and he wants to change the way the school runs. So all of that, too, could fit with him being the villain of the piece or just being this new law-and-order principal. It also sets him up nicely as maybe a season-long villain. Or a future villain because we don't know if Snyder is just law-and-order or if there's something more ominous about him.

Favorite Quotes

My favorite quote of this episode comes from Principal Snyder. He is talking to Giles about Principal Flutie and how Flutie would've said the students need understanding. Snyder says, "That's the kind of woolly-headed liberal thinking that leads to being eaten."

My next favorite quote of the episode is when Sid is explaining the demon hunting, how he got to be a ventriloquist dummy, and how the demon becomes human. Giles says, "I must say, it's a welcome change to have someone else explain these things."

Spoilers

MOST OF THE spoilers here relate to the next episode, Nightmares. When she and Buffy are talking about what they can do, Willow reveals that she plays piano. Buffy suggests Willow can play and sing and Willow looks absolutely petrified and shakes her head No. And then we see in the dramatic scene at the end how she runs off stage. All of this will come back next week when she experiences her worst nightmare of being on stage, singing in front of everybody.

We will also see echoes of some of those fears in Season Four in the very last episode, which is mainly dream sequences. Willow is late for a play. She doesn't even know what's going on, and she's very nervous about it. A lot of that has more to do with Willow feeling like she's never really gotten past who she is in high school, that she has been playing a part the whole time. But it does play a bit on her stage fright.

Likewise, we see Cordelia's obsession with how her hair looks. In this episode, it's perfect but she's worried about it. Giles is able to use it to distract her. In the next episode we'll see her hair just in this mess that she cannot even get a comb through. I see it as sort of Raggedy Ann hair. So that's kind of fun.

Also interesting, and perhaps more subtle, is Xander knowing exactly what Giles should say to distract Cordelia. That foreshadows what happens later in the series, where we start seeing this chemistry between Xander and Cordelia. On this watch, I noticed how often they're interacting. Also in this episode, he is the one who questions Cordelia. We are building this, maybe not a relationship, but the fact that they are getting to know each other and Xander is so aware of her.

Questions For Your Writing

- **Do characters other than the antagonist oppose your protagonist?**

- **If so, do they have strong motives for doing so?**
- **Can you sum up a new character in a line the way Giles did for the first reference to Principal Syder?**
- **Does your story need red herrings?**
- **If so, when you read it again knowing the truth, does everything each suspect says and does still fit?**

Next: Nightmares

NEXT, our characters face their greatest fears in Season One, Episode Ten, Nightmares.

CHAPTER ELEVEN

NIGHTMARES

This chapter talks about Season One, Episode Ten, Nightmares, written by Joss Whedon and David Greenwalt and directed by Bruce Seth Green.

In particular, we'll look at:

- **Indirect dialogue that heightens conflict and exposition**
- **Escalating conflict for maximum emotional impact**
- **Foreshadowing characters' emotional arcs**
- **A Midpoint reversal for Buffy that's personal yet relates to the main plot**

Okay, let's dive into the Hellmouth.

Opening Conflict

We start with Buffy in a shadowy cave, her hair in braids, candles on all the walls. The Master confronts her. He's this powerful vampire that was the antagonist in the pilot, and who has been lurking through many of these episodes.

He confronts her. She drops her stake and backs away. He grabs her. She says, "No, No, No." Buffy is still saying that when Joyce shakes her awake. So this is part of our opening conflict. It sets the stage for the episode, though we don't quite know why yet.

After Joyce shakes her awake, we get the initial conflict. Remember, the initial conflict may or may not relate to our main plot. It is a conflict that draws the reader into our story. That's what keeps the reader or audience member engaged while we set the stage.

Here, Joyce says to Buffy, "I spoke with your father." Buffy says, "He's coming right?"

And there is our emotional hook. We know nothing about her past with her father, but immediately we know that she is worried about this, whether her dad will show up or not. So along with Buffy's fears about the Master, which is our outer conflict, we have her inner conflict. Her fears about her dad.

At school, Willow asks Buffy about the divorce. Buffy says she's sure she wasn't a big help with her parents' marriage because she was always in trouble.

New Characters

We then see Buffy, Xander, Willow, and Cordelia in class. It looks like it's a psychology class. The topic is active listening. The teacher says that one of the most fundamental needs is to be heard.

At that moment Buffy sees a boy who is too young to be in high school lurking in the doorway. He's maybe ten years old, and he looks very sad. At the beginning of the scene we were also introduced to a new character named Wendell whom we hadn't seen before. Right after Buffy sees the little boy, Wendell opens his textbook. There's a large tarantula in it.

Story Spark

Seconds later, spiders are crawling all over Wendell. We get a close-up on this boy and he says, "Sorry about that." And there is a cut to credits.

This is our Inciting Incident or Story Spark, what sets off our main plot. Usually that comes about 10% into the episode, which is the case here.

Theme Of Nightmares

When we come back from the credits, we're in the Master's lair, and he basically gives us the theme, or the premise, of this episode. He says, "Fear is a wonderful thing. And it's the most powerful force in the world. We are defined by what we fear."

The Master also says he can feel something happening above, conflict and change. His lair is underground, so he is sensing something on the surface.

Buffy's Fears About Her Dad

In the next scene we have Joyce dropping Buffy off at school. There's wonderful dialogue here filled with conflict. We can tell exactly how worried Buffy is although she never says that. And she denies it when Joyce asks. But Buffy keeps asking what time her dad will pick her up. Is it 3:30? And Joyce says, "Are you worried about your dad not coming?"

Also, Joyce eventually responds to what Buffy isn't saying. She says, "Your dad loves you. He adores you."

Giles Dazed And Confused

Buffy stops to see Giles in the library. He comes out of the stacks looking dazed and disoriented, as if he got lost back there. Buffy says, "Hey, Giles wake-y wake-y!" That line foreshadows what is to come in our episode. Though at the moment it looks like she's just having a little fun with Giles.

Xander, Willow, and Buffy together go to talk to Wendell about what happened. But Cordelia walks by and tells Buffy about a history exam that Buffy had no idea was happening. Cordelia says it's no wonder, because Buffy has barely attended class this semester.

Buffy doesn't even know where the room is. Cordelia has to show her.

Nightmares Take Hold

This is a nightmare that I used to have when I was practicing law full time. I had a big hearing coming up, and I couldn't find the courtroom in my dreams.

However, when I first watched this episode, I think I was still in law school at the time. So I don't think I was having that dream. And I didn't recognize at that point that what was happening were nightmares.

That starts becoming clearer, though, when we go back to Wendell, Xander, and Willow. Wendell tells a story about how he had a pet spider, a tarantula, when he was a kid. And he went away on vacation and left his brother to take care of the spider. His brother left the heat lamp on, and the spider died. Since then he has felt that spiders hold this against him.

Nearing The One-Quarter Twist

At 11 minutes, 42 seconds in, Wendell says, "That's when the nightmares started."

This is about one-fourth of the way through the episode. Usually at the one-quarter point in a story we see something from outside that comes in and spins the story in a new direction. In this episode, I think that turn comes a little bit later, so I'll talk about it in a moment.

But I find it interesting that the first specific reference to nightmares – the title of the episode, and the ultimate explanation for why the strange things are happening – comes right at the one-quarter mark.

Buffy's First Full Nightmare Experience

Immediately after that, we see Buffy having her first full nightmare experience. Up to that point, even her not quite knowing where the classroom is feels almost believable given that we know Buffy often has to cut class because of being the Slayer.

But now she is in class taking a test. Her pencil breaks. She goes to sharpen it, and all this time has elapsed. She writes her name and looks up. It's already almost the end of the class. So time is moving strangely. Buffy sees this little boy again, and he once more looks sad.

The One-Quarter Twist

Now we cut to the hallway. A girl we haven't met before sneaks down into the basement to have a cigarette. The boy looks after her and says she shouldn't go there. 14 minutes, 53 seconds in this giant man (or maybe he's a monster) says, "Lucky 19." He beats up this girl.

I see that as the first major plot turn in the story. Before that we did have these nightmares coming true. But while Wendell was scared, and Buffy was anxious and frustrated, no one was physically hurt.

This shows our villain of the piece, this giant man, becoming active for the first time.

Hospital Visit

Our next scene is in the hospital. So this has definitely taken the plot in a new direction.

Buffy and Giles go to see Laura, the student who was attacked. She doesn't seem surprised that Buffy and Giles are asking questions. Which makes me wonder if people in school already are getting a sense that somehow Buffy and

Giles both deal with these weird things that happen in Sunnydale.

We don't know that for sure. But with a little prodding, Laura confides in them. She tells them about Lucky 19.

They then go talk to her doctor. (Apparently, there's no real doctor-patient confidentiality in Sunnydale because all they have to say is they're friends of Laura's.) The doctor tells them she has shattered bones but she'll recover. And she has it pretty easy compared to the other kid.

They are shocked by the "pretty easy" comment until he tells them this boy was brought in and he's in a coma. We don't see the boy's face. But now Buffy and Giles know that perhaps there were two attacks by this scary guy.

Back At School

Back at the high school we see this student we don't know. He's got dark sunglasses and a black leather jacket and is talking very tough to his friends. His mother comes in. She hugs him and kisses him and calls him Boo-boo. He is completely freaked out by this.

Willow separately starts making a connection to how all of this could be a nightmare. She and Xander are walking the halls seeing things going on around them. Xander disagrees with her until they walk into a classroom and he's standing there in front of everyone in his boxer shorts. He is now convinced.

Back In The Library

We switch to Giles and Buffy in the library. Giles confesses to Buffy that he can no longer read. Buffy looks at the newspaper articles he's pulled. She sees one about a kiddie league player who was badly beaten after the game and now he's in a coma.

From the photos, she recognizes him as the boy that she has seen lurking around the school when these strange things happen. When Giles asks her how she can explain that, she says, in my favorite quote of the episode, "What am I, knowledge girl now? Explanations are your terrain."

Buffy's Dad Appears

Buffy also sees the 19 on Billy's jersey. That is the name of the little boy: Billy. But she isn't following up on this right now because her dad comes into the library. She's surprised because he's supposed to be there after school. Now he's there in the middle of the day.

She introduces him to "Mr. Giles, the librarian." Her dad says, "Let's go talk outside." (Her dad's name is Hank. So it's Hank Summers.) He says he came early because he needs to talk to her. And he tells her he wants to explain why he and Joyce split up.

The Midpoint Of Nightmares

We're now at the Midpoint of the episode. 21 minutes, 47 seconds in of about a 43-44 minute episode. This is the point where, in a well-structured story, the protagonist either makes of vow to pursue the quest, throws caution to the wind, or suffers a major reversal, or both.

Here we get a major reversal for Buffy. And while it relates to the emotional story here, it isn't immediately obvious that it is part of the main plot.

Escalating Conflict

This reversal is so devastating emotionally because not only does it hit Buffy's worst fear, but the writers keep escalating this conflict.

Every time Hank says something, we think it's the most awful thing that he could say to Buffy. Then he makes it worse. And we're right there with Buffy as she goes through this.

It starts with Hank saying that it was having Buffy and raising her that caused the divorce. Then he doubles down on it and says, "Imagine what it would be like to have a child like you." He goes on to catalog Buffy's faults: "You never think of anyone but yourself. You're sullen and rude..."

When she reacts, saying, "Why are you saying this to me?" it gets worse. He says, "I'm saying it because it's true. Could you stand to live in a house with a daughter like that?" She becomes tearful, and then he tells her she's not being very mature to get "all blubbery" when he's trying to be honest.

At this point, even re-watching, I thought, "Okay, that has to be it. That is the worst he could say."

But he says, "I don't get anything out of these weekends, so let's not do them anymore."

Still Not The End

Now certainly that would be a place to end this scene. And to put Buffy out of her misery. But there is one step more. Before he walks away, Hank says, "I sure thought you'd turn out differently."

As an audience member watching it, or even as I'm telling it to you, it seems so over-the-top. It seems like too much. How could Buffy not realize that this isn't real, that it is a nightmare that is coming true?

But she doesn't see it. With the other things that she observed, even her exam, she might be able to say, okay, that was not normal. This is not normal what happened.

But because Hank is saying to her exactly what she fears, she believes it. She's been afraid her dad won't show up. Afraid he's not going to keep up the relationship and that she is the cause of the divorce.

She's afraid all these things he says are true. And so she believes every single one of them.

A Major Reversal In Two Ways

This is a major reversal both emotionally and in our main

plot. It affects the plot because it makes Buffy unable to be at her best and fight.

We will see her from here through the Three-Quarter Turn running and hiding. Saying she's not strong enough, she can't fight this big scary guy. It all stems directly from this reversal at the Midpoint. From this incident where Hank just hits at every awful thing Buffy thinks about herself. It undermines her.

And that is what we should see in a good plot. Whatever happens at the Midpoint drives the story from there forward, up until that three-quarter mark.

Realizing What's Happening

Right around now we also see Xander, Willow, and Giles concluding that definitely what's happening is people's nightmares are coming true. Giles figures out that Billy must've crossed over from reality to dreaming while he was in a coma and triggered this phenomenon. He says things like this are easy when you're on a Hellmouth.

So we see operating what Joss Whedon said in one of the DVD commentaries or interviews. That the Hellmouth was created to be this explanation.

It wouldn't be enough that this little boy is in a coma and is having these dreams. While it would affect him, it wouldn't affect anyone else. But because we have the Hellmouth, that will extend and amplify what's happening out into Sunnydale and all of reality.

Other People's Nightmares

We then have a number of quick scenes where we see other people's nightmares coming true. Including Cordelia who is appalled at her hair. This is what I mentioned in the last chapter that we got a little hint of in The Puppet Show. Her obsession with her hair and, more so, how she looks.

Back to Buffy. She sees Billy and for the moment that

does distract her from her emotional pain. And she follows him into the dugout at the ballpark. She's asking if something happened to him after his game or at his game. And he doesn't remember. He does tell her he plays second base, and she asks if he is Lucky 19.

He looks very frightened and says, "That's what he calls me." Billy calls this large, frightening man the Ugly Man. We see the Ugly Man break in. He's got a club, or maybe it's a bat, and he's coming after Buffy and Billy. Buffy says he's too strong, she can't fight him.

Worried About Buffy

Back with Giles, Willow, and Xander. They're worried because if nightmares are coming true, they know Buffy has very frightening nightmares. So this cannot be good. They need to find her. One of them says, "Well, it'll be faster if we split up to find her." And Willow says, "Faster, but not really safer."

We cut back to Buffy and Billy. They have run away. Billy says he can't help Buffy, they have to hide. That's how it works. She wants to go find her friends.

We are back to her friends momentarily. Someone is calling out to Willow. It sounds like it's Buffy. So it seems to connect with the previous scene.

Willow goes down into the basement, saying she's not afraid, she's not afraid. A hand grabs her.

Then we are with Xander. He's in the hall. There are swastikas all over it. Previously, he mentioned he was afraid of Nazis. He becomes distracted, though, when he sees a candy bar and starts following a trail of them.

Billy And Baseball

Back with Buffy and Billy, they have evaded the scary guy for now. They are watching kids play ball. And Billy comments that it's bad when you lose. In their conversation it comes out that in his last game he made the last play. The team lost. I don't know if he says the coach blamed him or not, but Billy says, "It was all my fault."

And Buffy says, about 30 minutes in, "What, you were the only one playing? There weren't eight other people on your team?"

Then Billy says, "He said it was my fault." And the Ugly Guy comes out again. Buffy says, "Let's go this way," pulls Billy with her, and they are in the graveyard.

Approaching The Three-Quarter Turn

About 31 minutes in we are approaching that Three-Quarter Turn. Which takes the episode, the story, and spins it in yet another new direction.

It also flows out of the Midpoint. So our protagonist is more active as to where the story goes, or what pushes the story toward, the Three-Quarter Turn. It comes out of her Midpoint reversal and her actions.

We're moving up to that. But first we see a series of scenes where what we think is going to happen – what we think is the great fear of the character and the nightmare – turns out to be something else entirely.

Surprising Fears

Here we have that hand that grabbed Willow. She's in the basement where that girl was beaten up. So we think Willow is afraid of some sort of monster. That perhaps following Buffy is putting her in the path of these monsters.

Instead, Willow is pulled onto a stage. She is with an opera singer. And she's introduced as the World's Finest Soprano, Willow Rosenberg. We talked about The Puppet Show and how Willow was so afraid of singing on stage. And how she ran off stage during that post-credit sequence. So here we have this – her worst nightmare – in front of everybody.

She's unprepared, she doesn't know the words. She refuses to sing when her partner keeps turning to her. When she finally does try to sing this awful squeak comes out.

Xander And The Clown

Then we are with Xander. He has seen these swastikas. he's afraid of Nazis. But he finds a chocolate Hurricane candy bar. (I don't know if that's a real candy bar. If anyone knows, let me know. I hadn't heard of it.)

He is so excited about it. But it leads him to a clown. He screams and he runs. And we find out later that this was the clown from one of his birthday parties that scared him so much as a little kid.

The Three-Quarter Turn

We are now at 33 minutes, 56 seconds in. At the three-quarter point in terms of the timing of the story. And we see an open grave, and Buffy is standing there. She wonders who died, and the Master appears.

Now this is starting to turn the story in a new direction. He says – in response to her wondering who died – "What's the fun of burying someone who is dead?" He also tells her, "I am free because you fear it. Because you fear it, the world is crumbling." And he asks what she's afraid of. "How about being buried alive?" We see her then, inside the coffin, pounding on the inside of the coffin lid.

We don't know it yet, but this is the Three-Quarter Turn. We're going to find out that it's not just that Buffy is buried alive, but she becomes a vampire. So this is her greatest fear: to become the thing that she has been fighting.

And this will turn the story, along with Giles figuring out that they need to wake up Billy.

Escalating Conflict In Nightmares

Even with Buffy's fears we see this wonderful escalation by the writers. First, we had her fears about her father and how that undermines her. Then we have her outside fears. First, that the Master is out, and he is. Then that he'll kill her. He doesn't do that, but we escalate it to he'll bury her alive. And that isn't the worst thing. It's becoming a vampire.

Fears Faced

Next we see Willow, Xander, and Giles reunited. Xander becomes disgusted by running from the clown and being afraid. He turns around and punches it. Tells it that it was a lousy clown. And he feels good after doing that.

This gives us our first hint that you have to defeat your fears by facing them. Not perhaps a super-original premise. But I like the way it plays out here, because everyone from then on has to face their fears, including Billy at the end.

There's complete chaos in the school. And Giles says that soon there will be no reality left. They need to try to wake up Billy.

They see the cemetery. And they know that there didn't used to be a cemetery there. So they go there and see Buffy's grave.

Xander says, "Whose nightmare is this?" and Giles says, "Mine." So we have Giles' greatest fear. He says, to the grave, "I should've taken more time to train you, but you had so much to face."

Buffy's hand comes out of the grave. When she gets out, she says, "Don't look at my face." She is a vampire, and she is in vamp face. And Giles says, "You never told me you dreamed of being a vampire."

He explains that they need to wake up Billy and everything will shift back. Buffy says they better hurry. She's getting hungry.

So now we have another escalation, which is not just that she'll be a vampire, but that she will start attacking and drinking the blood of her friends. And it makes sense that

Buffy would have this fear. We haven't heard her say it before or seen it in her dreams. But she knows Angel. She knows how he became a vampire and the first thing he did was kill his family.

There's chaos at the hospital. They find Billy, the real Billy, in a coma. Buffy is talking to dream Billy. But he says he can't wake up because he has to hide.

The Climax

We're now at the Climax. The scary guy is coming after them. He's talking about Lucky 19.

Buffy is a bit in the shadows. Until now she has been running and hiding, basically following Billy's approach. Now she says, "Yeah, there are a lot of scary things, a lot scarier than you." And she steps into the light and says, "And I'm one of them."

So she uses what she fears – being a vampire. And it makes her even stronger. She's able to defeat this guy and knock him out. He slumps against the wall.

This is our climax, the beginning of it, for Buffy. But she also has to help Billy do what he needs to do. She tells Billy, "Come here, you need to do the rest." And she holds his hand. Billy says, "No more hiding," and reaches out – or actually I think Buffy says, "No more hiding." He reaches out toward the scary guy, and then this light floods everything.

We don't see the face of this monster.

Emotional Growth

This is another great example of what we've seen throughout the series. Buffy prevails, not just based on physical strength, but on her emotional capabilities. Her emotional growth.

The real Billy wakes up. Buffy is not a vampire anymore. Everything has gone back to normal. And Billy has a Wizard of Oz movie moment where he says he had the strangest dream. "You were there, you were there." And then he says, "Who are you people?"

All of them are standing around the bed, blocking the view of anyone who walks into the hospital room. And who walks in but Billy's coach? He says, "Oh, Billy's got company." And he explains that he comes by every few days, hoping against hope that Billy will wake up.

"He's my Lucky 19. So how is he?"

This is really nice because it explains why dream Billy kept saying, "We have to hide, that's how it works." Because as long as the real Billy was in a coma, he was safe from the coach. He must have known or sensed that the coach was coming by to see if he woke up and, perhaps, finish the job on him.

I'm not sure I picked that up in my previous watches of the episode. So it was neat watching and taking notes and putting it together to see how that fit in.

The Finish

The coach is shocked that Billy is awake. Billy confronts him, not just about what he did, but about saying that it was Billy's fault. And he uses the words that Buffy said to him. That he was only one kid on the whole team and it wasn't his fault.

Xander stops the coach from running away. So we know the coach is going to face justice for what he has done. That is the end of our climax.

Falling Action

We are at the Falling Action. The group talks about Kiddie League. I forget which one says, "Wow, how could it be like that?" And I think it's Xander saying, "Have you seen those parents?"

And we see Buffy with her dad, who is really there this time to pick her up. She looks so happy and he hugs her.

Our last moment is Willow asking Xander if he was still attracted to Buffy when she was a vampire. He stutters and stumbles but he says "Yes."

Spoilers

First, some minor foreshadowing about Buffy's secret identify.

We have Laura in the hospital confiding in Buffy and Giles. This scene hints that people were starting to perhaps feel that Giles and Buffy (or at least Buffy maybe, they don't pay much attention to Giles) was someone who might be able to help them. And we will see that next in Out of Mind, Out of Sight. Cordelia comes to Buffy for help when she thinks she is being targeted.

This is also the start of kind of chipping away at the whole secret identity idea. People who haven't been specifically told don't seem to know Buffy's the Slayer. But they do start to get the feeling that Buffy can protect them. We will see that made explicit in Season Three, when Buffy gets the Class Protector Award.

Hank Summers

The other foreshadowing, or one of many others, is Buffy and her dad. Her fears about her dad. Despite her worries in this episode about whether he'll show up, without the nightmare sequence I might have been surprised when Hank Summers fades out of Buffy's life as the series goes on. Because in the beginning, when we get the real Hank here, he seems so happy to see Buffy. And she's happy to see him. Plus Joyce has told us, "Your dad adores you."

Also, in the pilot episode of Season Two we'll find out

that Buffy spent all summer with her dad. So they seem to be staying in touch. He seems to be close with her.

After that, though, I think it's in Season Three, we will see Hank starting to flake out on Buffy. And of course later he will completely abdicate his parenting role.

Knowing all of that is coming, and knowing how Giles becomes more and more of a father figure for Buffy, I found the meeting between Giles and Hank Summers almost heartbreaking. When Buffy is saying, "This is my dad," and then says, "This is Giles, the librarian."

It made me choke up just knowing how Giles will step in and really become her father. And how her father will disappear on her.

There are also a couple other fun spoilers.

Buffy's Fate

Finally, the most major spoiler is Buffy's grave. Giles' sadness, his feelings that he failed her. We will see all of that in the beginning of Season Six. That he was not a good enough Watcher, that he could not prepare her. Even though we know the lore that every Slayer dies young.

He of course is still going to feel this guilt and the sadness and this feeling of failure after Buffy dies at the end of Season Five. And for Buffy, the foreshadowing that she dies, that her friends will see her tombstone. Also, that she will be stuck inside the coffin and have to fight her way out – something we'll also see at the beginning of Season Six.

And I wonder, was that already planned?

Because obviously given what Buffy's life is like, I completely believe her fearing that she would die, be buried alive, or become a vampire.

Then there's something I somehow missed mentioning when I did the Buffy and the Art of Story podcast episode on Nightmares. The opening dream Buffy has. It foreshadows the scene in Prophecy Girl when she confronts the Master in his lair and he kills her.

Questions For Your Writing

- **Look at one of your scenes with dialogue between two characters. Is it based in conflict?**
- **If not, what can you do to change that?**
- **If so, how can you escalate the conflict?**
- **What are your characters' greatest fears? Regardless whether you are writing speculative fiction like Buffy, can those fears serve as a basis for a storyline?**

Next: Out Of Mind, Out Of Sight

NEXT IS OUT OF MIND, Out of Sight where an invisible girl targets Cordelia.

CHAPTER TWELVE

OUT OF MIND, OUT OF SIGHT

THIS CHAPTER TALKS about about Season One, Episode Eleven: Out of Mind Out of Sight, written by Joss Whedon, Ashley Gable, and Thomas A Swyden and directed By Reza Badiyi.

In particular, we'll look at:

- **Crafting excellent transitions from scene to scene**
- **Incorporating theme into plot**
- **A weak Midpoint that undermines the story**
- **Whether the flashbacks serve a purpose or slow down the story too much**

Okay, let's dive into the Hellmouth.

Opening Conflict

As we should, we begin with our opening conflict. Cordelia and her friend Harmony are talking and walking in the halls of Sunnydale. This might be the first time that we get Harmony's name. I'm not positive on that, but it's noticeable because it's right at the beginning.

Cordelia is talking about getting her dress specially made for the spring dance because off the rack gives her hives. Though she hasn't been elected May Queen yet, she is confident she will be. Buffy, coming from off to the side, trips and falls right in front of Cordelia and Harmony. All her weapons fall out of her bag. She tries to explain, saying it's for history class and Mr. Giles.

Cordelia and Harmony make fun of her and walk away.

Buffy is still on the floor as she watches them leave. This is one of many times when Sarah Michelle Gellar's expression is so clear. Her eyes look so sad as she watches and listens to them make fun of her.

This conflict is not our main plot, but it does foreshadow it. We always want in the beginning of a story to have some kind of conflict to hook the reader or audience member. It can be completely unrelated to the plot. It can start the main plot. Or, as here, it can reflect it or give us a hint of it.

In Class

Doubling down on the theme of our episode, we switch to the classroom where a teacher is talking about Shylock. (I had to look this up because I did not read Shakespeare's Merchant of Venice. I didn't know that's where it came from.) The teacher is asking about Shylock and the anger of the outcast in society. So this is a bit of an echo of that first scene where Buffy is the outcast. It further sets up our main plot about an outcast invisible girl.

Cordelia says Shylock is too self-involved and argues that

he is not seeking justice. As I understand it, based on my reading, this is an ongoing debate among critics. Whether Shylock was seeking revenge or justice. Is he the hero or is he the antagonist?

It is a compelling theme. But for whatever reason, in this episode, it doesn't quite play out for me in a way that feels satisfying or that keeps my interest. I always remember the episode is one that I don't love. I thought perhaps as I went through it and analyzed it for the podcast that would change. But I'm sorry to say it didn't really.

But I'll try to dig into why that is. (If you love this episode, please let me know what you loved about it and why. Contact information is in the Appendix.) There are definitely things I think are amazing here, as always with Buffy as a whole, though it didn't quite come together for me.

Cordelia And Her Teacher

After class the teacher tells Cordelia it's always exciting to know someone did the reading. I'm sure when I first saw this I felt annoyed because Cordelia seemed to be expressing a somewhat shallow take on it. Particularly because she compares it to when she ran over a girl "just a little." And the girl tried to make it all about her and her hurt leg instead of about Cordelia's trauma.

Looking into it further, though, I can see how that conversation echoes the theme.

Also, now that I teach, I understand the teacher's comment more. It's more that someone at least took the time to read something and comment on it. Sometimes it can be difficult to get students to do that.

Cordelia asks for help with her paper. She and the teacher plan to meet the next day after class.

We then see Cordelia and Harmony again walking in the

hall. Cordelia tells Harmony her dress is ready, and it's so great Mitch is gonna die.

We cut to yet another dimly lit Sunnydale locker room. This time the boys' locker room. (So apparently they don't have any bigger budget than the girls do for lightbulbs.) And we see Mitch, who has just been mentioned. Given Cordelia's line, which links these two unrelated scenes, we think that he'll probably die.

Story Spark

So no surprise when strange things happen. We hear a girl laughing but we don't see her. At 4 minutes, 30 seconds in a baseball bat appears to rise by itself and start beating on Mitch. This is the Inciting Incident or Story Spark that gets our main plot rolling.

Here, it happens exactly where it should, at 10% into the episode. So even if our initial conflict had not foreshadowed our main plot and was something unrelated, around 10% we would expect to see that spark or incident that puts our main plot in motion.

And we cut to credits.

Cordelia Wants Your Vote

When we return Cordelia is handing out candy with a C on it and asking for votes. She refuses to give Buffy one and says, "Oh I don't think I need the loony fringe vote."

Buffy is clearly hurt by this. It doesn't really help when Xander and Willow start laughing about something Cordelia did in grade school that was similar. They are laughing so hard they can't get out what happened. And they don't really need to because they keep setting each other off by just saying a few words.

Buffy, though, doesn't get the In jokes and now feels left out even with her two friends.

Buffy As Outsider

Trying to offer some comfort, Xander says what kind of moron would want to be May Queen anyway? And Buffy says, "I was." Xander tries to backpedal a bit. Buffy comments on how nice it was when she was queen. It was fun. We get this wistfulness, and sadness, again from Buffy at how now she is in this very different position. While she doesn't say it, even with Xander and Willow she is still a bit of an outsider. Because she hasn't gone to school with them their whole lives.

I also feel like I need to comment that this is twenty-some years later. So quite a few times in this episode we get language that I don't think we would hear now. Generally, people are not using the term "moron" to refer to people anymore. And some references to mental illness like the "loony" and the "lunatic fringe" make me cringe. I'm using them only as quotes. I'm not suggesting this is how we should talk.

An Injured Mitch

At 7 minutes, 8 seconds in we find out that Mitch is not dead after all. He is badly beaten up. As he's being taken out on a stretcher, he tells Buffy what happened and that the bat moved by itself.

We now get one of our quotes of the episode, one of my favorites. Principal Snyder says, "No dead students here. This week."

He then tries to keep Buffy from going into the locker room and says she's always sticking her nose into things. Willow and Xander distract him by talking about how Mitch's father might sue.

A Possessed Bat?

In the still dim locker room, Buffy sees a message on the locker room doors: Look.

We cut to Xander and Willow talking about this in the cafeteria. Giles joins them. He says that, assuming the bat itself is not possessed, this could be telekinesis, an invisible creature, or an angry ghost.

Willow is tasked with looking for records of missing or dead students. Giles asks Xander for help. We get another great candidate for quote of the episode. Xander says, "What, there's homework now? When did this happen?"

Our First Flashback

We switch to Cordelia. She's talking about how depressed she is about Mitch. He's all black and blue and will look bad in the photos.

We then get out first flashback. It is black and white. We see Cordelia and Harmony once again talking about Mitch. In addition to the black and white, we know it's in the past because Cordelia's talking about how Mitch just broke up with someone else, and he's nosing around her.

We hear a girl off screen say, "Hi, guys." Cordelia turns and says, "What do you want?"

Then, in present day, we have her turn to look at Buffy. Buffy has asked if she can talk to her, and she gives Buffy that exact same look.

Flashbacks Can Be Tricky

Flashbacks, like dreams, can be tricky to use in fiction. The flashback happened in the past, so we are pulling the reader away from the main plot. Some writers really hate flashbacks. Some readers really hate them, too.

I'm not as opposed to them in principle. But sometimes a flashback is a sign that the writer's lacking confidence. So rather than letting the readers figure it out and infer what's happening based on the present, the writer is saying, "Hey, let me tell you about this thing that happened in the past."

I feel like here is an example of a flashback that, at least for me, doesn't quite work. As the episode goes on, we can figure out that there was this girl who was ignored. Who was an outcast. And who is now trying to get back at Cordelia.

Also, I feel like the parallels to Buffy, which is partly what this flashback is for, have already been shown to us. We've already gotten that, though we don't know that is going to be the driving force for the antagonist yet. I might have been more engaged with this episode if I needed to figure that out along with Buffy.

I also think maybe the writers here were trying to add emotional weight by having us see through the antagonist's eyes.

As Cordelia and Harmony are being mean to Buffy, Harmony is hit by an invisible force. She falls down the stairs and is hurt. This is about 11 minutes, 20 seconds in. We hear laughing. This is the same laughing we heard in the locker room with Mitch. Of course, Buffy didn't hear it then.

The One-Quarter Twist

This incident is our One-Quarter Twist in the plot. I call it that because it comes about one-quarter of the way through, though sometimes you'll see it a bit earlier or a bit later. Here it's about right on target.

It is the first major plot point, and it generally comes from outside the protagonist. So here, it's nothing really to do with Buffy. Maybe her being there contributed to our antagonist's feelings. But for the most part the antagonist has a grudge against Cordelia and is first going after Mitch and now Harmony.

This turns the story because it's the first time Buffy witnesses something. Here's the laughter and now she is beginning to track our antagonist, though not knowing who or what she is.

But she is on the trail. She follows the laughter. And she ends up in the band room. She thinks she's following a ghost, but then the ghost bumps into her. She tries to talk to what she now thinks is probably an invisible girl, but gets no answer.

And we have a commercial break.

When we get back, we see two guys in black suits standing around the school. Nothing more than that right now with them. I don't know that I noticed them the first time that I watched this episode or that I thought that they were significant if I did.

Invisibility Powers

Buffy tells Giles what happened. And because whatever it is bumped into her, they all conclude it is an invisible girl. Or maybe an invisible girl ghost. Xander says that's so cool, the power of invisibility. And he would use it to protect the girls locker room. Which is another one of those things that I hope would not be thrown in there to be funny now. Even at the time I don't think Willow and Buffy and Giles could've loved that, but it kind of gets glossed over, not commented on.

They talk about Cordelia being the common denominator of Mitch and Harmony.

Xander and Willow walk away. They're talking about ordering dinner, and Buffy is with Giles and again looks a little sad as she watches her two friends, who've known each other forever, walk away.

Outside Looking In

Buffy is going to try to watch over Cordelia. We see her that evening in the school hallway. And she is watching through a small window in a closed door as Cordelia and her friends get ready for the dance. There is laughing. Cordelia's dress is very pretty.

It's a little bit of an obvious metaphor for Buffy feeling like she is on the outside looking in, but I don't mind. It seems fairly realistic, and it represents much of what Buffy's life is like at Sunnydale. She is doing all these things to protect everybody. Yet, most of them are not her friends and don't know she's doing it. Or, like Cordelia, perhaps think she's weird.

This is also why I don't necessarily think we needed that flashback to link Buffy with our antagonist. To kind of hit us in the face with the idea that Cordelia is similarly mean to Buffy the way she was to the invisible girl.

Flute Scene Transitions

Buffy hears a flute playing and follows it again to the band room. And we cut to Giles in the library, and he also hears the flute. This is another nice thing that I admire in this episode despite that it doesn't quite work for me as a whole. I love the way these unrelated scenes are linked together.

So here we have the flute, and then we have Giles. At first I thought, "Oh, he's going to follow the flute." But instead Angel comes to see him in the library. Giles is startled because he's looking into the pane of glass and seeing his own reflection, and he doesn't see anyone next to him. Then he turns and Angel is there.

Angel And Giles Meet

Angel says, "Don't worry, I didn't come here to eat." Giles figures out this must be Angel, whom he hasn't met before but whom he has heard about from Buffy. Angel wants to help with defeating the Master, our season antagonist. We haven't seen him in this episode, but this reminds us that he's around.

It also reminds us about Angel. And we get another great quote. Giles sums up a central conflict in the season so far, the sort of romantic subplot. He says: "A vampire in love with the Slayer. It's rather poetic in a maudlin sort of way."

They talk about the Master. Giles says he wishes he had more volumes of Slayer prophecies. He's read everything that he can find, but many are lost. Angel says he knows about one of them Giles is missing. A particular codex that was just misplaced, but he can get it. (When researching one of my Awakening novels I learned that a codex usually means a manuscript or book that's handwritten. Before that, I thought it might be a term Joss Whedon made up to refer to books with Slayer history or prophecies.)

Giles mentions the invisible girl and says it's a wonderful power. Angel says he doesn't know about that. Looking in the mirror and seeing nothing is an overrated pleasure.

Another Flashback

We get another flashback in black-and-white. For the first time we actually see Marcy, the invisible girl. We don't know her name yet. She is looking in a mirror. So again we have that link, the reference to the mirror after Angel talked about one and about lacking a reflection. It's another connection between the scenes.

Marcy is trying to take part in a conversation between Cordelia and Harmony. They are making fun of a speaker that just talked for what they say is two hours and was so boring. Marcy throws in things about the man's toupee. And they completely ignore her as if she is not there. Cordelia even repeats the comment about the toupee, and everybody laughs.

Themes In Out Of Mind Out Of Sight

These two scenes encapsulate additional themes running through this episode. One is the difference, and it's often a gender difference, between views on the imagined power of invisibility. You've probably heard the question: if you could choose the power to be invisible or to fly which would it be?

I read an article suggesting that women more often choose the power to fly because they already feel invisible and it doesn't feel like a great power. It feels like a negative.

Because it is so much harder to be heard in the workplace or in mixed groups or in many different situations.

I feel like we see this reflected when Xander says, cool – invisibility, and we see Willow look really troubled.

Also between Giles and Angel. Giles says invisibility is a wonderful power. Angel in many ways is invisible. He can't see himself in a mirror, he skulks around outside society. He is saying no, it's not great.

So it clearly isn't only splitting along gender lines, but I found it interesting that we have this theme there. This idea of what it's like to be invisible. That is doubled down where Marcy is talking and says something and then Cordelia says it and everybody laughs.

Which reminds me of the cultural phenomenon that often happens in business. At least, I've experienced it. I know many other women who have. When everyone's talking, and the woman advances a theory or an idea or a solution. Everyone just keeps talking past it until a male colleague says the very same thing, and then everyone listens.

And here we see that happening with Marcy among a group of women. But it is the higher status woman, Cordelia, who says something and everyone listens. So there are these themes about power, visibility, and being ignored. And I really like that, and it's part of why I really want to like this episode. Yet I'm not sure we ever come to any real conclusion about this or say anything about it.

This last flashback doesn't really move our plot forward. It gives us the back story about Marcy, which I feel like we could get through present day conversations. In fact, we will have one soon about Marcy's yearbook when we get back to the main plot.

The Schoolyard

We are in the school's courtyard. Cordelia is being

applauded as the Queen. She has been elected, and she's giving a speech. We're about 20 minutes into the episode, so we are moving toward its Midpoint. Buffy and Xander are off to the side. Willow has that list of dead or missing students. She also notices the two guys in black suits who are standing near the stage and asks if Cordelia has bodyguards now.

Buffy notices that the most recent missing student, Marcy Ross, played the flute. And she connects it to the flute that she heard in the band room. This is the first time we've gotten Marcy's name.

Buffy goes to the band room and sees a footprint on a chair. She climbs on the chair, pushes a ceiling tile out of place, and gets up into an overhead crawlspace. She discovers that someone is living there. There are many things, including a flute and a teddy bear.

The camera angle tells us that Marcy is watching. It zooms in as Buffy looks at Marcy's yearbook. Buffy reads it and says, "Marcy Ross, so it is you." And behind her a knife is hanging in the air. That's halfway through the episode at 22 minutes, 42 seconds in. So I guess it's maybe a little more than halfway, because episodes are generally 42-44 minutes.

But we have what I see as our Midpoint commitment. At the Midpoint, we will see either a major reversal for our protagonist or a major commitment. Our protagonist commits to the quest, throws all in. Think about if you've read or watched Gone With The Wind. Scarlett O'Hara, starving, finally gets to her faraway neighbor's garden, and there are no edible vegetables or other crops left. And she says, "As God is my witness, I will never be hungry again." And that is the literal Midpoint of the movie, this vow by Scarlett.

You can also have both a reversal and a commitment.

Buffy Takes A Yearbook

Here, I looked for that moment. We don't have a reversal

for Buffy here. We do have her identifying Marcy for certain. I feel like the most we have in the way of a commitment is when Buffy takes that yearbook. So she doesn't just observe Marcy's things. She takes the yearbook and she climbs out. Buffy has put herself directly opposed to Marcy. But this isn't a super-strong commitment. And I feel like it's another reason why perhaps this episode just doesn't grab me.

Though I do like the yearbook and it is definitely key. Not long at all later in the episode we will see how the yearbook helps Buffy and her friends figure out what's going on and why.

Attack On The Teacher

The next scene we have is the teacher who was so kind to Cordelia. She looks up, thinking Cordelia has come to see her after class. Instead, the invisible Marcy laughs and puts a plastic bag over the teacher's head to suffocate her.

Now Cordelia does walk in. She gets the bag off of the teacher, who survives. Marcy writes on the blackboard. All Cordelia and the teacher see is this chalk moving by itself, and it writes: Listen.

And we cut to commercial.

Invisible Marcy

When we're back, Buffy is in the library showing Giles, Willow, and Xander Marcy's yearbook. Every single person wrote: "Have a nice summer." Giles thinks this seems like Marcy has lots of friends. But everyone explains to him that this is the thing people say when they don't know anything about the person, don't remember them, and don't care. "Have a nice summer."

Xander says it's the kiss of death. He and Willow both say they didn't know Marcy. Buffy points out that they wrote it, too, although Willow I think wrote "Have a great summer." They still think that maybe they never had classes with her, didn't interact with her until she asked for the yearbook signatures. But Willow finds out they had four classes with her. They realize that no one noticed her and she became invisible.

Flashbacks Not Needed?

So this scene right here is part of what I'm talking about, that I don't think we needed those flashbacks showing us what happened with Marcy. Because this library scene pretty much fills us in as our characters figure it out.

Giles says it's quantum mechanics. We get another great quote when Buffy says, "I think I speak for everyone here when I say, 'Huh?'"

(I was really surprised how many quotes I wrote down from this episode. It's another example of how one episode can still have so many amazing things in it, and it's why I keep saying though it didn't grab me, I still pretty much enjoyed watching it.)

Giles elaborates on physics and quantum mechanics and how because people perceived Marcy as invisible, she became it. With a little help from the Hellmouth.

We Flash Back Again

We then get another black-and-white flashback. In this one, the teacher, the same teacher, is calling on people. Marcy keeps raising her hand. The teacher never calls on her. Marcy looks at her hand, and you can see she's feeling very afraid and shaky as the hand gradually disappears.

I want to have this great sympathy for her at this point. And yet it doesn't really hit me emotionally that much. Maybe because we've already been told this happened, maybe because we don't know anything about Marcy other than that everyone ignored her. I understand, and I don't know how you do that, how you share more about her, because who would tell us about her? No one noticed her.

Although Buffy does see some things that belong to Marcy up in that space. Maybe we could've had her getting to know Marcy better or learning more about her as part of the story. But we don't get that.

I don't like to try to take apart a story based on, "Oh, I think the author should've done some other thing." I want to look at the story as it is. So I'm just throwing that one idea out there as maybe that would've been something that might've been more engaging for me. Obviously, it wasn't the way the writers decided to go with it.

What Does Marcy Want

Xander asks what Marcy wants. And Buffy shows a marked-up photo of Cordelia. She says, yes, it's what they thought. It's Cordelia. At that moment Cordelia walks in the door of the library. Another nice transition because, though our characters stay in the same place, this is a new scene.

Cordelia first insults Buffy and her friends, saying Buffy is weird and her friends are losers. But she wants Buffy's help, and she thought Buffy might be in a gang because of all those weapons and because she's always around when strange things happen.

And remember at the end of our pilot, Cordelia was talking about the vampires who broke into the Bronze. She said it was some kind of gang, and Buffy knew them. So we see this theme from Cordelia. This is how she is making sense of Buffy and what she sees as the weirdness of Buffy.

All About Cordelia

Cordelia says, "It's all about me. Me, me, me." And Xander says for once she's right.

Buffy explains what is happening, what they think Marcy is doing. We hear Marcy ranting as Cordelia insults her picture in the yearbook. Then we're back to Buffy, who says this might be about the May Queen.

Cordelia is determined to be crowned. She says otherwise Marcy wins. And we get another great quote, one of my favorite Cordelia quotes. She says, "She's evil, okay, way eviler than me."

They all kind of have to agree with her. Buffy says, well, this will be good, Cordelia will be bait to draw Marcy out.

Is Cordelia Lonely Too?

Next Cordelia and Buffy walk down the hall in the high school. Cordelia is going to get her dress on and get ready for the dance. They talk about loneliness.

Cordelia says she can be surrounded by people and be completely alone. And how people just want to be in the popular zone, and they're so busy agreeing with her that they don't even hear what she's saying. And Buffy asks, okay, then why do you try so hard to be popular?

And we get another great quote. Cordelia says, "It beats being alone all by yourself."

Cordelia and Buffy find a broom closet or janitor's closet that Buffy thinks will be safer for Cordelia to change in. Cordelia goes in to change, and Buffy stands outside. That Buffy would stand outside rather than being in there with Cordelia seems a little shortsighted given that she knows that Marcy has been up in this space between the ceiling tiles and the ceiling. On the other hand, I guess she might think it's better to be outside and keep watch.

Whatever the reason, we hear this flute music again. We see Xander, Giles, and Willow trying to follow it, and we cut between them and Buffy and Cordelia.

Buffy Tries To Bond

Buffy is talking to Cordelia through the door about how she felt when she was popular and how sometimes she did feel something was missing. Cordelia reacts with surprise and almost scorn. She can't believe Buffy was ever popular, or at least that's what she's saying. And Buffy has a great quote here, something like, "How about we have this heart-to-heart with a little less heart from you?"

But then there are noises and Cordelia's muffled screams. Buffy has trouble getting in. The door is locked. She breaks in and sees Cordelia's feet going through the ceiling.

Popularity, Theme, And The Outcast

This conversation about popularity and aloneness seems to be yet another theme through the episode, or an elaboration on our theme of the outcast. Where we're saying okay, there's the outcast, but people who are surrounded by people can also feel lonely.

An interesting thing to explore, yet I don't know that we really explore it here. So while I love the quote and I love the conversation, I feel it just isn't picked up on in the story itself.

(If you have other thoughts on that, I would love to hear them. I just am not seeing it.)

And it's not that everything our characters say, or every theme we touch on in a story, has to be played out in that story. That would lead to: "The moral of the story is...." I'm not looking for that. But I feel like there are a number of intriguing concepts in this episode that are not really played out in the plot, and yet we spent all this time on these flashbacks.

Maybe that too is part of what is not quite working here.

The Three-Quarter Turn

We now have another change in direction, or we just saw another change in direction, with Marcy grabbing Cordelia. That was about 33 minutes, roughly three-quarters through the story. Usually we see a plot turn there.

It typically grows out of the protagonist's action at the Midpoint or out of the reversal to the protagonist. So it shouldn't be like the first major plot point that comes from outside the protagonist. This one should grow organically from that Midpoint, and yet still spin the story in another direction.

We have that here with Marcy grabbing Cordelia, but also with Buffy. Because Marcy knocks Buffy out and injects her with something. She ties up both Buffy and Cordelia in the Bronze to these thrones for the spring dance.

Growing From The Midpoint

I feel like this does come from that Midpoint because that is when Buffy took the yearbook after she invaded Marcy's space. That put her in Marcy's sights in a way that she hadn't been before.

Marcy will even tell us that she thought Buffy would understand. Because she had been seeing Buffy as a sort of sister outcast. Then Buffy started opposing her, so this does grow from the Midpoint. And it takes the story in a new direction. Because now we're not hunting Marcy, we're in direct confrontation with her. Buffy is directly trying to protect Cordelia and stop Marcy.

At The Bronze

As Buffy wakes up, Cordelia is panicking. She can't feel her face. It's numb. The word Learn is written on the wall, and Marcy is taunting them. She says Cordelia will be the lesson. That she will give Cordelia what she's always wanted. Everyone will look at her. Marcy unveils a cart with a tray of scalpels and knives and surgical instruments.

In between the Marcy, Buffy, and Cordelia scenes we get Giles, Willow, and Xander. They have followed the flute, thinking they're following Marcy. But it's a recording she made. It lures them into a room where they become trapped. The gas has been turned on. They will pass out and ultimately die if no one saves them.

Buffy obviously can't save them because she is tied up,

literally. They can't help her. So we are cutting between them, and they're talking about how crazy Marcy is. But they're unable to do anything about it because the gas is overcoming them.

Buffy inches her fingers forward to get the scalpel. As Cordelia is pleading with Marcy and arguing with her, Buffy gets the scalpel and saws at the ropes while Marcy yells at Cordelia. She gets free and kicks and fights with the invisible Marcy.

Angel To The Rescue

In the meantime, Angel has come to the school to bring the Codex to Giles. He finds our three friends and drags them out of the room, then goes back to turn off the gas because he doesn't need to breathe.

This subplot with Xander, Willow, and Giles tracking the flute feels a little flat to me. We obviously needed a reason why they aren't there to help Buffy. So it gets them out of the way and gives Angel something to do. Also, in an episode earlier in the season I talked about how Angel would just show up, look good, and say cryptic things. So this time he does come and save the day.

But there's just not that much to it. Even having him come to bring this Codex that is going to be important (more in the spoilers about it), not that much is happening there. And again we are stepping away from our main plot.

Maybe it could've just been done more quickly. Because it didn't feel to me like it raised the tension very much to flip back and forth between the scene in the room with a gas leak and Marcy and Cordelia. For one thing, there's no way that I believe that these three can die. Yes, Joss Whedon has set out that important characters can die. But there's no way I think he's going to wipe out three of our four main characters. (Or I guess out of five if we count Angel.)

Buffy And Marcy

Buffy tells Marcy she used to feel sorry for her, but then she realized Marcy is a thundering loony. This is more language we probably wouldn't use today. But even if we set that language aside, it feels to me like not enough of an explanation for Marcy.

Yes, we have the mystical-science explanation of no one paid attention to her and she became invisible. That is heartbreaking. Yet we don't, at least I don't, really feel bad for her. Part of it is because the story dismisses her as, okay, and then she just went crazy.

Well, she's isolated. Even more so, she's invisible. This would be terrible for anyone's mental health. And yet it's treated as, well, she's just crazy. I had sympathy for you, but you're crazy, so now I don't.

That doesn't feel authentic to Buffy. As I talked about before, part of her power is her empathy for others. Her ability to help give them voice. Like when she basically gave Billy the words to stand up to his coach.

Wishing For A More Complex Antagonist

I get it. Buffy needs to defeat Marcy. She's not about to let her carve up Cordelia's face. But I feel like it's a real missed opportunity here to have a nuanced and complex antagonist. Maybe some of my feeling on this point is that we know the writers can do this. They do it so much and will do it so much throughout Buffy. It's part of what I love about the show.

But the reality of network TV is that, as I understand it, often things go very fast. A writer is given a plot, a storyline, and sent off to write it. There isn't always the time to do everything you would like to do. So perhaps that is what happened here, and that's why we don't get as layered and as rich an antagonist in this one-off episode as we get with many of our season-long antagonists.

Though even with some of our single-episode antagonists in Buffy, we sometimes see more development. Or, as in The Puppet Show, we don't really get much about the antagonist, but we get this intriguing other character, Sid.

The Climax

So back to Buffy fighting. We're at the Climax. This big confrontation between the protagonist and antagonist.

Cordelia is screaming and crying. And Buffy tells her to shut up. Buffy, up to that point is kind of losing to Marcy, who is taunting her about how do you fight someone you can't see? But when Cordelia is silent, Buffy stands still and listens. And we have this nice moment with this noise like a breeze, and it's blowing Buffy's hair, and it's sort of mystical all around her. She holds very still and listens. We hear something creaking, and she turns and punches Marcy.

Marcy becomes tangled up in the curtains for the stage. Now Buffy can see her and fight her, and she does.

Men In Black

Then these two guys in black suits sweep in and say that they're FBI. They'll take it from here. Buffy says, "You can cure her?"

They say they can rehabilitate Marcy. She'll be a useful member of society. They refuse to answer when Buffy asks, or states, "So this has happened to other kids."

This climax also feels a bit unsatisfying to me.

Yes, Buffy does defeat Marcy, and she calls on something in addition to her physical strength to do it. So we see a little bit of growth here in the sense that stillness and listening are important to her winning the fight.

Yet these two FBI guys coming in feels strange. Maybe because they're from a different kind of story. Until now, we've been dealing mainly with the supernatural, even when we brought in the robot. It was as part of this demon who is now in our present-day world.

Here, we have this intrusion of a government agency and law enforcement into what is normally a supernatural story. And we didn't get a lot of set up here. We did see these two guys around. So they're not completely out of the blue. But it just feels a bit off to me and anticlimactic to just have them whisk Marcy away.

Falling Action

We then go to the Falling Action part of the story. This is where we tie up loose ends. Or in this case untie Cordelia.

We see Buffy and her friends together with Giles. They fill her in on the flute and the gas leak. But Giles stops them from telling her that Angel is the one who saved them.

I think this is in deference to Angel saying it's too hard to be around Buffy. And Giles knowing it's probably hard for Buffy as well. So he must think it's better that he doesn't mention Angel's visit.

Maybe he also doesn't want to mention anything about the Codex until he looks into it, so he doesn't want to say why Angel was there.

Cordelia finds our group of four at the library and very sincerely thanks them. She doesn't just say thanks or thank you, she really talks about what they did for her and what it meant to her. Willow says, "Hey, we were just gonna go get some lunch, want to join us?"

Before Cordelia can answer, Mitch comes up and says, "You're not hanging out with these losers?" Cordelia says, "Are you kidding?" She was just helping them with their fashion problems, and of course she's not joining that leper colony.

Xander says, "Where's an invisible girl when you need one?"

The plot threads have been resolved, and we get what I see as an epilogue.

Epilogues

I've been thinking about epilogues lately because Shiromi Arserio, the producer/narrator of three of the audiobooks in my Awakening supernatural thriller series, listens to the podcast. After hearing my comments about prologues, she asked what I thought about epilogues. She said a number of books she's been narrating lately have very long epilogues.

First, I had to look up the definition of epilogue. It's one of those things that of course I know what it is. I've seen it in books. I've included them in mine, although I can't remember if I ever actually labeled one "epilogue." But when it comes to definition, I had to resort to the dictionary.

I think this is a pretty good one. Miriam Webster on line says an epilogue "is a concluding section that rounds out the design of a literary work." Also, it's the final scene of a play that comments on or summarizes the main action.

Out Of Mind, Out Of Sight Epilogue

So here we have invisible Marcy and the FBI bringing her into this classroom. I see this as an epilogue because it does somewhat comment on our main plot. And it rounds out the story in the sense that we knew the FBI took her away. We didn't know what was going to happen to her.

I don't know that we needed to know because our protagonist's arc has resolved. Buffy did protect Cordelia. She did stop Marcy. I guess I like that we at least see what happened to Marcy if we're going to bring in these FBI guys that otherwise don't seem to fit.

So they bring her into a classroom. We see a teacher. On all the students' desks, books are open in front of them. But they're all invisible. Marcy sits down and opens her book to the chapter on assassination and infiltration. And we hear her say, "Cool."

Theme And Message

I found this disturbing the first time I watched it. And I continue to find it disturbing. Which I'm sure is the point. These government guys had been watching and watching, and they didn't intervene when Marcy was doing any of these things. In fact, Buffy called them on that when they came in, and they said, well, we came in as soon as we could.

Really? Because they'd been standing around. Though I guess you could say they were trying to figure out what was going on.

Weaponizing Marcy

Now we find that they are wanting to weaponize Marcy. That there is no real attempt to help her mentally or emotionally but just to use her. I have a little trouble with this in terms of the episode as a whole. Because how does this fit with any of those themes that we raised? Is the answer that the outcast becomes a weapon against society?

You can certainly make an argument for that. That being an outcast, that the way others treat someone, can both be wrong and have these terrible consequences. But I don't know if that's what the episode was trying to say or not.

We have Buffy, who is something of an outcast but who nonetheless is putting her life on the line all the time to protect other people. We haven't really explored what the difference is between her and Marcy.

I am sort of on the fence with this epilogue, as I am with the entire episode.

Spoilers

THE CODEX

The major foreshadowing here is this Codex that Angel says he will get, and Giles talking about the prophecies about the Slayers. This is done so quickly and almost feels like an aside in this episode. Or like it's just an excuse to briefly see Angel. And to remind us about the Master. But that Codex will have the prophecy that drives the entire finale: that Buffy will face the Master and she will die.

Part of me wants to say the scene didn't need to be in this episode. It felt kind of shoehorned in. We could have just put it in Episode Twelve, Prophecy Girl.

Setting Up Giles' Diligence

Then I thought about it, and I suspect the authors wanted to do this earlier so that when we get to Prophecy Girl we feel like Giles has been studying the Codex. Because in no way do we want to feel like Giles leaps to the conclusion that Buffy is going to die. He needs to have time to really study this Codex. To cross-reference, to be in a place where he is very authoritative and very certain about this prophecy. So I think that's probably why we get it in this episode.

And maybe the reason partly for the whole gas leak, in addition to getting Willow and Xander and Giles in a place with they can't help Buffy, is to kind of obscure the importance of that Codex.

I still would've liked to have seen Angel come in for maybe another reason. But it's intriguing as it is because we have set up now this idea that there are these prophecies about the Slayer.

Zen And Buffy

There is some foreshadowing for the entire series here

when we see Buffy holding still and listening. This is part of her training. We will see over the course of the series that she develops more and more of this sort of inner calm, this connection to everything. This kind of Zen-like approach.

She doesn't focus on that all that much. Here and there we see it. Then in Season Five she really doubles down on it when she is dedicated to truly studying and learning about being a Slayer and wanting to give herself the best possible chance to survive. We will see her working with crystals, meditating, and doing a handstand on one hand and concentrating.

This was a nice little bit of foreshadowing for that aspect of being a Slayer.

Season Four Foreshadowing

We also have some pretty heavy Season Four foreshadowing. I said we aren't used to seeing government agencies in Buffy. And I talked about the idea of weaponizing the supernatural. Here, weaponizing our antagonist.

In Season Four we will see an entire arc where we have the Initiative. It's a branch of the military that is all about studying demons and modifying their behavior. But a segment of the military wants to use them as weapons. Now here we have a girl being used as a weapon in total disregard to her mental health.

The Initiative will be focusing on vampires and demons, not humans. So in some ways I feel like they're not quite as bad as the FBI is depicted here. But it does definitely give us a little hint of that. Whether that Initiative story acc was already planned, I don't know. But it is interesting to me that so early on we see a bit of this concept, that perhaps there are people in government who are aware of all this going on and who want to use it.

Questions For Your Writing

- **Take a look at your scene or chapter breaks. Can you use a line of dialogue, a sound, or some other element to connect the end of one to the beginning of the next?**
- **What happens at your Midpoint? Is there a major reversal or commitment? If not, can you create one or the other or both?**
- **If the protagonist makes a major commitment somewhere else in the story, does it work better if you move it to the Midpoint?**

Next: Prophecy Girl

NEXT I'LL TALK about the Season One finale, Prophecy Girl, where Buffy faces the Master and attempts to defy a prophecy that decrees her fate. It remains one of my favorite episodes of Buffy the Vampire Slayer.

CHAPTER THIRTEEN

PROPHECY GIRL

This chapter talks about Season One Episode Twelve Prophecy Girl, written and directed by Joss Whedon.

In particular, we'll look at:

- **How this huge story for Buffy is wrapped in Xander's experience**
- **Different characters we identify with emotionally**
- **Actions that express and emphasize the characters' feelings**
- **A very layered Story Spark**
- **A strong Midpoint and Three-Quarter Turn**

Okay, let's dive into the Hellmouth.

Opening **Internal Conflict**

We begin in the Bronze, a classic Buffy location. And we start with conflict – Xander's conflict.

It's mainly internal. He is struggling over whether to, or how to, ask Buffy out. Specifically, for the Spring Fling, which is what they call the prom. He's practicing his lines on Willow, as she looks on adoringly. What I love about Willow in this scene is that she is such a good friend to Xander. Though her feelings are so clear on her face, and we know she has this crush on him, she really does her best to encourage him about what to say. But mostly to be a sounding board for him.

Xander wonders what Buffy is doing right now. And we cut to Buffy.

Opening External Conflict

Buffy's fighting a vampire outside in what looks like a field. There are people parking there, including Cordelia, who hears noises. Buffy eventually defeats the vampire. When it's over, she says, "Three in one night. Giles would be so proud." She sounds so weary, and we cut to Giles.

He's in the library, and he's translating Latin. He says to himself as he's parsing through the words, "The Master shall rise...this is it...and the Slayer... My God." Everything starts to shake. Giles' teacup falls to the floor and shatters. We see the earthquake shaking the Bronze, toppling over bookcases in the library.

The Master in his lair feels it and says, "Yes, yes," and holds his hands up in a very dramatic way. Then the shaking stops and we get some humor. Because he says, "What you think? 5.1?"

What Is The Inciting Incident?

All of this is part of our Inciting Incident or Story Spark. I had to think about what the Spark was here. On the surface, our story is about this prophecy that Buffy will face the Master and she will die. Everyone is certain it is going to come true even as they struggle against it.

But if the prophecy foretells the future, and is going to come true regardless, which it does, then there almost is no Story Spark within the episode. Because that story was already in motion.

Yet we will see the Master later will say that Buffy set this in motion. For that reason, I see the Spark as when Giles translates that part of the prophecy about the Anointed One, and how Buffy will face the Master and die.

Coffee Reveals Character

Before we move on, though, a quick note about Giles' teacup. I think he was drinking coffee. It looked a lot like coffee in that cup. And we will find out throughout the series – hopefully this is too minor spoiler for anyone to care – that Giles is quite the tea drinker. I can only think of one other time when he drinks coffee. So I think it's coffee in the cup, and it shows how he's staying up all night and he's struggling with this. And he is so distressed.

The Tension Escalates

After the credits, Buffy comes to the library to tell Giles about the vampire fighting and her close call. He is so disheveled and distracted. And he doesn't really listen to her, which is rare. She says, "Giles, care," and jokes about breaking a nail.

In the next scene we are outside the school, and we get Xander's conflict again. He gets Buffy alone, and he asks her to the dance and says he wants to date her. She says she doesn't know what to say. He says, "Well, you're not laughing, that's a good start."

But she doesn't feel the same way as he does, and he takes it very badly. He says something like: "I guess a guy's gotta be undead to make time with you." Buffy tells him that's harsh. He kind of apologizes but says, "I don't handle rejection well, which is funny because I've had so much practice."

Buffy looks very sad when he leaves. And remember, last week she was feeling very isolated in the school, even from Willow and Xander. Giles wasn't really listening to her this morning. And you get the feeling all she's been doing outside of school is slaying vampires.

So she's feeling very alone. And now Xander, one of her two friends, is angry at her.

A Side Character's Point Of View

Having Xander's perspective so strong in this episode shows one of the strengths of the show. As I've mentioned before, we have different characters we all can identify with for different reasons. In Xander you get – I won't say every man because I'm not saying every guy or every person is like Xander. But he is the one who has no special powers here. Yes, Willow is an ordinary girl, but it is clear she's supersmart. She's really good at research.

Xander is struggling kind of with everything. So he is that person who is easy to feel for. Yes, he reacts badly when Buffy turns him down. We'd like to see him handle it better. But he's human and very flawed and he is one entry point in this series.

Bringing Out Characters' Emotions

In this episode we get so much emotion from each of the characters. We have Willow and her feelings about Xander, and later her feelings about what's happening in the world. We have Giles and his fears about losing Buffy.

We don't get Angel's emotions quite as much, but you get his anger over this prophecy and his devastation about losing Buffy. And of course we have Buffy herself, who was struggling both emotionally and with first the slaying and then the prophecy.

This is the best type of story to me. Because while it includes action, it is about the human story and Buffy's feelings.

Anxious Giles

We are back in the library. Giles is on the phone saying, "I need to see you. I understand, come after sundown." We realize he's talking to Angel. Which tells us – we don't yet know what that prophecy says – it tells us how important it is. Because I just don't picture Angel even having a phone. The idea that Giles would call him when normally he just turns up tells us how serious this is.

Plus, Giles' appearance. Jenny comes in and she overhears him. And she comments on him wearing the same clothes as the day before. She knows something is going on. People have been sending her reports of things like a cat giving birth to a litter of snakes, and some messages from a monk about the Anointed One.

These messages further rattle Giles because he and Buffy both believe that she killed the Anointed One. When we find out the full prophecy, we'll understand why he is so spooked. Because the idea that the Anointed One was gone probably was giving him some small amount of hope that this prophecy would not come true.

Jenny Offers To Help

Jenny wants to help. And we get another nice moment, which we saw so much of in the pilot, where we get quick exposition, but it is through genuine conflict. So it works on both levels. Here, we have Jenny offering to help. Giles says, "I don't know if I can trust you." And she says something like, "I helped you cast that demon out of the Internet. I think that warrants some trust."

So for those who haven't caught an episode with Jenny in it, we get a very fast sense of who she is.

Jenny has gotten all these reports about things. We know it's something about that she's involved with magic, and that she cast out a demon. So there are reasons Giles should trust her, but we also know that he doesn't, not quite.

Building To The First Major Plot Turn

We next see Cordelia with her new boyfriend. They're being very cute and happy and she's kind of unCordelia-like. She seems so relaxed. And she asks Willow to help her at the Bronze to get ready for the dance, something with the sound system. Willow says yes, but she's distracted. She sees Xander in an empty classroom throwing a ball against the wall, very unhappy.

He tells her what happened with Buffy. He is so upset. And then he says, "Hey, I know, we'll go to the dance together."

I love Willow here. She is so strong. And she says, "No. Do you think I want to go to the dance and watch you wishing you were with her? You should know better." And she's very quiet about it and very firm. She takes care of herself and she points out what he has done in taking her for granted.

This works on two levels. It works if we think that Xander does recognize Willow's feelings for him. It also works if he doesn't. Because she has been being this great supportive friend, and he does take her for granted. It's like an afterthought: okay, we'll go together. They have always done so many things together. Even if she didn't have feelings for him, it's just sort of, "Oh, you can help make me feel better." He's suggesting going to the dance without thinking about her feelings at all.

The One-Quarter Twist

We are now just over 14 minutes in. So sometimes we would see the One-Quarter Twist in the episode coming earlier. In a book or movie, it almost always happens right at the one-quarter point through the story. Some books will put it about one-third of the way through. In TV, it varies, I suspect because in network TV we have the commercial break issue. But regardless of where it is, what matters is that it turns the story in a new direction. And it comes from something outside the protagonist.

Here, we have exactly that because Buffy overhears this conversation between Giles and Angel. If she hadn't overheard, it's possible Giles wouldn't have told her of the prophecy. At the very least, it would likely have played out differently because he might've found some other way to tell her. As it is, she hears this conversation, which is another great example of getting information to the reader through conflict.

A Dramatic Reveal Though Conflict

The way Buffy finds out makes the reveal of exactly what this prophecy says so dramatic. Giles is saying to Angel that it's clear what will happen. Angel argues with him. Giles says he's read the text, The Codex. And Angel says, "Then you're reading it wrong."

This pushback from Angel, and his refusal to believe the prophecy, forces Giles to speak angrily and so strongly, in a way that perhaps he would not have done even to Angel. That he might not have wanted to say aloud this way to himself for that matter. He says, "I wish to God I were. But it's very plain. Buffy will face the Master and she will die."

This telling of what the prophecy says, and that Buffy is going to die, is so much stronger than if Giles had said that while reading it to himself and maybe thrown down his glasses or knocked over his cup. It's also stronger than if we saw the actual text of the prophecy on the screen. Or than if he simply read it out of a book to Angel or to Buffy. It is such a strong statement, and this adds to the effect on Buffy.

Buffy Reacts

Buffy reacts to the prophecy that she'll die, but also Giles' certainty. He seems so strong and so certain. She gives this shaky laugh that pulls in so much emotion. So desolate, and so on the edge. Sarah Michelle Gellar does an amazing performance here.

Her lines are another example of that escalation that was in Nightmares where each line is that much more heartbreaking than the last. She says she knows the drill, when one Slayer dies the next one is called. And she asks will Giles train her, or will they send someone new. Does it say how the Master will kill her? "Do you think it will hurt?"

Using Actions To Show Emotions

We also see through her actions how she feels. And this is key in any story. If you're writing a novel, this is a good thing to either do in your first draft or on rewrite. I often look when rewriting at what action the character would take. It's particularly key in visual mediums like movies, television shows, and plays because we can't be inside the character's head, and we can't feel the character's sensations.

Here, Angel moves toward her to comfort her. And she yells at him, "Don't touch me," and jerks away. She keeps the physical distance from him. And in a few moments, she'll say, "What do you know about it – you're never gonna die."

She says she'll quit. Giles tries to say it might not be that easy and says something about the signs. She throws books at him and says, "Signs. Read me the signs. Tell me my fortune."

This is the quote I mentioned in the pilot episode (in the spoilers) where we had an earlier scene between Buffy and Giles very much like this. And this is escalated to the nth degree because she's going to die. She says, "I'm sixteen. I don't want to die." She also yells at Giles that he's so useful with his books. He's really a lot of help. (Obviously meaning that he's not.)

He looks so devastated and says he supposes he's not.

When she says she doesn't want to die, she throws the cross Angel gave her onto the floor. In our next scene we get more of what she's feeling through action because she's sitting on her bed looking through her photo album. Looking over her life as she's contemplating dying.

Joyce Sensing Something Wrong

Her mom, Joyce, comes in. Joyce clearly knows Buffy is upset about something. Buffy won't tell her what it is. She makes a comment, and Joyce, in a great quote, says, "You're probably just full from that bite of dinner you nearly had."

Buffy tries to get Joyce to go away for the weekend, thinking that getting away from the Master will help. Joyce says she can't get away, and isn't the prom or Spring Fling this weekend, and did nobody ask Buffy. Buffy tells her somebody asked. And Joyce says, "Not the right someone."

What's ironic is that is sort of true. That isn't Buffy's problem right now. But, yes, the wrong person asked — someone she doesn't want to go with. And she has fallen for Angel, who isn't exactly the boyfriend who's going to take her to the Spring Fling.

Joyce says, "See, sometimes I do know what you're thinking." She takes out a dress, acknowledging this might not be the right time for it, but she shows Buffy this beautiful dress that she bought for her. Even though they can't really afford it. But she saw Buffy eyeing the dress in the store window.

Subtext In Dialogue

Buffy loves it. But she says she can't go to the dance. And then we get this line that I love from Joyce. We talked about it at a Buffy discussion group at a bookstore in the Andersonville neighborhood in Chicago, Women And Children First. We had one meeting where we talked about Joyce and Buffy and the different scenes between them throughout the series. I thought this one really showed how Joyce connected with Buffy and did understand her.

Others thought it showed how disconnected and clueless Joyce was about Buffy's life.

My feeling is that while Joyce is talking about a different situation – she thinks the issue is the dance – she gives Buffy exactly the advice that Buffy needs to hear. Maybe my saying the advice drives the rest of Buffy's decisions is a bit strong, but it definitely informs the choices that Buffy makes.

When Buffy says she can't go to the dance, Joyce says, "Who says? Is it written somewhere? You should do what you want."

This goes right to the prophecy. Yes, it's written, and we'll see Buffy echo that at the end when she's talking to the Master. But she defies it.

The World Changes

For now, we switch to Cordelia and Willow in the school. They're heading for the audiovisual lab because Cordelia's boyfriend never showed up. I think he was supposed to be there for a sound check. She's mad, or trying to be mad. She normally would be. But she likes him so much that she thinks it's cute.

There's a window in the door. They look through. At first it looks like a group of students is watching cartoons. Willow and Cordelia go in, though, and see these students have been slaughtered. There's blood everywhere. And there is a bloody handprint on the TV. We see it with cartoon dancing pigs behind it. Such a strong visual of what has happened.

At Buffy's house again, she is trying on the dress and

looking at herself in the mirror. Looking wistful. Joyce calls to her and says there's something on the news about Willow.

The Midpoint Of The Plot

We see Buffy in Willow's bedroom. Buffy's wearing the dress with her leather jacket over it. Probably the jacket Angel gave her. Willow tells her what happened. Willow is so shocked and stunned. She says, "I've seen a lot of terrible things, but this was different." And she says something like, "It wasn't our world anymore. It was theirs. What are we going to do?"

This is 22 minutes, 39 seconds in, almost exactly at the Midpoint.

And Buffy says, "What we have to." We know she has decided that she will face the Master even though she'll almost certainly die.

Buffy's Philosophy And The Show's Theme

This choice Buffy makes encapsulates the theme of the show. There is no higher power telling Buffy to fight. She's not acting out of some threat of eternal punishment, like you might find in many religions, or for a reward. She doesn't know. She does what she does because she can, and because she doesn't want to live in the world where it's what Willow says: It's not our world anymore. It's theirs.

Buffy has the power to try to change that, to fight. And her philosophy, whether she says it or not, is that it's better to fight and probably die than to live in that world and not try to change it. She cannot live with that.

Right before Buffy leaves, Willow says, "I like your dress." Buffy looks down as if she forgot she was wearing it. She tells Willow to take care. And the way she says it, we know that she does not think she will see Willow again.

Preparing To Face The Master

Back at the library, Giles and Jenny are talking about the

Anointed One being a child. Giles quotes the prophecy where it says the Slayer will not know him, and the Anointed One will lead her to the Master. Buffy comes in, once again having overheard, and says, "Okay, I'm looking for a kid."

She and Giles argue. Giles say he's been among his books too long. He's going to face the Master. She's not. Buffy can't talk him out of it, so she punches him and knocks him out. She tells Jenny to think of something cool to tell him that she said when he wakes up.

Jenny says, "You'll die." And Buffy says maybe she will, but maybe she'll take the Master with her.

Outside it's dark. The Anointed One comes up to Buffy and says, "Help me." Pretending to be this helpless little boy.

She says, "It's okay, I know who you are."

And I have always wondered, is this part of what changes things? Because the prophecy says she will not know him, yet she does know him. I also like that because if that's true, that's something that Giles did to help her. Telling her who the Anointed One is. Who she's looking for.

Character-Based Conflict

Back in the library, Xander and Willow get really angry and upset at Giles that Buffy left. Xander in particular says how could Giles let her do that? In a great quote, Giles says, "As the soon-to-be purple area of my jaw will attest, I did not *let* her do anything."

Both Xander and Willow get mad at Jenny because she is trying to tell them yes, Buffy is important. But hey, there's an apocalypse, that's what we should focus on. Willow says, "Why does she get to be in the club?"

Xander Challenges Angel

Xander goes to see Angel and ask for Angel's help. Xander is saying the two of them will go face the Master and help Buffy. Angel tells him he's way out of his league, that the

Master will kill him. And Xander says, "I don't like you. At the end of the day, I pretty much think you're a vampire," but "Buffy thinks you're a real person. So prove her right."

I love Nicholas Brendan's delivery here. Those lines, and the whole argument with Angel, could have come across as being all about Xander's jealousy. But they don't. He is truly concerned for Buffy.

And I get the feeling that his distrust of Angel – sure, there's a bias there, this is the person Buffy wants. But it also feels genuine. I'm sure that was intentional, given what we see as we go through the episode. Xander is written and directed as having complex motives and feelings. He's not just sulky and angry because Buffy rejected him. He definitely feels that way. But he does put that aside, and he wants to save Buffy. And he will go to Angel even though he's jealous of Angel, and though he also in his gut does not trust Angel.

Entering The Cave

Buffy is in the Master's candlelit layer. The scene looks very much like the one from her nightmare in the episode Nightmares. There isn't a lot of physical fighting here.

There is some hunting – what Buffy calls cat and mouse.

The Master is able to draw her to him without even touching her through his own mystical power. As he is gripping her, he tells her it was noble of her to try. But prophecies are tricky, they don't tell you everything. She is the one who set him free. If she hadn't come into the lair, he couldn't have left.

So this is why, going back to the Story Spark, I see it as Giles translating that prophecy. This line from the Master suggests that if Giles never translated the prophecy and never told Buffy, perhaps this whole story wouldn't have happened.

Though we still had the Anointed One around. Probably

there would've been some confrontation at some point. But not this specific story on this day.

The Three-Quarter Plot Turn And Death

We are also have a Three-Quarter Turn in the story that comes from the protagonist's actions, but spins the story in a new direction. The Master kills Buffy. He bites her. He exults in the power of drinking her blood and drops her face down into a pond or lake. And says, "By the way, I like your dress."

He's now free.

Xander and Angel, who have been heading for the lair and are underground, feel the shaking and know that the Master has become free. They run down and they find Buffy. But she is dead. She drowned. Angel holds her in his arms, looking devastated. And we cut to commercial.

When we're back, Xander is saying CPR, we need to try CPR. Angel can't do it because he has no breath. So Xander revives Buffy.

The Hero's Journey

These scenes echo parts of the story structure The Hero's Journey. At some point I'll have to go through that entire structure because probably this whole episode follows it. But a couple parts stood out in particular. There's a point where the hero goes to the inmost cave. And this can be literal, as it is here. Buffy is in a cave.

Or if you think about one of the Star Wars movies, I want to say Return of the Jedi, but maybe it's Empire Strikes Back. Where Luke literally goes into the cave. And he doesn't know what's in there.

It is the hero facing something that she has avoided to this point. Something the hero has been fearing and dreading. So we have that here.

And the next scene is typically a death. It can again be

metaphorical or literal. Here, it is a literal death and rebirth. After the death, the hero goes back into the world with the elixir or the Holy Grail or whatever it is.

We have that very literally here. Alive again, Buffy says, "I feel different." She says she feels strong. And she is no longer operating out of fear.

She heads for the school. She kicks a vampire on the way. She is no longer afraid of the Master.

More Obstacles For The Protagonist's Friends

Jenny and Willow are caught out in the parking lot behind the school. They planned to go to the Bronze. Everyone thought the Hellmouth would open there. (The Master's supposed to get free and open the Hellmouth and take over the world.)

Hordes of vampires come toward them. And they realize the Hellmouth must be in the school, because all the vampires would be coming to the Hellmouth. But more important, they're in great danger. It's just the two of them when Cordelia drives up in her car.

They get in and say they need to get to the library. Cordelia drives right through the double doors of the school, down the hall, and crashes at the library doors. I love this because Cordelia is so strong and acts so quickly. Without asking any questions, she gets it. She may not know the details, but she knows what to do.

Buffy Returns

The Master is on the roof above the library. There is a skylight. He is looking down through it and calling forth the Hellmouth. Inside the library is chaos. Vampires, parts of the Hellmouth (these snaky little arms) are grabbing at people and breaking through. And then this three-headed slimy monster with teeth. I'm never sure if that is the actual Hellmouth or if the Hellmouth is the opening. But anyway, it's pretty awful. Lots of screaming, running, fighting. It does not look good.

Buffy leaves Xander and Angel outside the school as a line of defense. She goes up on the roof and comes up behind the Master. Much as she did not hear him in the lair behind her, he does not register that she is there until she says something. He turns and says, "You're dead."

And in a great quote she says, "I may be dead but I'm still pretty." (If you listen to other Buffy podcasts you probably know this is where the title comes from for one of them: Still Pretty.)

Is It Written Somewhere?

I love that the Master then says that it was written that Buffy died. I feel like this is a little call back to Joyce saying "Is it written somewhere?" and telling Buffy to do what she wants.

And Buffy says, "What can I say? I flunked the written." Which is another fun quote.

She pretends to let him draw her over. He grips her throat, so he thinks he's winning.

Then she insults him and breaks away and does a flip over him.

This is a nice call back to the pilot, where we saw a fair amount of Buffy doing her somersaults and flips and acrobatics. In the DVD commentary for the pilot, Joss Whedon mentioned that was pretty close to the end of that. We definitely see Buffy fighting throughout the season. But we don't see her doing so many of these sorts of gratuitous flips that don't really accomplish anything.

The Climax Of Prophecy Girl

So here we get this flip and somersault. I guess it does something because it gets her on the other side of the Master. She grabs him, or actually he grabs her again, but she is clearly in control. She's looking down behind her through the skylight and sees this big shard of wood (from one of the tables or the bookshelves or something). And she flips the Master over.

He plunges down and lands directly on that shard of wood, and he is dusted. His dusting is far more dramatic than other vampires. It is slower. We see what looks like dirt. Just pieces of dirt flying off of him as his body disintegrates. But unlike other vampires there is this large skeleton left.

So that was our climax. All of this action where everything comes together and closes off our main plot.

Falling Action

We have brief Falling Action. Down in the library, Cordelia lets Angel and Xander in. Xander says to Giles, "Buffy died and everything."

Giles says, "I should've known that wouldn't stop you." And he gives her this look of admiration and love.

Xander says they need to party. They should go to the dance. And Cordelia says, "Yeah!" I love this too because we get this arc for Cordelia. Just last episode she was thanking them for saving her, and then she immediately turned on them and said, "I'm not hanging out with those lepers," when Mitch came up to her.

Now she helped save the day. And she let Xander and Angel into the library, which I think was kind of symbolic, and she's excited about going to the dance with them. So it's a really nice moment where I think Cordelia has become part of the group. Though we will certainly see that she will struggle with that.

The Three Beat

On the way out, Angel says to Buffy, "By the way, I like your dress." And she says, "Yeah, yeah, it's a big hit with everyone."

This is what's known as a three beat. When you come back again and again to an aspect of the story. Here, it is a line of dialogue – I like your dress. It is said three times by three different people in very different circumstances, and in very different ways. And each time it has a different meaning in the story.

So we have Willow saying it sincerely, and then we have the Master being kind of sarcastic. Now we have Angel saying it in the context Buffy would've liked in the beginning of the episode. When she was feeling sad and probably thinking about how Xander asked her to the dance and was mad at her, and on some level thinking about how Angel was never going to take her to a dance. Here he is saying, by the way, I like your dress.

And at this point it just doesn't matter.

The End Of Prophecy Girl

We end on a long shot of the Master's skeleton in the library. So it's leaving a little something eerie at the end after our hero has a great triumph and celebration.

Spoilers

THERE ARE QUITE a few things in this episode that foreshadow Season Two in particular, and some later parts of the series.

I really like that.

An End That Still Foreshadows

This could have been a series finale. I feel certain it was written that way. I don't remember the timing of Buffy being renewed, but it seems very likely that with a twelve-episode Season One, they wrote it to be a series finale just in case. I really appreciate that. It's hard to watch a show that you love end. It's bad enough if it doesn't get renewed. But if it doesn't reach any conclusion it's so disappointing.

There was a very short-lived show called, I want to say, Happy Town. (Amy Acker, who plays Fred in the series Angel, was in it, which is how I came across it.) And it raised so many intriguing things. I still think about how it might've ended. They did kind of throw in a bit of a wrap up, but it felt tacked on. I know there was so much more to that story, so it still bugs me.

Spoilers About Jenny Calendar

So we have Jenny. Giles not trusting Jenny. And Willow and Xander asking what she's doing there.

I had not realized until this rewatch how many flags there were that Jenny maybe wasn't trustworthy. And we see next season that she does have her own agenda. While she doesn't do it purposely, she hurts Buffy very badly. And here we have this suspicion.

I'm uncertain about how genuine Jenny is being here. When she finds out Buffy is the Slayer, she truly appears surprised and comments that Buffy's "so little." And I wonder. If Jenny was sent to watch Angel, wouldn't her family have told her that Buffy is the Slayer? Or maybe they don't know. It all makes me wonder if the writers knew there'd be something about Jenny but perhaps not quite what yet.

Or maybe she is pretending. But I think the performance doesn't suggest she's pretending. Perhaps the actress was told to play it either way.

Giles Might Fight

We get a quick foreshadowing for Giles when he says to Buffy, "I've been in the books too long." Something like it's been too long since he's been in the real world and fighting.

So I guess this does give us a hint that perhaps Giles wasn't always the book guy.

We definitely find that out next season, that he had quite a past and dabbled – more than dabbled – in the occult. And he is a really good fighter.

In this season, we have seen him be very about the books. We don't see him fight. In fact, we get suggestions that he's not a good fighter. So maybe, too, the writers were still developing Giles. But this gives us a hint that there is more to him in terms of being able to do battle himself.

Foreshadowing Future Conflict

The Xander-Angel scene really struck me this time. Because Xander says, "Yeah, I pretty much think you're a vampire," and next season that will be the issue. That Angel turns evil, becomes Angelus again. And Xander was right. How much of Xander's feelings come from jealousy and how much are a real grasp of the issues, and/or a gut level instinct, hard to say.

But it turns out he was correct.

Of course we know there's an issue about Buffy and Angel as Slayer and vampire. But we don't know that there's any reason really to fear Angel. He hasn't fed on humans in, I think he told us, 100 years. So it's a nice moment that Xander flags that and foreshadows the Season Two arc.

Dracula And The Master

We also have the Master drawing Buffy to him. And we will see Dracula do the same thing in the beginning of Season Five. I had forgotten that the Master did this, and that Dracula kind of echoes that. Which makes sense because Dracula likewise is a very old vampire.

Not as old as the Master, though, because we see that the Master looks different because of his age. He's from this earlier time when presumably all vampires were much more powerful. And we will find that out later as well. So the Master looks a little bit like the Turok-Han that we will see in Season Seven that Buffy at first is unable to defeat at first.

So we get these calls forward to these other powerful vampires. Buffy, in response, pretends to be under the Master's power. Then she insults him and breaks away. And she does, I think, a very similar thing with Dracula.

That also makes sense to me. It doesn't feel repetitive because these are tools in Buffy's toolbox. This is what she does. It works well with the Master, and she does it again with Dracula.

The Master's Bones

Finally, that last shot of the Master's skeleton – so telling because in Season Two, Episode One we will deal with the Master's bones. And this tells us the Master is different. Buffy has defeated him, and yet there is this tiny question. Why is there still a skeleton there when other vampires turned to dust and they're gone? That will be key from almost the very beginning of the Season Two pilot episode.

Questions For Your Writing

- **The moment with Giles drinking coffee is subtle and yet very telling. Is there anything similar one of your characters does when stressed?**
- **Do you know your protagonist's philosophy of life? Faced with a choice like Buffy's at the Midpoint here, what would your protagonist do? Why?**

- **Xander's motives for challenging Angel to help are mixed, which makes his words powerful. Do any of your characters have mixed motives?**

Next: Season One Overview

NEXT I'LL TALK about Season One as a whole, including favorite plot turns, scenes, and characters.

CHAPTER FOURTEEN

SEASON ONE OVERVIEW

I'M so excited to talk about the whole of Season One, including some favorite moments.

In particular, I'll cover:

- **Strongest plot turns**
- **Best villain in a one-off episode**
- **Most interesting red herring**
- **Favorite single episode character who gets killed**

Okay, let's dive into the Hellmouth.

BEST OPENING CONFLICT: Prophecy Girl

Starting with (of course) my favorite opening conflict. I want to say that it is Xander asking Willow out in Prophecy Girl, where he isn't really asking her out. He is practicing to ask out Buffy. It's such a wonderful character moment for Willow in particular, and I really enjoy that.

However, probably the strongest opening in the sense of truly signaling our main plot and bringing us into Buffy's experience, is the one in Out Of Mind, Out Of Sight (the invisible girl episode). Other than that, it wasn't my favorite episode, or the one I found the strongest. But I was surprised how often it came up as I put together my Season One overview for the podcast.

In the very beginning, we have Cordelia with her popular friends talking about the Spring Fling. She's so excited about her dress she's having made. And so certain she'll be Queen that she's already planning for it. And then we have Buffy almost crashing into the scene. Literally. She stumbles. She falls on the floor in front of Cordelia and her friends. Her bag of weapons spills out and she struggles to explain it. Cordelia and her friends laugh at her.

It is such a moving moment for Buffy. It really epitomizes the conflict of the entire series. Maybe saying the entire series is really strong, but certainly of the first season, and we will see it return.

It's not just the normal girl or the normal life versus the supernatural, but also her loss of her old life. The life where she was the girl getting ready for Spring Fling or the prom with nothing but dresses and boys on her mind. And where her peers saw her as that popular girl, rather than as Cordelia would probably say, "this weirdo." It just encapsulates that theme for the season and for the episode, which is all about the outcast in society.

Second Choice Opening Conflict

My close second for Opening Conflict is The Witch. Giles is almost ranting at Buffy, lecturing to her about her sacred duty and the importance of it. And now she's gone and enslaved herself to "this cult." Then we switch to Buffy in a cheerleading outfit.

The looks on both their faces are just so wonderful. Giles looks so annoyed. At this point he doesn't know Buffy that well, and he's seeing her as frivolous and not taking this seriously. Buffy is giving this pouty sort of look.

It does really draw in the conflicts of the series in such a fun way.

Favorite Story Spark: I, Robot…You, Jane

Moving on to our Story Spark or Inciting Incident. The one I thought was the strongest again, interestingly, was in an episode that I didn't overall think was one of the best: I, Robot…You, Jane.

In it, Willow is scanning the book where Moloch, the demon, has been trapped. But she's not really looking at the book she's scanning. So she doesn't see that it's strange that the writing disappears off the page. But we see it as the audience member.

We get this close up of the screen of this big old clunky computer. (Which at the time would not have been old. It was cutting-edge.) And we get the words Where Am I? across the screen in that old-style text. When that was the only font that there was. I love that as the opening conflict because there is so much there in the scene.

Now we know that Moloch, who was bound into this book for centuries, was released. But not just released — released into the Internet. Something that did not exist, that he couldn't even have imagined.

Also, it sets off Willow's opening conflict for the episode. Her feelings of isolation. She's here alone in the library. It's dark, like so many places in Sunnydale often are. But our library usually is not. It is usually lit in warm tones. We have a number of people there. We feel that our core characters feel very safe there.

And here we have Willow, this time by herself. It's late, it's dark, she scanning books. While I am sure she really is glad to be helping and doesn't mind doing it, it highlights how she too is set apart and isolated.

We focus a lot in the series about Buffy being isolated. Or at least that is what is talked about. The one girl in all the world. But aside from Xander and Buffy, we don't see Willow having other friends either. She has this crush on Xander, and he doesn't return her feelings. So she is in that sense left out and alone. It is this perfect set up for Moloch, this demon, to pose as a boy and win Willow's heart.

That is why I see this as such a strong Story Spark. It begins both stories. Our main plot about Moloch trying to wreak havoc and take over the world, and what I think is the real plot in the episode. His drawing Willow in, and Willow having to step back and reject him.

Favorite One-Quarter Twist: Angel

On to my favorite One-Quarter Twist. This is the first plot turn, generally coming from outside the protagonist and spinning the story in a new direction. In Angel, Episode Seven, Angel stays the night with Buffy. They talk as he is lying on her floor. She's lying in bed, he's lying on the floor. It is the first long conversation they've had. It's the first one we've seen them have that goes in depth about anything personal.

Up until that point, he is just dropping by, warning her about something, looking good, and disappearing. This really starts to bond them beyond just that they both are intrigued by the other and find the other attractive.

Even though we find out later so much about Angel that Buffy wishes she didn't know, if you trace back, everything he says to her is true. He is definitely editing the truth. But there is some real intimacy there. And it is pivotal to turning the episode in a new direction.

It turns Buffy's and Angel's relationship. It leads to the reveal that he is a vampire. And it pushes him on this path of having to face how he is going to live. That also plays into the Master's goal of both defeating Buffy and bringing Angel back into the fold.

Second One-Quarter Twist: The Pack

My close second is The Pack. It is the first part of the dodgeball scene in gym class where the pack, the hyenas, are with Xander on one side. Willow and Buffy are on the other. Xander up to this point has been acting strangely. He sniffs Buffy's hair, he's been a little bit mean making fun of other kids. But this is the first time he is so mean to Willow.

He throws the ball straight at her, really hard to get her out. That is such a key thing in their relationship arc in that episode. And it turns the story because Willow reacts to it by thinking, okay, he doesn't want me around anymore, which he then tells her. On the other hand, when Buffy sees him being so mean to Willow, that is what makes her believe Xander isn't in control.

Favorite Midpoint Commitment

My favorite Midpoint commitment really has to be Prophecy Girl. I had to try hard not to name Prophecy Girl for everything. Part of it is because it is such a pivotal episode. Also, it's the one I watched most recently, so it came most readily to mind. But after looking through my notes and thinking about the episodes, I feel Prophecy Girl really earns this Midpoint.

We see Buffy truly committing to her quest and throwing caution to the wind. Because she's been trying to get her mother to leave town. She is saying that she'll quit, she's not going to face the Master because she doesn't want to die. But she sees Willow, how disturbed Willow is. She hears what Willow says about it not being our world anymore, it being theirs. And when Willow says what are we going to do, Buffy says, "What we have to."

That's the moment when she vows that she will probably die but she will take the Master with her if she can. There is no greater commitment than that.

Reversal In Retrospect: The Pack

I noticed something when I was going through the transcript of The Pack. I realized there is a major reversal in there that I did not point to as a reversal when I was doing the episode because it comes much later. It is not at the Midpoint. It's closer to the three-quarter point where the pack attacks Principal Flutie.

This is really a major reversal for Buffy. You're probably thinking, yes, pretty big reversal for Principal Flutie as well. And yes, of course, it's the most key for him. Also for the pack. It's a commitment for them. They're going all in on the hyena thing.

But it is a major reversal for Buffy because she was not able to sort it out and stop this terrible thing from happening. We don't deal with this in the episode, but it's a reversal that she could not stop these students, and it really is a point of no return for them. So I think that's a major reversal that is in an odd place.

Maybe because that isn't the story that the writers were focused on telling. In retrospect, that's maybe another reason why that episode, much as there's lots of good in it, for me doesn't quite work as well as so many other Buffy episode.

Favorite Midpoint Reversal

My favorite reversal in terms of emotional arc and the overall story of Buffy is the Angel episode's reversal. When

Buffy discovers that he is a vampire. Because it really just seems like there is no answer to that. He vamps out; she sees it for herself. She can't deny this.

That is such a strong reversal. It's not just Buffy trapped in this coffin and this vampire's looming over her. We can imagine how she is going to get out of that, imagine there's some way she can fight. She can use some great move for dodging away.

But with Buffy and Angel, she's the Slayer, he is a vampire. It's hard to see how that can ever be worked out.

Best Three-Quarter Turn: Buffy Dies

Moving on to the Three-Quarter Turn. (This is the plot point, generally about three-quarters through the episode, sometimes a little bit later earlier, that comes from the Midpoint, typically from the actions of the protagonist. And yet it turns the story in another new direction.) Again here I have to go back to Prophecy Girl. Because Buffy dies, and I don't know how you get a stronger Three-Quarter Turn than our protagonist dying.

That turn comes directly from her commitment at the Midpoint to go down and face the Master. She does it though she knows it's foretold that she will die, and Giles thinks there's no wiggle room around that. And she does in fact die. In most stories, at least at the time that episode aired, that just would never happen. You know you can't kill your protagonist at the three-quarter point of your story.

And it does spin everything in a new direction. Xander revives her. She feels renewed and has more strength and purpose, and she's not afraid anymore. And she confronts and kills the Master.

Subtle Second Three-Quarter Turn

My close second – oddly, I think, given that it wasn't one

of my favorite episodes — is The Pack. I really like this turn because it is subtle.

It's when Giles and Buffy and the zookeeper are talking, and Giles inadvertently gives the zookeeper the missing piece. Because he and Buffy don't know the zookeeper is the one who drew the designs on the floor outside the hyena cage. Or that he is the one who has been trying to purposely create the spell so that he can harness that power for himself.

But the zookeeper didn't know that there needed to be a predatory act to complete the spell. So that turn drives the rest of the story, spins it in a new way. Now we have the zookeeper figure out ways to lure in all the hyena kids to the area of the cage. And it's what pushes him to do a predatory act. I don't know that this guy needed much pushing to do one, but it is what tells him that's what he needs to complete his spell.

Three-Quarter Turn For Willow

The Pack is also a wonderful episode for the Three-Quarter Turn because there is a very strong one in the Willow-Xander friendship subplot. Three-quarters is right around where Willow is going closer and closer to the cage where they've imprisoned Xander. We don't know this, but she is trying to figure out in her heart how much in there is Xander and how much is the hyena. And he is trying to lure her closer, saying everything that she wants to hear from him. He thinks he's tricking her. But she is purposely getting close so that he will lunge for the key and try to hurt her if he is the hyena. And that is what he does. And Willow says, "Now I know."

So I love that as well because it shows how smart Willow is. Her actions get her the answer, but it had to just be so hard for her to do that.

Last Plot Point: Climax

Our last plot point is the climax. It was so hard to pick one.

Nightmares

I love the climax in Nightmares because it's kind of a double one. There is the Buffy part where she literally has to face the ugly guy, this giant guy with a club, and she's been turned into a vampire, which is one of her greatest fears. She's been hiding in the shadows both to get away from him and to kind of hide from herself. Not wanting to accept that this has happened to her. But she embraces the power of that and fights him off.

She also is able to help give the little boy, Billy, the strength. Because of that, he's able to come out of the coma and see who did this to him, who he is really afraid of, and confront his coach.

The Witch

I also love the climax of The Witch because we get this true teamwork. We see Giles casting out the spell to put Amy and her mother back and save Buffy, who is dying. We see Buffy immediately gather her strength, fight Amy's mom, and do it in such a way that she is not killing a human. Willow and Xander don't do that much to fight off Amy's mom. But they do everything they can, from trying to fight her, running after her, grabbing the axe or fire extinguisher.

Willow and Xander are a great example of how your characters do not have to be super people. Rather, at a certain point in the story they need to do everything they possibly can with the strength, the power, and the resources they have. And both Willow and Xander are really acting at their capacity here.

Prophecy Girl

I love the climax of Prophecy Girl for obvious reasons. We have Buffy confronting this villain who has been there throughout the season. Whom she has been so afraid of, and she gets past that and wins the fight. That of course is a wonderful climax.

She faces death, although that actually happens before the climax. So I guess we can't technically put that in the climax of Prophecy Girl.

So let's just say she fights the Master and prevails after dying and coming back to life.

And the Winner Is

If I have to pick a favorite, I think I need to go with Nightmares because I feel like that particular fight was so hard for Buffy. She became something she really feared – a vampire. Being able to embrace and use that power, I think was amazing.

Absolute Favorite Falling Action

My favorite Falling Action, where we tie up the loose ends, absolutely has to be The Puppet Show. On two counts.

First, after the demon is killed, Sid — the guy who's trapped in the ventriloquist dummy – stabs it in the heart, so he's released and now his spirit is gone. He's dead. It's just a dummy again.

And we get this wonderful moment where the curtain comes up. They're on the talent show stage. You have what does look, as Principal Snyder says, like some sort of abstract art performance piece. They're all frozen. Buffy's holding the dummy. And there's this demon with his brain chopped off, and a knife in his heart, lying in guillotine, and I think Willow's holding an axe. All of them have this deer in the headlights look.

Then, two, the cherry on the sundae. We get the post-credit sequence where Buffy, Xander, and Willow are doing their dramatic scene reading. And they are just so bad.

So that is no question my favorite Falling Action in all of Season One.

Falling Action In The Pilot

My close second is The Harvest, part two of the pilot. We hear Giles saying that people forget what they can and rationalize what they can't forget so that they can make sense of these things. So they're not going to remember that Buffy was slaying vampires. And then we get an example where Cordelia is talking to her friends and doing exactly that. She says there was a gang, and Buffy knew them and everything.

I love it because it's an illustration and it contains so much foreshadowing. We get that hint of admiration. Cordelia liked Buffy in the beginning, then thought she was really weird and strange. And both those things are still there. But she also has this admiration for Buffy. It suggests that they will perhaps connect again.

And we see that Cordelia keeps this idea in her head that maybe Buffy knows gang members or is in a gang because in Out Of Mind, Out Of Sight she comes to Buffy for help when she realizes that people around her are being hurt. And says, "Oh, I thought maybe you were in a gang."

Favorite Quotes Of The Season

Moving on to some other favorite things.

My favorite quote of the season comes from Prophecy Girl. It is when Joyce tells Buffy to go to the dance. Her saying to Buffy why can't you go, is it written somewhere, you should do what you want.

And I love this for all the reasons I said in that chapter. It really speaks to who Buffy ultimately it is. As does her later line, "I flunked the written." Buffy is not going to just accept what authority figures tell her, or what has been decreed for her. She will use what she can to fight and do what she needs to do. She's not going to ignore what could help her, but she is going to find her own way.

Favorite One-Off Villains

My favorite one-off villain in a single episode story arc is from Nightmares. But it isn't the ugly guy or the coach. It's the real villain there, which was fear. It was the characters' own fears being used against them, and I thought that was such a strong villain.

My second favorite is Amy's mom (Catherine).

I love it because it layers in so much about parents and children. And because her motives are ones that many people have. That desire to push someone else to do something that you could not do, or that you did do but wish you could continue. That kind of inability to separate what you want from this other person.

Here it's taken to the extreme, and I think that it's done so well.

Favorite Red Herring

My favorite red herring is Principal Snyder in The Puppet Show. All mysteries have various suspects whom we consider could be the ones who did it. Principal Snyder works so well because he is so antagonistic to Buffy, but that antagonism has a real basis. I also think he's my favorite because he's just so open about how he doesn't like students. Overall, Snyder's very well motivated. If we look at that episode knowing that he is not the villain, everything he says still works.

And it all gets across who he is so clearly. He is law-and-order – his order – over chaos. He sees teenagers as sort of intrinsically agents of chaos, and he distrusts them all. He particularly focuses on Buffy and her friends because he sees them as part of the problem. And he doesn't distinguish between, or doesn't care about, motives. He wants order. And this all fits with everything he says and does.

He could be the villain in that piece. Or he could be the principal that he is, with views that he has. So that's why I like him so much as a red herring. It makes him such an interesting character.

Favorite One-Off Victim

My favorite character who is killed off in a one-off episode is Doctor Gregory. He is from Teacher's Pet, the praying mantis episode. He was the teacher who encouraged Buffy. I like him so much when he tells Buffy she's smart and imagine what she could do if she did the homework. It comes after a moment in class where he's asking questions. Buffy hasn't done the reading, and Willow is trying to signal her the answers. Buffy is mostly figuring them out. What I love is that Doctor Gregory could have yelled at her for not doing the reading. He could consider it cheating that she is pretending she's done the reading and her friend is trying to give her the answers. Some teachers might have yelled at her for that.

Instead, he sees that Buffy is smart. He looks for what her talents are, what her strengths are. Rather than coming down on her for what she doesn't do, he highlights what she is good at, how smart she is. He motivates her that way. And it truly does motivate her.

He isn't saying: You're letting me down. He's saying: you are smart, you have the strengths, you can do so much. So of course he gets killed. (I guess the lesson in Buffy is: Don't be that great teacher.)

Favorite Character Who Doesn't Survive Season

My favorite character who doesn't survive the season is of course Principal Flutie. And yes, I really created this category just for him. I don't know that there is another character who is killed off in the season who wasn't part of a one-off episode.

We had Jesse, but he was killed in our pilot, which was a self-contained story. I think all the other victims, like Doctor Gregory, were killed off as part of a one-episode story. They aren't ongoing characters through the season.

Principal Flutie, we see him a few times. Which is why I started thinking of him as a regular. And I liked him so much. He, too, encouraged Buffy and seemed like someone who really cared about the students. He had a lot of integrity. As much as I enjoy Principal Snyder – he is a great character – I am sorry we didn't get to see Principal Flutie a little bit longer.

And maybe Herbert the pig is my close second for one-off death. Because he was very cute and Principal Flutie was a little afraid of him. But you could see that there was no reason to be. Herbert the pig, we hardly knew ye. I really enjoyed him as a one-off character who gets killed in a single episode.

Those are all of my favorites that I drew from Season One.

Spoilers

Fear As A Villain

Going back to my favorite villain from Nightmares, which was fear, we will see fear as more or less as the villain in Season Four in the Fear Itself episode. That was the Halloween episode where our characters go to a haunted house put together by a fraternity.

In my recollection, I do not love that episode nearly as

much as I liked Nightmares. It does deal with some very real fear. Willow's simultaneous fears about maybe being more powerful with witchcraft than she can handle, and that she's not learning enough, that she isn't very good at magic. We see all those fears manifested. Oz fears that he will turn into a werewolf when he isn't expecting it. He is learning to manage it at that point by locking himself up. But his fear is that it will take over, and he won't be able to stop it.

Xander's fears about his life being different from that of his friends. They're in college, he's not. And they no longer can hear him or see him in that episode.

Those are all real fears.

And we have Buffy's abandonment fears. I feel like for me, that's where that episode falters a bit. That goes into the whole first year of college, Parker Abrams thing. Where Buffy just cannot get over this guy. I figure I have to wait and talk about that then. There's a lot there, but I'm blaming Parker for my not loving that episode.

And for Buffy's fear not quite ringing true for me.

Angel Season Two Arc

Angel (the episode) has one of my favorite Midpoints. And as the Midpoint of the season, it's so telling. I feel like that had to be deliberate, that the writers and creators must've known that Angel was going to be the focus of Season Two.

Because the episode occurs at such a key spot in Season One. Right in the middle of the entire season we get that reveal that Angel is a vampire. And we understand that vampire-Slayer conflict that will drive Season Two and also a large part of Season Three.

Ambiguous Snyder

Principal Snyder is not only a great red herring but a great character. I feel like The Puppet Show in particular really sets the tone and foreshadows the ambiguity about

Snyder. Throughout the next couple seasons we will wonder – Is he evil?

We start to see that, yes, the authorities in Sunnydale put him in charge specifically because they know all these things are going on and they want someone who can handle it or manage it. But it is not clear, are those authorities good or evil? What are Snyder's motives? Yes, he wants order. But there's a point where you question if he's being willfully blind to the fact that Buffy truly is fighting the forces of darkness. Or does he really just not care, it's irrelevant to him? Or is he outright evil?

I'm not certain that's ever really answered. Maybe the answer is that he cares about order above all things, and nothing else matters to him.

We have a great back and forth between him and the mayor in Graduation Day. It encapsulates that whole issue for Principal Snyder. So I love that right from the start we get that conflict with him.

Buffy's Choice

Finally, our biggest foreshadowing is Buffy's choice to fight and probably die versus to let it be a world that belongs to the vampires and the Master. Because in The Gift she will make that same type of choice.

But she is in such a different place in Prophecy Girl. She's sixteen, and she doesn't want to die. Yet she ultimately realizes she would rather fight and die than live in the Master's world. In Season Five, though, she is so worn out and exhausted by what she is lost. It has been so hard for her.

In Prophecy Girl, she becomes resolute and determined. She feels a certain amount of peace when she says to Willow, we'll do what we have to. In The Gift she says that if these are the choices, she doesn't know how to live in the world. And it's a very sad, defeated, weary place that she is in when she ultimately must face the choice to sacrifice herself.

We do briefly get back that sense of peace and wonder – her feeling like this is the work she was made to do, this is her purpose. She again feels this is the right thing as she's diving in to close up that portal between the worlds. She doesn't know what will happen to her. But she knows it is the right thing.

So that is such a great foreshadowing in Prophecy Girl of what's to come in The Gift, which also might have been the end of the series. Because after that Buffy shifted to a new network, and it wasn't a certainty that would happen. So The Gift was written as the series finale.

And I feel like this early Prophecy Girl episode really foreshadows that. It gives us that clue that, as a hero, Buffy will more than once lay down her life.

Overall, it's pretty amazing because you wouldn't necessarily think the writers could top what was in Prophecy Girl when it comes to showing that happening. Or maybe top is the wrong word. But that they could have Buffy sacrifice herself again, but have it be a different character arc and different issues and yet return to that theme.

Questions For Your Writing

- **What character in Season One speaks most to you? Why?**
- **Can you incorporate aspects of how that character develops into your own story?**

- **Which episode do you feel had the strongest plot? Did you like that episode the best?**
- **Why or why not?**
- **Have you learned more about writing from closely watching Buffy Season One?**
- **If so, how can you use what you've learned to improve your current writing project (or your next project)?**

Coming Soon: Season Two

THANK you so much for reading Buffy and the Art of Story Season One.

Can't wait for Season Two to release in book form? Listen to the Buffy and the Art of Story podcast, a production of Spiny Woman LLC.

And read on for resources, contact information, and a few more thoughts on Buffy that don't directly relate to writing.

APPENDIX

Sarah Michelle Gellar As Cordelia?

Another fun thing from the DVD commentary for Welcome To The Hellmouth:

Joss Whedon talked about how Sarah Michelle Gellar initially got the part of Cordelia, but the network said, "Let's see if she can be Buffy."

I would love to know more about why that was. I had seen Sarah Michelle Gellar on All My Children. It's the one soap opera that I used to watch on and off. I would not have imagined her in the role of Buffy. It was part of why I might not have watched this show had my screenwriter friend not encouraged me to do it. I imagined her character on All My Children, and it didn't make me want to watch a whole show about her.

So I find that kind of fascinating that somebody said, let's see if she can be Buffy.

Maybe it was just because she was a known quantity. She had been acting I think since she was three, and she probably had a fan base from All My Children. And it's not that I didn't like her on that. I did, but she was just a very different type of character.

Old Technology On Buffy DVDs

There isn't any interview on the Teacher's Pet DVD or any commentary. For that podcast episode I looked at other DVD features. And found such a retro thing. There was a menu item for DVD-rom.

When I clicked it (and I don't think that I ever clicked on it before, but maybe I did), it said, "Put the DVD into a DVD-Rom drive." And it specifically said, "Not a CD-Rom drive," which is what most computers had at the time. Put it in a DVD-Rom drive to access the official Buffy website and a screen saver.

And I thought, wow, could you not just go on the Internet to the official Buffy website?

I'm sure you must have been able to by then. But maybe most people just didn't know how to find it. Then it has a note: Must run Windows 95 or up. As in 1995.

Typewriters And Mutant Enemy

In the DVD commentary for Nightmares Joss Whedon said that he got the name Mutant Enemy, which is his company name, from his very first typewriter. Which he had at age 15.

I just enjoyed that because I remember having my first typewriter. It was a manual typewriter. I was typing on it in the yard. And I thought it was so cool. I was a real writer. I had a typewriter now.

Joss also talked about the logo for Mutant Enemy. And he didn't have one. He didn't know he needed one. I forget who he said came to him, but when everything was almost finished for the show they came to him and said, "You need a logo."

So he had 20 minutes to come up with one.

He drew the little monster man. He had a postproduction guy make the little monster guy go across the screen and recorded himself saying, "Grrr...argh." That's why we get that at the end of the shows.

Emotional Basis For Buffy

Also, Joss Whedon talked about the emotional basis for creating Buffy. We've heard already about the horror stories. Joss wanted to turn the blond girl trope on its head – the girl who's always a victim.

But here he talked about when he was growing up he always felt like he was in the world, but not of it. He felt isolated. And he wanted to write a story about someone who feels that way. That became Buffy.

Was I, Robot… You, Jane Predictive?

Giles says (of the future world Jenny describes) in I, Robot… You, Jane, "Where human interaction is all but obsolete? Where people can be completely manipulated by technology? I'll pass."

So was this predictive of our culture?

Now information is so much more readily available if you have access to the Internet. It's true not everyone has that. So there is still a divide between people who can easily get all that information and those who can't. But perhaps not as much of one as when the only way to find a lot of information was in books.

And we do have these issues Giles raises. Human interaction, of course, continues. You get more interaction in a way. I can keep in touch with people who are all over the world so easily. In contrast, I remember my dad almost never talked to his siblings. They lived in Pennsylvania, we lived in the Chicago area, and that was a long-distance telephone call. Too expensive to do other than for dire circumstances.

So you can have much more interaction. And yet less in the one-on-one, same-room sense.

Giles also critiques what he sees as a lack of context: "Computer knowledge is there and it's gone. There's no texture, no context." Also, "If it's to last, the getting of knowledge should be tangible, it should be smelly." That goes with this idea that information is so much more readily available now. But from twenty years ago, Giles makes his point about the need for more context. A lot of times now we are seeing quick blips of things with no context. No texture, no richness, it's there and it's gone.

As to Giles saying people can be completely manipulated by technology, we see now that there's more info out there, but it's perhaps harder to tell what is accurate. At least, it takes diligence to find out what's accurate and what's not.

But Jenny might say it's a plus that we have lots more points of view out there.

Spoilers

Fun Spoiler: Musical Comedy

When Xander and Willow realize the nightmares are coming true (in the episode Nightmares, of course), one of them says, "Nightmares, not dreams. That would be a musical comedy."

And of course in Season Six we'll get Once More With Feeling, the Buffy musical episode. Maybe not quite a comedy, but there are many comic moments in it. And it makes me wonder if they were thinking ahead to that. Or if that just came later and it just happens they mentioned it here.

I thought that was fun.

Fun Spoiler: Faster Not Safer

Another thing (which was probably not in Joss Whedon's mind at the time, but maybe) from Nightmares is when Xander and Willow and Giles split up. They're saying it'll be faster to find Buffy that way. Willow says, "Faster, but maybe not safer."

And so many years later Joss Whedon creates the movie Cabin in the Woods. Which explains why people in horror movies do such stupid things like split up.

So that seemed like a tiny bit of a hint that perhaps there would be more to come on that theme.

Connect

If you'd like to connect, you can find me on Twitter: @LisaMLilly (search #BuffyStory for Buffy and the Art of Story podcast episodes).

You can find my novels, non-fiction, and more contact information at my author website **www.LisaLilly.com**.

For books and articles on writing, productivity, publishing, and time management visit **WritingAsASecondCareer.com**.

Help With Your Story

If you want to learn more about the story structure that I've been using throughout the Buffy and the Art of Story podcast and in this book, and you would like to hear it in audio, my book **Super Simple Story Structure: A Quick Guide To Plotting And Writing Your Novel** is available in audiobook form. You can find it wherever you buy audiobooks or ask for it at your local library.

If you'd like to try walking through the plot points that I talk about in this book with your own story, screenplay, novel, or other project you can get free Story Structure worksheets at **WritingAsASecondCareer.com/Rewriting.**

For feedback on your plot outline or for individual coaching visit Help With Your Story at **WritingAsASecondCareer.com.**

ABOUT THE AUTHOR

An author, lawyer, and adjunct professor of law, L. M. Lilly's non-fiction includes The One-Year Novelist: A Week-By-Week Guide To Writing Your Novel In One Year; Happiness, Anxiety, and Writing: Using Your Creativity To Live A Calmer, Happier Life; Super Simple Story Structure: A Quick Guide to Plotting & Writing Your Novel, and Creating Compelling Characters From The Inside Out. She is also the host of the podcast Buffy and the Art of Story.

Writing as Lisa M. Lilly, she is the author of the best selling Awakening supernatural thriller series about Tara Spencer, a young woman who becomes the focus of a powerful religious cult when she inexplicably finds herself pregnant, and of the Q.C. Davis suspense/mystery series.

A member of the Horror Writers Association, Lilly also is the author of When Darkness Falls, a gothic horror novel set in Chicago's South Loop, and the short-story collection The Tower Formerly Known as Sears and Two Other Tales of Urban Horror, the title story of which was made into the short film Willis Tower.

Lilly is a resident of Chicago and a member and past officer of the Alliance Against Intoxicated Motorists. She joined AAIM after an intoxicated driver caused the deaths of her parents in 2007. Her book of essays, Standing in Traffic, is available on AAIM's website.

ALSO BY L. M. LILLY

Super Simple Story Structure: A Quick Guide To Plotting And Writing Your Novel

The One-Year Novelist: A Week-By-Week Guide To Writing Your Novel In One Year

Happiness, Anxiety, and Writing: Using Your Creativity To Live A Calmer, Happier Life

Creating Compelling Characters From The Inside Out

As Lisa M. Lilly:

The Worried Man (Q.C. Davis Mystery 1)

The Charming Man (Q.C. Davis Mystery 2)

The Fractured Man (Q.C. Davis Mystery 3)

The Awakening (Book 1 in The Awakening Series)

The Unbelievers (Book 2 in The Awakening Series)

The Conflagration (Book 3 in The Awakening Series)

The Illumination (Book 4 in The Awakening Series)

The Awakening Series Complete Supernatural Thriller Series Box Set/Omnibus

When Darkness Falls (a standalone novel)

The Tower Formerly Known As Sears And Two Other Tales Of Urban Horror